McGraw-Hill's

CBEST

McGraw-Hill's

CBEST

The Editors of McGraw-Hill

New York   Chicago   San Francisco   Lisbon   London   Madrid   Mexico City
Milan   New Delhi   San Juan   Seoul   Singapore   Sydney   Toronto

The **McGraw·Hill** Companies

Copyright © 2011 by The McGraw-Hill Companies, Inc. All rights reserved. Printed in the
United States of America. Except as permitted under the United States Copyright Act of
1976, no part of this publication may be reproduced or distributed in any form or by any
means, or stored in a database or retrieval system, without the prior written permission of
the publisher.

1 2 3 4 5 6 7 8 9 10   QDB/QDB   1 9 8 7 6 5 4 3 2 1

ISBN 978-0-07-171803-5
MHID 0-07-171803-6

This publication is designed to provide accurate and authoritative information in regard to
the subject matter covered. It is sold with the understanding that neither the author nor the
publisher is engaged in rendering legal, accounting, securities trading, or other professional
services. If legal advice or other expert assistance is required, the services of a competent
professional person should be sought.

> —*From a Declaration of Principles Jointly Adopted by a Committee of the*
> *American Bar Association and a Committee of Publishers and Associations*

Cataloging-in-Publication data for this title are on file at the Library of Congress.

McGraw-Hill books are available at special quantity discounts to use as premiums and sales
promotions or for use in corporate training programs. To contact a representative, please e-mail
us at bulksales@mcgraw-hill.com.

CONTENTS

McGraw-Hill's

CBEST

CHAPTER 1

THE CALIFORNIA BASIC EDUCATION SKILLS TEST

Congratulations on your decision to work toward becoming a teacher! There are few, if any, professions more rewarding to yourself or more helpful to others. This book is designed to help you achieve your goal by helping you to pass the California Basic Educational Skills Test (CBEST).

Passing the CBEST is one of the first steps to becoming a teacher in California and Oregon. You must pass the test in order to teach in these states as either a regular or substitute teacher; you must also pass the CBEST if you wish to be a school counselor or administrator. Teacher education programs in California and Oregon generally require that you pass the test before being admitted to their teacher-credentialing programs.

The requirement to take the CBEST is waived if you have passed another recognized test of basic skills, such as a similar test in another state. For information about what test scores will be accepted in lieu of the CBEST, go to www.cbest.nesinc.com or check the official CBEST registration booklet.

WHAT IS THE CBEST?

The CBEST is divided into three sections: mathematics, reading, and writing. It tests your proficiency in the basic math, reading, and writing skills that you'll need to be an effective teacher. The test only measures proficiency in basic skills, not your teaching methods or skills. Thus, passing or failing the test doesn't give any indication of your abilities to teach. Remember that passing the CBEST does not give you the credentials you'll need to teach; it is only a first step in the process of meeting the requirements in order to become a credentialed teacher.

The Commission on Teacher Credentialing (CTC) is responsible for the CBEST and its overall administration. It has contracted with Pearson Education, which is a private company that develops the questions, administers the test, and scores each test-taker's performance.

Sections of the CBEST

The CBEST consists of the following three sections, each of which is scored separately.

- The **mathematics section** consists of 50 multiple-choice questions. The questions require you to solve a variety of practical problems similar to ones you may face as a teacher. Most of the questions in this section involve word problems. Three skill areas are included: (1) computation and problem solving; (2) numerical and graphic relationships; and (3) measurement, estimation, and statistical principles.

- The **reading section** also consists of 50 multiple-choice questions. The questions require you to understand information presented in a variety of forms, including tables and graphs, as well as written passages. The information included in the questions comes from a variety of subject areas and represents a variety of levels of difficulty. All the information needed to answer the questions is contained in the test. You do not need to review subject areas to prepare because no outside information is needed to answer any of the questions.
- The **writing section** requires you to write two essays. There are no multiple-choice questions, only two topics that require a written response. Each written response should be about four to five paragraphs in length. One topic is based on a personal experience; the other topic requires you to take a position regarding a situation or statement. Here, too, you do not need to review any subject content; just be able to provide a well-organized, coherent essay that develops a position or idea. Each essay is graded by two independent scorers who rate each essay on a scale of 1 to 4. These scores are added to create a raw score on this section.

Timing

You'll have 4 hours to complete the entire test. If you are only taking one or two sections of the test, you still have 4 hours. Most people find that 4 hours is ample time to get through all three sections of the test. The challenge is to keep up your energy level and focus in order to use the time remaining after completing the test to check answers and proofread the essay.

REQUIREMENTS FOR PASSING THE CBEST

Scaled scores are used for reporting CBEST results. The scores are derived from the number of questions you get right and wrong. The scores don't tell you specifically how many questions you got right or how many you got wrong. For each section scaled, scores range from 20 to 80 (20 being the lowest score possible and 80 the highest). Your score on the CBEST is derived by adding the scores on all three sections; thus, the highest possible score is 240 and the lowest possible score is 60.

California and Oregon require a total CBEST score of 123. This works out to an average of 41 on each section. However, you can score lower than 41 on a section and still pass the CBEST if you get a high enough score on another section to offset the low score. However, if you score below 37 on any section, you fail the CBEST, regardless of how high your total score was.

If you don't do as well as you had hoped, all is not lost. You can retake the test as often as you need to in order to get a passing score. See "Retaking the Test" at the end of this chapter.

TAKING THE CBEST

If you need to take the CBEST, you'll need to make some decisions. Are you going to take the computerized test or a paper-and-pencil test? When and where will you take the test? Then you need to take some actions, including registering for the test, paying your fee, and showing up at the right place and time. Below is a summary of the information you need to know. More information is available at www.cbest.nesinc.com.

Computerized Test or Paper Test?

The CTC, which oversees the CBEST, conducted a pilot of a computer-based CBEST in the 2009–2010 academic year. It is likely that CTC will move further in this direction in future years.

At the time of publication of this book, test-takers can choose to take the CBEST as a paper-and-pencil test or as a computer-based test. In the 2009–2010 academic year, an additional fee of $64 is applied for persons wishing to take the computer-based test. As long as this additional fee is in effect, it is likely that most people will continue to take the CBEST as a paper-and-pencil test. However, because the paper-and-pencil test is only administered in California and Oregon, persons from other states who can't readily travel to these states must take the computer-based test, which is administered at Pearson Professional centers nationwide.

Registering for the Test

The paper-and-pencil CBEST is administered six times per year, usually on the first or second Saturday in February, April, June, August, October, and December. Go to www.cbest.nesinc.com to find the specific dates for test administration. You can also find information about locations where the test is given on this site.

The computer-based CBEST is available during 12 testing "windows"; within each window, there are five or six days available for testing. You can schedule a time and a Pearson Professional center at which to take the test based on your schedule.

You can obtain registration information and register for the test at www.cbest.nesinc.com. The 72-page booklet "CBEST Registration Information" can be downloaded from this site or you can request that the booklet be mailed to you along with registration forms. Registration for the paper-and-pencil CBEST can be completed online or by mail. Late registration for the paper-and-pencil CBEST (after the deadline for regular registration has passed) can be done online, by mail, or by phone (800-262-5080); an additional fee applies to all late registrations. For the 2009–2010 academic year, the basic registration fee is $41 with an additional $64 for computer-based testing.

Registration for the computer-based CBEST can only be done online at www.cbest.nesinc.com. After your registration has been processed, you will be sent an e-mail message with an authorization to test. Then you'll be instructed to go to another online site (for Pearson Education) to schedule the time and place for your test.

When registering, you may also request special accommodations needed due to a disability. Alternative testing arrangements deemed reasonable and supported by documentation may be provided for test-takers who cannot take the test under standard conditions. See www.cbest.nesinc.com or the registration information booklet for more information.

On Test Day

After registration, you will receive an admission ticket that lists your test site, the test date, and the reporting time. Be sure to arrive on time and to bring the ticket with you on test day. You will also receive instructions on providing acceptable proof of identity, which you will be required to present in order to take the test. If you are at a paper-and-pencil CBEST site, your thumbprint will also be taken as part of the identity verification process. At a computer-based testing site, finger or palm scan, photo, and signature will be taken. These are required before you are allowed to take the test.

If you are taking the paper-and-pencil CBEST, you will also need to bring several sharpened no. 2 pencils with erasers. Pencils will not be supplied at the test site. (Pens are not acceptable.)

No cell phones, electronic communication devices, calculators, paper, packages or bags, and food or drink are allowed at the test center. Water is permitted in approved containers only. No smoking or use of tobacco products is allowed. If you are taking the computer-based test, you will need to store all personal items, including watches, wallets, and purses, in a locker outside the testing room.

▬▬ AFTER TAKING THE TEST

Obtaining Your Scores

If you take your CBEST on computer, your unofficial results for the reading and mathematics sections will be available at the conclusion of your test. If you take the paper-and-pencil test, your unofficial results will be posted online two to three weeks after the test date. Instructions for retrieving your scores online and the dates on which the scores will be available online can be found at www.cbest.nesinc.com or in your test registration booklet. Your official results will be mailed to you about three weeks after the test date.

Retaking the Test

You can retake the CBEST as often as you need to until a passing score is achieved. Candidates who obtain a passing score (41 or higher) on any of the three sections of the test need not repeat that section. However, it may be advantageous to repeat a section that you passed in order to reach the total score of 123 required for the entire test (see "Requirements for Passing the Test" above). The highest score you obtain on a section—no matter when you earned that score—will be the score used to compute your total CBEST score.

Whether you plan to retake all three sections or only one or two of them, the procedures and fees for test registration remain the same as for the initial registration. However, you'll receive a $4 refund if you do not take the writing test on the test date. Check the official Web site, www.cbest.nesinc.com, or the official registration booklet for more information.

CHAPTER 2

STRATEGIES TO RAISE YOUR SCORE

A good test-taking strategy is the key to doing well on the California Basic Educational Skills Test (CBEST). Knowledge of how to approach the test will give you an advantage and enable you to get your best score possible. Many of the strategies discussed below are simple and based on common sense, yet few people follow them. Now is the time to think about how to approach the test and develop your plan of attack. Don't let the test attack you and leave you surprised and wishing that you had done things differently.

This chapter describes the broad strategies you'll need to score your best. In the review chapter later in this book, you'll find specific strategies for specific types of questions.

STRATEGIES FOR PREPARING FOR THE CBEST

Being prepared for the test is the best way to ensure success. Review the content to be tested and become familiar with the test structure. This will ensure that you get your best possible score. It's also the surest way to build confidence and conquer stress. The following strategies can help you prepare for the test:

- **Develop a plan and a schedule.** In order to make the most effective use of your time, develop a study plan that is personalized for your needs. Focus on your weakest areas; the diagnostic test in Chapter 3 can help you identify these. Figure out how much time you can devote to studying for the test and then use the time you have available wisely. Map out a plan with a specific schedule of what you want to accomplish each week and stick to it.
- **Familiarize yourself with the CBEST.** Nothing should come as a surprise on test day. Knowledge of what to expect will increase your confidence and help you tackle the test. Use the practice tests in this book to become familiar with the types of questions you'll face and the instructions you'll encounter.
- **Review the content tested on the CBEST.** It's important to brush up on your math skills, especially if you haven't had a math class in a while. You can also refresh your comprehension skills for the reading test, including reading graphs and charts. Use Chapters 4 through 10 to refresh your memory regarding the content you'll need to know for the CBEST.
- **Practice taking the test.** Use the practice tests in this book and the official practice test available at www.cbest.nesinc.com to prepare for the real thing. The practice tests will help you determine if you have mastered the content and become familiar with the test. Take the practice tests under conditions that closely approximate to the actual test administration. Take as many practice tests as you can; this will build the confidence you need to master stress and succeed.

▬▬ STRATEGIES FOR THE MULTIPLE-CHOICE SECTIONS

Except for the writing section, all questions on the CBEST are in multiple-choice format, a format that you have undoubtedly seen many times before. However, multiple-choice tests are not as cut-and-dried as they might seem at first. The way in which you approach these questions will affect your test score. Plan your strategy now to ensure that you do your best. Use the following strategies when you take the practice tests:

- **Answer every question.** There is no penalty for choosing a wrong answer. Therefore, if you do not know the answer to a question, you have nothing to lose by guessing. Make sure that you answer every question. If you are taking a paper-and-pencil exam and find that you are running out of time, enter an answer for the questions that you have not tackled. With luck, you may be able to pick up a few extra points, even if your guesses are totally random.

- **Take advantage of the multiple-choice format.** All questions are multiple choice in the math and reading sections of the CBEST. This means that for every question, the correct answer is right in front of you. All you have to do is pick it out from among the four incorrect choices. Consequently, when you aren't sure of the answer, use the process of elimination to rule out incorrect answer choices. The more answers you rule out, the easier it is to make the right choice. If you're having difficulty on a math problem that involves an equation (e.g., solving for x), try plugging in different answer choices to see which one works. The answer is right there, you just need to pick it out.

- **Skip the hard questions and come back to them later.** Keep in mind that there is a time limit; don't waste time trying to figure out the answers to harder questions until you've answered the easy questions. Every question counts the same when scoring the exam. This means that you are better off spending time carefully answering the easier questions, where you are sure to pick up points. If you're really stumped by a question, skip it and come back to it later when you can devote more time to it without worrying about not finishing the easy questions. As you proceed with the test, you may come to a question or a set of answer choices that jogs your memory and helps you to answer the question(s) you skipped. When you come back to a question, it's usually not as hard as it first seemed.

- **Be careful on the answer sheet.** There is nothing more harmful to your score than mistakes in using the answer sheet. Be sure to mark the answers in the correct row and keep checking this as you go, especially when you skip questions. Also, be sure you have penciled in the answer space completely and have no stray pencil marks.

- **Go with your gut.** In cases where you are not 100 percent sure of the answer you are choosing, it is often best to go with your gut feeling and stick with your initial answer. If you decide to change that answer and pick another one, you may pick the wrong answer because you thought too much about the problem. More often than not, if you know something about the subject, your first answer is likely to be the correct one.

- **Use extra time to check your work.** If you have time at the end of the test, go back and check your work. This is the surest way to improve your score; yet many test-takers, tired by the testing process, don't do it. The CBEST is a test of endurance; don't quit if you have time to check your answers. You'll be surprised at the simple mistakes you can catch. Make sure that you have marked your answer sheet correctly. Check any calculations and make sure that they are correct. However, resist the urge to second-guess too many of your answers; this may cause you to change a correct answer to an incorrect one.

STRATEGIES FOR THE WRITING SECTION

Most of the people who fail the CBEST do so because of low scores on the writing section. If writing is not your strong point, much of your test preparation should focus on the writing section. Below are some strategies that will help you to do your best on the writing section of the CBEST.

- **Reserve plenty of time for the writing section.** Reserve at least 1 hour and 20 minutes for the writing section of the CBEST. You can't pass the essays by scribbling down a quick answer. You will need time to think and plan and then time to write a carefully worded, coherent response that communicates the point you are trying to make.
- **Think first, write later.** The biggest mistake you can make is to begin to write before you have carefully thought out your response. Successful test-takers often spend up to 10 minutes thinking, jotting down ideas, planning, and outlining before they even begin to write a response to one of the writing prompts.
- **Stay focused on the central idea you want to communicate in each essay.** An essay needs a central idea or a point that you want to get across. If there is no central idea to communicate, then there is no reason to write the essay or for someone to read it. Choose a position or idea you want to communicate and develop it with supporting information, examples, and explanations. Avoid rambling. Keep your writing focused on the key idea(s) you want to get across.
- **Outline your response before writing.** Arrange your thoughts in a logical, coherent way. A good essay develops an idea step-by-step to arrive at a conclusion. Outlining your essay is one way to ensure that the essay is logical and coherent and develops ideas to arrive at a conclusion. But don't get overly concerned about the outline itself. The outline can be rough because it is only a tool to help you write; no one else will read your outline.
- **Focus on quality, not quantity.** Your essay need not be lengthy; four or five short- to medium-length paragraphs are sufficient. The focus should be on clarity, not length. Make your points by communicating what's important without rambling or repeating yourself. Make sure that you use complete sentences, that the sentence structure is correct, and that the words you use are clear and precise. A focused, well-written essay will earn you more points than a long, meandering one.
- **Proof and edit your work.** You're not done when you get to the end of your essay. To get your best score, you need to go back and reread your essay and make sure it makes sense and that it is as clear and coherent as possible. Feel free to delete or replace words or phrases or even add a new sentence if necessary to make your idea clear. In fact, when you first write your response, leave a little room between lines or in the margin for revisions and insertions. Just make sure that all your changes are clear and legible.

■■■ STRATEGIES FOR TEST DAY (AND THE NIGHT BEFORE THE TEST)

Following are the steps you can take to ensure you'll be at your peak on test day. Remember to plan and prepare, not only for the test itself but also for the logistics of taking the test. Good planning will ensure you don't get distracted or stressed out.

1. **Know where to go.** Be sure you know where to go to take the test. Take a practice run so that you know how to get to the testing location, where to park (if you're driving), and the amount of time you'll need for the trip. If you arrive late, you are likely to start off on the wrong foot. Stressing out on the trip to the testing location will not help you control your nerves and channel your adrenaline to master the test. Most paper-and-pencil tests start at 8:00 a.m. Start out early and allow yourself plenty of time to get there.

2. **Gather the documents you'll need the night before the test.** Review the registration instructions and materials you've received to make sure that you have the required documents, including the admission ticket and the documentation needed for proof of identity (see Chapter 1 for more information). Have these items ready to go so that you're not rushing around the next morning trying to locate them. If you're taking the paper-and-pencil CBEST, don't forget the no. 2 pencils!

3. **Relax and try to get a good night's sleep the night before the test.** You may want to watch a movie or do something else to relax. Avoid cramming; it will only heighten your stress level and keep you from getting a good night's rest. Do a physical workout to burn off nervous energy if you feel wound up and unable to relax and get to sleep. Keep a positive outlook and envision yourself succeeding on the test.

4. **Eat a good breakfast.** If you normally eat a healthy breakfast, go ahead with your regular breakfast on the day of the test. Don't drastically change your eating habits or your coffee or sugar intake. Even if you don't normally eat breakfast, have a light, but healthy, breakfast so you can stay energized and alert for the 4-hour CBEST.

5. **Stay calm.** Once test day comes, you are as prepared as you are going to be. There is no point in panicking. If your heart or your mind starts to race, take deep, relaxing breaths. Banish negative thoughts and imagine yourself succeeding. If you're still stressed out, remind yourself that only your best scores will count and you can always retake the test (see Chapter 1 for more information on policies regarding retaking the test).

CHAPTER 3

DIAGNOSTIC TEST

The practice test in this chapter gives you a very good idea of what you will face on test day. It's called a diagnostic test because it helps you "diagnose" how well prepared you are right now for the real exam and what subjects you need to review and study.

All the questions on the diagnostic test are modeled after the questions in the actual California Basic Educational Skills Test (CBEST). This chapter includes the same number of questions and the same types of questions as on the actual exam. The questions cover the same topics and are designed to be at the same level of difficulty. Explanations for the answers to the multiple-choice questions are given at the end of the diagnostic test.

The diagnostic test includes separate tests for the three subject areas included on the CBEST: mathematics, reading, and writing. The questions for the reading and mathematics tests are in the multiple-choice format that you will encounter on the actual exam. For the writing test, you'll find two essay questions or writing prompts similar to the ones you'll be required to respond to on the actual exam.

This test includes an answer sheet that you should remove from the book. Use this sheet to mark your answers to the multiple-choice questions.

When you are finished with the test, check your answers against the answer key provided at the end of the diagnostic test. For any questions that you answered incorrectly or had difficulty with, carefully read the answer explanations provided at the end of this chapter. If you don't understand what you did wrong, you can use the review chapters of this book for review and further explanation.

Pinpoint your weak areas by determining the topics for which you made the most errors. This knowledge will help you focus your study as you work your way through the subject review chapters in this book. Build your study plan around the areas you most need to review and practice.

This test best helps you to gauge your test readiness if you treat it like an actual examination. Here are some hints on how to take the test under conditions similar to those of the actual exam.

- Find a 4-hour time period when you will not be interrupted.
- Fill in the bubbles on the answer sheet with a no. 2 pencil; make sure the bubble is filled in completely and that there are no stray pencil marks.
- Complete the entire test in one 4-hour session. If you want to take each subject area test contained in this diagnostic test separately, you should allocate about 1 hour and 20 minutes per test. The actual test provides 4 hours, which you can allocate to the three tests in any way you wish.

Good luck!

ANSWER SHEET

PRACTICE TEST 1: DIAGNOSTIC
Answer Sheet for Multiple-Choice Questions

READING TEST

1 Ⓐ Ⓑ Ⓒ Ⓓ Ⓔ	18 Ⓐ Ⓑ Ⓒ Ⓓ Ⓔ	35 Ⓐ Ⓑ Ⓒ Ⓓ Ⓔ
2 Ⓐ Ⓑ Ⓒ Ⓓ Ⓔ	19 Ⓐ Ⓑ Ⓒ Ⓓ Ⓔ	36 Ⓐ Ⓑ Ⓒ Ⓓ Ⓔ
3 Ⓐ Ⓑ Ⓒ Ⓓ Ⓔ	20 Ⓐ Ⓑ Ⓒ Ⓓ Ⓔ	37 Ⓐ Ⓑ Ⓒ Ⓓ Ⓔ
4 Ⓐ Ⓑ Ⓒ Ⓓ Ⓔ	21 Ⓐ Ⓑ Ⓒ Ⓓ Ⓔ	38 Ⓐ Ⓑ Ⓒ Ⓓ Ⓔ
5 Ⓐ Ⓑ Ⓒ Ⓓ Ⓔ	22 Ⓐ Ⓑ Ⓒ Ⓓ Ⓔ	39 Ⓐ Ⓑ Ⓒ Ⓓ Ⓔ
6 Ⓐ Ⓑ Ⓒ Ⓓ Ⓔ	23 Ⓐ Ⓑ Ⓒ Ⓓ Ⓔ	40 Ⓐ Ⓑ Ⓒ Ⓓ Ⓔ
7 Ⓐ Ⓑ Ⓒ Ⓓ Ⓔ	24 Ⓐ Ⓑ Ⓒ Ⓓ Ⓔ	41 Ⓐ Ⓑ Ⓒ Ⓓ Ⓔ
8 Ⓐ Ⓑ Ⓒ Ⓓ Ⓔ	25 Ⓐ Ⓑ Ⓒ Ⓓ Ⓔ	42 Ⓐ Ⓑ Ⓒ Ⓓ Ⓔ
9 Ⓐ Ⓑ Ⓒ Ⓓ Ⓔ	26 Ⓐ Ⓑ Ⓒ Ⓓ Ⓔ	43 Ⓐ Ⓑ Ⓒ Ⓓ Ⓔ
10 Ⓐ Ⓑ Ⓒ Ⓓ Ⓔ	27 Ⓐ Ⓑ Ⓒ Ⓓ Ⓔ	44 Ⓐ Ⓑ Ⓒ Ⓓ Ⓔ
11 Ⓐ Ⓑ Ⓒ Ⓓ Ⓔ	28 Ⓐ Ⓑ Ⓒ Ⓓ Ⓔ	45 Ⓐ Ⓑ Ⓒ Ⓓ Ⓔ
12 Ⓐ Ⓑ Ⓒ Ⓓ Ⓔ	29 Ⓐ Ⓑ Ⓒ Ⓓ Ⓔ	46 Ⓐ Ⓑ Ⓒ Ⓓ Ⓔ
13 Ⓐ Ⓑ Ⓒ Ⓓ Ⓔ	30 Ⓐ Ⓑ Ⓒ Ⓓ Ⓔ	47 Ⓐ Ⓑ Ⓒ Ⓓ Ⓔ
14 Ⓐ Ⓑ Ⓒ Ⓓ Ⓔ	31 Ⓐ Ⓑ Ⓒ Ⓓ Ⓔ	48 Ⓐ Ⓑ Ⓒ Ⓓ Ⓔ
15 Ⓐ Ⓑ Ⓒ Ⓓ Ⓔ	32 Ⓐ Ⓑ Ⓒ Ⓓ Ⓔ	49 Ⓐ Ⓑ Ⓒ Ⓓ Ⓔ
16 Ⓐ Ⓑ Ⓒ Ⓓ Ⓔ	33 Ⓐ Ⓑ Ⓒ Ⓓ Ⓔ	50 Ⓐ Ⓑ Ⓒ Ⓓ Ⓔ
17 Ⓐ Ⓑ Ⓒ Ⓓ Ⓔ	34 Ⓐ Ⓑ Ⓒ Ⓓ Ⓔ	

MATHEMATICS TEST

1 Ⓐ Ⓑ Ⓒ Ⓓ Ⓔ	18 Ⓐ Ⓑ Ⓒ Ⓓ Ⓔ	35 Ⓐ Ⓑ Ⓒ Ⓓ Ⓔ
2 Ⓐ Ⓑ Ⓒ Ⓓ Ⓔ	19 Ⓐ Ⓑ Ⓒ Ⓓ Ⓔ	36 Ⓐ Ⓑ Ⓒ Ⓓ Ⓔ
3 Ⓐ Ⓑ Ⓒ Ⓓ Ⓔ	20 Ⓐ Ⓑ Ⓒ Ⓓ Ⓔ	37 Ⓐ Ⓑ Ⓒ Ⓓ Ⓔ
4 Ⓐ Ⓑ Ⓒ Ⓓ Ⓔ	21 Ⓐ Ⓑ Ⓒ Ⓓ Ⓔ	38 Ⓐ Ⓑ Ⓒ Ⓓ Ⓔ
5 Ⓐ Ⓑ Ⓒ Ⓓ Ⓔ	22 Ⓐ Ⓑ Ⓒ Ⓓ Ⓔ	39 Ⓐ Ⓑ Ⓒ Ⓓ Ⓔ
6 Ⓐ Ⓑ Ⓒ Ⓓ Ⓔ	23 Ⓐ Ⓑ Ⓒ Ⓓ Ⓔ	40 Ⓐ Ⓑ Ⓒ Ⓓ Ⓔ
7 Ⓐ Ⓑ Ⓒ Ⓓ Ⓔ	24 Ⓐ Ⓑ Ⓒ Ⓓ Ⓔ	41 Ⓐ Ⓑ Ⓒ Ⓓ Ⓔ
8 Ⓐ Ⓑ Ⓒ Ⓓ Ⓔ	25 Ⓐ Ⓑ Ⓒ Ⓓ Ⓔ	42 Ⓐ Ⓑ Ⓒ Ⓓ Ⓔ
9 Ⓐ Ⓑ Ⓒ Ⓓ Ⓔ	26 Ⓐ Ⓑ Ⓒ Ⓓ Ⓔ	43 Ⓐ Ⓑ Ⓒ Ⓓ Ⓔ
10 Ⓐ Ⓑ Ⓒ Ⓓ Ⓔ	27 Ⓐ Ⓑ Ⓒ Ⓓ Ⓔ	44 Ⓐ Ⓑ Ⓒ Ⓓ Ⓔ
11 Ⓐ Ⓑ Ⓒ Ⓓ Ⓔ	28 Ⓐ Ⓑ Ⓒ Ⓓ Ⓔ	45 Ⓐ Ⓑ Ⓒ Ⓓ Ⓔ
12 Ⓐ Ⓑ Ⓒ Ⓓ Ⓔ	29 Ⓐ Ⓑ Ⓒ Ⓓ Ⓔ	46 Ⓐ Ⓑ Ⓒ Ⓓ Ⓔ
13 Ⓐ Ⓑ Ⓒ Ⓓ Ⓔ	30 Ⓐ Ⓑ Ⓒ Ⓓ Ⓔ	47 Ⓐ Ⓑ Ⓒ Ⓓ Ⓔ
14 Ⓐ Ⓑ Ⓒ Ⓓ Ⓔ	31 Ⓐ Ⓑ Ⓒ Ⓓ Ⓔ	48 Ⓐ Ⓑ Ⓒ Ⓓ Ⓔ
15 Ⓐ Ⓑ Ⓒ Ⓓ Ⓔ	32 Ⓐ Ⓑ Ⓒ Ⓓ Ⓔ	49 Ⓐ Ⓑ Ⓒ Ⓓ Ⓔ
16 Ⓐ Ⓑ Ⓒ Ⓓ Ⓔ	33 Ⓐ Ⓑ Ⓒ Ⓓ Ⓔ	50 Ⓐ Ⓑ Ⓒ Ⓓ Ⓔ
17 Ⓐ Ⓑ Ⓒ Ⓓ Ⓔ	34 Ⓐ Ⓑ Ⓒ Ⓓ Ⓔ	

1 **1**

READING TEST

TEST DIRECTIONS: Read each passage and answer the multiple-choice questions that follow. For each question, choose the one best answer from the answer choices provided. Mark each answer on the answer sheet provided.

You may work on the questions in any order you choose. You have 4 hours to complete all three sections (mathematics, reading, and writing) of the CBEST.

1 ██ **1**

Read the passage below and answer the four questions that follow.

Lie out in the sun too much today—and get skin cancer 20 years from now. Smoke too many cigarettes now—and get lung cancer decades down the road. _____ there is potentially a third danger to add to this list: be exposed to too much lead, pesticides, or mercury now—and have your aging brain become seriously confused during your senior years.

A new area of medical research is one that studies how exposure to toxic elements in younger years can result in serious health problems in senior years. It is difficult to research these problems because the only way to do so is to observe people over many years to determine results. _____, there is increasing evidence that a part of what has been called normal aging might, in fact, be due to exposures to toxic substances such as lead.

1. Which words, if inserted *in order* into the blank lines in the reading selection, would best help the reader understand the idea the writer wants to communicate?
   A. However; Nowadays
   B. So; Finally
   C. As a result; Without a doubt
   D. On the other hand; Furthermore
   E. Now; However

2. What is the best title for this passage?
   A. There Is Lead Everywhere
   B. The Difficulties of Identifying Long-Term Health Threats
   C. Toxins Today, Health Problems Tomorrow
   D. Avoid the Sun—and Cigarette Smoke
   E. Lead—Even More Dangerous than Sun Exposure

3. You might infer from this passage that
   A. people might be exposed to lead and other toxic substances more than they realize.
   B. doctors are increasingly concerned about the natural process of aging.
   C. lead is the most serious toxin affecting the aging process.
   D. blood tests are the best way to measure an individual's lifetime lead exposure.
   E. cigarettes are more dangerous than too much sun exposure.

4. Why is the effect of exposure to known toxins hard to study?
   A. It is difficult to trace in the body.
   B. Today, exposure to lead and other toxins is no longer a serious problem.
   C. Toxins are discarded from the body at a rate that is too rapid to measure.
   D. Scientists have to observe exposure to toxins in subjects over a long time period.
   E. It is not possible to identify many of the toxins present in the body using medical tests.

Read the passage below and answer the three questions that follow.

[1]There are several disadvantages associated with living in a city apartment rather than a house. [2]The lack of space is the most important of these, because most city apartments are considerably smaller than houses. [3]Privacy is another problem. [4]Even if one lives in an apartment alone, people who share a building can hear each other closing doors, walking up stairs, and moving furniture around. [5]Some neighbors can be loud! [6]However, houses have their own disadvantages. [7]Lawn care, for example, is generally not something that is expected of apartment dwellers, but homeowners and even tenants of rental homes generally have to do some lawn maintenance in the summer months. [8]And a house has more space to be cleaned and, if you are the homeowner, more systems that need to be maintained.

5. Which of the following sentences is least relevant to the development of the paragraph?
   A. Sentence 3
   B. Sentence 5
   C. Sentence 6
   D. Sentence 7
   E. Sentence 8

6. Which of the following sentences expresses an opinion rather than a fact?
   A. Sentence 2
   B. Sentence 3
   C. Sentence 6
   D. Sentence 7
   E. Sentence 8

7. What is the author's purpose in writing this paragraph?
   A. Convince people to live in a house rather than an apartment.
   B. Provide advice on problems of living in an apartment in the city.
   C. Convince people to live in an apartment rather than a house.
   D. Explain the responsibilities of home ownership to first-time home buyers.
   E. Compare the advantages and disadvantages of living in an apartment to living in a house.

GO ON TO THE NEXT PAGE.

1 ███████████████████████████████████ **1**

Refer to the pie chart below to answer the question that follows.

Ethnic Composition of State X

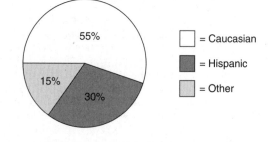

8. According to the pie chart above, what is state X's second largest ethnic group?

A. Caucasian
B. White and Other combined
C. Other
D. Hispanic and Other combined
E. Hispanic

Read the passage below and answer the five questions that follow.

Science involving particles no greater than 100 nanometers in length is called *nanotechnology*. A *nanometer* is one 100 billionth of a meter in length, or about 10 times the length of a hydrogen atom.

Nanotechnology is often referred to as the "Next Big Thing" that will make the Internet revolution *pale* in significance. Nanotechnology is already used to make a variety of new and improved consumer products, from televisions and computer monitors to wrinkle cream and sunblock. Scientists working with nano-sized particles are developing super-fast and energy-efficient computer chips, ultra-strong fabrics and building materials, and, more crucially, faster-acting medicines for the treatment of diseases.

When it comes to human health, however, nanotechnology might prove more hazardous than helpful. Studies with laboratory animals suggest that contact with nano-sized particles can cause various forms of cancer. These particles are so small that they easily enter a person's bloodstream and central nervous system. Only time and further medical research will tell whether the full potential of nanotechnology will be realized.

9. A hydrogen atom is

A. about 1 nanometer in length.
B. longer than a nanometer.
C. impossible to measure in comparison to a nanometer.
D. larger than a non-sized particle.
E. shorter than a nanometer.

10. As used in the passage, the word *pale* most nearly means

A. shrink
B. boast
C. faster
D. continue
E. expand

11. The author implies that in the future nanotechnology may play its most important role in the

A. development of consumer products.
B. exploration of outer space.
C. development of faster computer processors.
D. treatment of medical problems.
E. development of cosmetics.

12. According to the passage, nanotechnology is now used to develop

A. cosmetics
B. genetically modified grains
C. alcoholic beverages
D. household cleaning products
E. genetically modified soybeans

13. The author seems worried about

A. the safety of scientists who work with nano-sized particles.
B. the use of nanotechnology in agribusiness.
C. government putting a stop to nanotechnology research.
D. the use of nanotechnology to make weapons of mass destruction.
E. the long-term impact of nanotechnology on human health.

Read the passage below and answer the four questions that follow.

When I was young I used to think that older people recalled their youth as something seen through a haze. _____. Although I am now an old man, the last years that I spent in my native land and my first years in America come back to me with the *clarity* of yesterday.

14. Which sentence, if inserted into the blank line in the selection above, would best fit the development of the paragraph?

A. I know better now.
B. That may well be true.
C. That haze now envelops my memories.
D. In fact, many senior citizens have problems remembering things.
E. I now find this to be correct in most instances.

GO ON TO THE NEXT PAGE.

1   1

15. As it is used in the passage, the word *clarity* is best defined as

   A. clearness
   B. transparency
   C. perfection
   D. colorfulness
   E. reflection

16. The author of the paragraph

   A. was born in the United States and spent his first years in America.
   B. apparently immigrated to the United States when he was still quite young.
   C. moved back to his native land when still quite young.
   D. is a Native American.
   E. was born in a foreign country and visited the United States for 10 days.

17. What is the main idea of the paragraph?

   A. Older people have hazy memories.
   B. Older people are hazy about where they were born.
   C. Older people can often clearly remember their youth.
   D. Older people can clearly remember only yesterday.
   E. Older people have trouble remembering most things.

Read the passage below and answer the five questions that follow.

   The last known case of the smallpox virus occurred in 1978. However, the world is not necessarily rid of the virus forever; it lives on in science laboratories, and the threat of bioterrorism today has caused new concerns about a smallpox epidemic.

   Smallpox originated in Africa. The virus traveled to Europe from Arabia via Egypt. The first English-language description of the disease is in an Anglo-Saxon manuscript written during the tenth century. The name "smallpox" was given to the disease in the sixteenth century to distinguish it from chickenpox and from the Great Pox, or syphilis, both of which had already spread across Europe.

   Smallpox bacteria could be carried through the air for considerable distances and could cling for long periods to clothes, books, furniture, and other items. Europeans came to accept an attack as *inevitable*. In Russia, 2 million people died from smallpox in one year. At the end of the eighteenth century, so many faces were permanently pitted from severe smallpox that any woman who had no smallpox marks was considered beautiful. It's no wonder that our public health officials today are so worried.

18. According to the passage, smallpox was

   A. easily preventable.
   B. rarely fatal.
   C. primarily a women's disease.
   D. transmitted through the air.
   E. first diagnosed in England.

19. As used in the passage, the word *inevitable* most nearly means

   A. painful
   B. powerful
   C. certain
   D. widespread
   E. possible

20. Which of the following questions does the passage best answer?

   A. How many people have died from smallpox?
   B. Why did people fear smallpox?
   C. Why is smallpox no longer a common disease?
   D. How did smallpox spread to Russia?
   E. Was smallpox painful?

21. The name "smallpox" was given to that virus

   A. in an Anglo-Saxon manuscript.
   B. to distinguish it from syphilis.
   C. before chickenpox became a problem.
   D. because it affected children.
   E. because most people infected had very few marks from it.

22. In the passage, the author's underlying purpose is to

   A. caution
   B. summarize
   C. predict
   D. amuse
   E. argue

Review the table of contents below and answer the two questions that follow.

GO ON TO THE NEXT PAGE.

1 ■■■■■■■■■■■■■■■■■■■■■■■■■■■■■■■■■ **1**

23. A reader is looking for information about which foods are good sources of calcium. The reader could probably find this information most efficiently by looking in which part of the book?
    A. Part One
    B. Part Two
    C. Part Three
    D. Glossary
    E. Index

24. In which part of the book would information about the nutritional value of chicken most likely be found?
    A. Part One
    B. Part Two
    C. Part Three
    D. Part Four
    E. Part Five

Read the passage below and answer the four questions that follow.

   It sounds contradictory, but here is some new advice for people who are feeling unusually tired: get out and get some exercise. Studies have shown that regular, low-impact workouts such as short strolls or brief bike rides can help increase overall energy levels by 20% and decrease fatigue levels by 65%. In other words, if you are feeling tired, the best way to feel more energetic is to get some exercise.
   This advice is based on a study done at the University of Georgia. Three dozen people who did not get any kind of regular exercise yet consistently felt exhausted were divided into three groups. One group did not exercise at all. A second group worked out fairly intensively on an exercise bike three times a week. The third group also worked out but at a slower pace. Of the two groups that exercised, both reported a 20% increase in energy levels. However, the group that exercised at a more leisurely pace stated that they experienced far less fatigue than the high-intensity group.
   This was not the first study to point out a link between regular exercise and increased energy levels. Clearly, it is time to get off the couch and onto the *track*.

25. What is the main idea of this passage?
    A. Low-impact exercise is always better for people than intensive exercise.
    B. The best way to address fatigue is to get out and exercise hard every single day.
    C. If people feel tired, they can best improve their energy levels with regular exercise.
    D. Low-impact exercise helps people with serious conditions such as heart disease and cancer.
    E. Intensive exercise will cause fatigue.

26. According to the passage, which group experienced the greatest benefit from this experiment?
    A. The group that did not exercise at all
    B. The group that rode exercise bikes intensively
    C. The group that stuck to low-impact exercise
    D. The group that took additional daily naps
    E. The group that rode exercise bikes intensively and the group that stuck to low-impact exercise

27. What type of people participated in this study on fatigue and exercise?
    A. Athletes wanting to get more rest
    B. Sedentary people who were always tired
    C. Scientists interested in proving their various theories
    D. Patients with life-threatening diseases who were exhausted
    E. Doctors interested in curing heart disease

28. The word *track* as used in the last paragraph of the passage can best be defined as
    A. keep a record of.
    B. a new attitude.
    C. follow carefully.
    D. a paved, circular path.
    E. following a trail of.

Read the passage below and answer the five questions that follow.

   We've all known people who are convinced that their pet dog or cat possesses extraordinary intelligence for its species, as demonstrated by an ability to speak, to perform arithmetic, or some other intellectual feat that we humans generally assume is reserved for ourselves.
   These people can learn a lesson from the story of Hans the horse, whose owner had convinced not just himself but many other people as well that Hans could add and subtract numbers and even multiply them. Hans would signal his answers by repeatedly stomping his hoof. Hans even fooled the scientists . . . except one, who tried recruiting questioners who were bad at math and didn't know the answers to their own questions. The results: Hans consistently gave *wrong* answers for these questioners!
   As it turns out, Hans *was* intelligent . . . very intelligent. But could he perform arithmetic? Of course not. Hans had

GO ON TO THE NEXT PAGE.

1   1

become an expert at reading body language! When Hans reached the correct number, every questioner who knew the correct answer responded with a subtle, involuntary change in posture, head position, or breathing. Hans had learned to pay close attention, no doubt largely because his owner rewarded him with a treat whenever he gave a correct answer.

29. Hans's owner believed he had trained Hans to
    A. accept treats from strangers who asked him to perform arithmetic.
    B. observe the body language of a person asking him for an answer to an arithmetic problem.
    C. perform simple arithmetic such as addition and subtraction.
    D. stomp his hoof upon the owner's command.
    E. pay close attention to questioners.

30. Which of the following is probably NOT a reason that Hans learned to respond correctly to arithmetic questions?
    A. Hans was extremely intelligent for a horse.
    B. Hans was punished for giving wrong answers.
    C. Hans was very observant of the humans around him.
    D. Hans was rewarded for his behavior.
    E. Hans liked treats.

31. The article's author seems skeptical about the
    A. claims of people who brag about the intelligence of their pets.
    B. intelligence of scientists who study animals.
    C. claim that only humans can develop high-level language skills.
    D. ability of animals to understand the body language of humans.
    E. ability of animals to respond consistently to rewards.

32. The article strongly supports the claim that animals
    A. pay close attention to their owners' behavior.
    B. are more intelligent than most people think.
    C. can be trained to do almost anything.
    D. mimic the behavior of their owners.
    E. have limited range of responses to rewards.

33. This article is most likely to appear in a magazine catering to
    A. veterinarians
    B. pet owners
    C. horse trainers
    D. zookeepers
    E. zoologists

Read the passage below and answer the three questions that follow.

According to the American Society for Aesthetic Plastic Surgery, 11.7 million cosmetic procedures were performed in the United States in 2007. _____.
The most popular surgical cosmetic procedure was liposuction, and the most common nonsurgical cosmetic procedure was Botox injections.

Between 1997 and 2007, the number of regular surgical procedures went up by 114%, but the number of nonsurgical procedures went up by an amazing 754%. Although men still make up less than 10% of the patients undergoing cosmetic procedures, their numbers are growing at a faster rate than women's.

34. Which sentence, if inserted into the blank line in the selection above, would best fit the development of the paragraph?
    A. The television show *Nip/Tuck* helped people understand and accept cosmetic surgery.
    B. However, these figures may not be reliable.
    C. Cosmetic procedures can be very expensive, so only wealthier patients can afford them.
    D. Cosmetic procedures are generally divided into two broad categories: those that require surgery and those that do not.
    E. Cosmetic procedures are not usually covered by health insurance plans.

35. The author is most likely addressing which of the following audiences?
    A. Men who might not otherwise consider cosmetic surgery
    B. People trying to decide whether or not to have cosmetic surgery
    C. Cosmetic surgeons
    D. People interested in trends in American society and culture
    E. Women who want to feel better about having had cosmetic surgery

36. What is the most common surgical cosmetic procedure?
    A. Botox injections
    B. Eyelid surgery
    C. Liposuction
    D. Laser hair removal
    E. Face lift

37. Which of the following best presents the organizational structure of the main topics addressed in this passage?
    A. I. An introduction to cosmetic procedures
       II. Growing use of cosmetic procedures
    B. I. Official statistics on cosmetic procedures
       II. Statistics for men and women compared
    C. I. Surgical cosmetic procedures
       II. Nonsurgical cosmetic procedures
    D. I. Rapid growth of cosmetic procedures
       II. Even more rapid growth of nonsurgical cosmetic procedures
    E. I. Official statistics on cosmetic procedures
       II. Even more rapid growth of nonsurgical cosmetic procedures

GO ON TO THE NEXT PAGE.

1 ███████████████████████████████████████ **1**

Review the excerpt from a book's index below and answer the two questions that follow.

```
Trees, 121–175
     Classification, 121–124
          Carboniferous Period, 125–132
               tree ferns, 126–127
               horsetails, 127–128
               lycophytes, 129
          Triassic Period, 133–142
               conifers, 134–135
               ginkgos, 136–138
               cycads, 139–141
               other gymnosperms, 142
          Cretaceous Period, 143–155
               flowering plants, 145–150
               leafy trees, 151–155
     Flower-producing trees, 170–175
     Fruit trees, 164–169
     State trees, 156–163
Tree Farms, 176–188
     types of wood, 178–181
     uses, 181–188
Tree Ferns, 189–201
```

38. Which of the following best describes the organizational pattern used in the section of the book dealing with individual tree species?
    A. By physical characteristics
    B. By scientific name
    C. By size
    D. By region
    E. By scientific period

39. On which page should one look to find information about growing trees in large quantities?
    A. 181–188
    B. 189–201
    C. 145–150
    D. 164–169
    E. 129

Read the passage below and answer the three questions that follow.

It wasn't very long ago that environmentalists were a frequent target of public ridicule; however, now the idea that pollution and carbon produced by humans can have a big impact on Earth's environment is much more widely accepted. One reason for this could be that eco-friendliness has been taught in many schools for so long now that today's young adults grew up with an awareness of environmental issues that their parents didn't have. Another reason could be that the amount of media attention devoted to these issues has increased, thanks in part to celebrities and other public figures who have

espoused this cause. Of course, still another reason could be that on a global scale, world leaders are taking more steps than ever before to lessen humanity's negative impact on air, water, climate, and animal populations. Whatever the reason, environmental issues are coming to the forefront as a topic of serious public debate.

40. With which of the following statements would the author be most likely to agree?
    A. Environmentalism is easy to ridicule because it is based on unproven science.
    B. Everyone now agrees that environmental issues are important.
    C. Media attention is not usually helpful to environmentalists.
    D. World leaders are taking more steps than they have in the past to protect the environment.
    E. Environmental issues are only addressed by politicians during election seasons.

41. As used in the passage, what does the word *espoused* mean?
    A. Married
    B. Refused
    C. Accepted
    D. Brushed aside
    E. Promoted

42. The author probably feels
    A. sad that answers probably cannot be found to environmental problems.
    B. despondent that more is not being done to help the environment.
    C. glad that environmental concerns are being taken more seriously than before.
    D. angry that people are not educated better about environmental issues.
    E. disappointed that environmentalists used to be mocked.

Read the passage below and answer the five questions that follow.

Margarine, a butter substitute marketed today for cholesterol-conscious eaters, has a long and controversial history. It was created in response to a prize being offered in 1869 by Emperor Napolean Bonaparte for a butter substitute that could be produced cheaply for the soldiers and lower classes. The winner was a substance called oleomargarine, invented by French chemist Hippolyte Mège-Mouriès. The name was eventually shortened to margarine.

The dairy industry reacted with vigorous force against the margarine trade in many countries; the sale of margarine was banned or heavily taxed by most U.S. states almost as soon as it was introduced. However, the most

GO ON TO THE NEXT PAGE.

1 ████████████████████████████ **1**

effective measure taken against margarine has been to control the color. Margarine is nearly white by nature, which makes it less appealing to consumers who are used to yellow butter. Prohibitions on selling colored margarine existed well into the twentieth century in the United States, though margarine producers fought back by selling color tablets that could be worked into the margarine at home.

43. According to the passage, who would be a likely consumer of margarine in Napolean's day?

   A. The French navy
   B. The royal classes
   C. Visiting dignitaries
   D. Citizens of Pennsylvania
   E. The upper classes

44. According to the passage, who would most likely object to margarine being widely available to consumers in the United States?

   A. A corn farmer
   B. A policeman
   C. A sharecropper
   D. A dairy farmer
   E. A doctor

45. According to the passage, which of the following makes margarine less appealing?

   A. The ban on its sale and production
   B. Its color
   C. Its French origins
   D. Its taste and texture
   E. Its level of trans saturated fats

46. The author is most likely a

   A. student writing a research paper on margarine.
   B. dietician writing an article about the dangers of margarine.
   C. heart patient writing a plan for lowering his cholesterol.
   D. chemist writing an analysis on the production of margarine.
   E. representative of the dairy industry.

47. Which of the following is the best title for the passage?

   A. Margarine: A Colorful Past
   B. Dietary Guidelines for Lowering Cholesterol
   C. The Dangers of Artificial Foods
   D. Napolean's Big Contest
   E. Margarine vs. Butter

Read the passage below and answer the three questions that follow.

Without a doubt, one of the biggest risks to the elderly today is falling. It is also one of the most common accidents that people age 65 and older experience. Some receive just a few bumps and bruises, while others are hurt so badly that they cannot ever fully recover.

U.S. health officials surveyed thousands of elderly people and found that approximately one in six Americans have fallen in the past three months. A third of these people sustained considerable injuries, including the most dreaded break of all, a hip fracture. Approximately 16,000 people even died from the injuries they suffered, whereas even more were left completely disabled. Centers for Disease Control and Prevention (CDC) epidemiologist Judy Stevens stated, "It's a tremendous public health problem because so many older adults are affected."

Along with an admonition to move slowly and carefully, the CDC also recommends that the elderly get enough gentle exercise or physical therapy to help strengthen their muscles and improve their balance. This not only will reduce the number of falls but also give a real boost to older adults' self-esteem.

48. What is this passage primarily about?

   A. Most falls experienced by the elderly are either disabling or fatal.
   B. Falling is one of the biggest health risks for older people.
   C. Elderly people's self-confidence is threatened by falling.
   D. The CDC claims that regular exercise will help prevent falls.
   E. Hip fractures are the most prevalent injury among the elderly who experience a fall.

49. Why does the author include a quote from a CDC official?

   A. To support the basic idea of the passage
   B. To provide a controversial point of view
   C. To demonstrate current and relevant statistics
   D. To show that treatment for falls is readily available
   E. To provide a differing opinion from the main point of the passage

50. Gentle exercise is recommended to do all of the following EXCEPT

   A. improve balance.
   B. reduce the number of falls.
   C. maintain proper weight.
   D. boost overall self-esteem.
   E. strengthen muscles.

MATHEMATICS TEST

TEST DIRECTIONS: Carefully read the multiple-choice questions that follow. For each question, choose the one best answer from the answer choices provided. Mark each answer on the answer sheet provided.

You may work on the questions in any order you choose. You have 4 hours to complete all three sections (reading, mathematics, and writing) of the CBEST.

2 ████████████████████████████████████ **2**

1. Karen's average score for two tests is 90. What score must Karen earn on a third test to raise her average to 92?

   A. 96
   B. 93
   C. 95
   D. 94
   E. 97

2. Linda is buying a remnant of fabric that is marked $12.00, but there is a sale at the fabric store and everything is 30% off. How much will the remnant cost? Assume there is no sales tax.

   A. $3.60
   B. $4.00
   C. $8.00
   D. $8.40
   E. $8.50

3. If 1 mile is equivalent to 1.6 kilometers, then 10 kilometers is equivalent to

   A. 9.2 miles-
   B. 16 miles-
   C. 1.6 miles-
   D. 6.25 miles-
   E. 6.3 miles-

4. Which of the following is the most appropriate unit for expressing the space inside the trunk of a car?

   A. Feet
   B. Square feet
   C. Cubic feet
   D. Square inches
   E. Inches

5. There are 16 ounces in 1 pound. If 30 ounces of coffee beans are removed from a 5-pound bag of coffee beans, the new weight of the bag of coffee beans is

   A. 50 ounces.
   B. 20 ounces.
   C. 40 ounces.
   D. 60 ounces.
   E. 70 ounces.

6. What is the total unit area of the figure below?

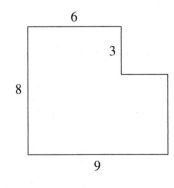

   A. 52
   B. 72
   C. 68
   D. 57
   E. 63

7. If you increase the perimeter of a square by 50%, you increase its area by

   A. 200%-
   B. 50%-
   C. 100%-
   D. 125%-
   E. 75%-

8. Jane started her stamp collection exactly one year ago, and in that time, she has collected 132 stamps. On average, how many stamps has she collected per month?

   A. 10
   B. 11
   C. 12
   D. 20
   E. 13

9. If Melanie can complete 6 forms in 15 minutes, how long will it take her to complete 30 forms?

   A. 12 minutes
   B. 60 minutes
   C. 75 minutes
   D. 120 minutes
   E. 85 minutes

10. Among 10 playing cards, 2 are spades, 1 is a heart, 3 are diamonds, and the rest are clubs. What is the probability of randomly selecting a card that is a club?

    A. $\dfrac{3}{10}$

    B. $\dfrac{1}{3}$

    C. $\dfrac{2}{5}$

    D. $\dfrac{1}{2}$

    E. $\dfrac{3}{5}$

11. Of 27 animals at the zoo, 15 are monkeys. Which of the following fractions expresses the ratio of monkeys to all other animals at the zoo?

    A. 5:4
    B. 5:9
    C. 4:5
    D. 4:3
    E. 5:14

GO ON TO THE NEXT PAGE.

2 ███ **2**

12. There are 8,751 students in the school district and 832 teachers and administrators. How many more students are there than teachers and administrators?
    A. 8,129
    B. 8,919
    C. 9,229
    D. 9,538
    E. 7,919

13. $3.98 \times 0.72 =$
    A. 3.26
    B. 2.8656
    C. 4.7
    D. 5.0293
    E. 3.7

14. $3.8 - 0.38 =$
    A. 3.42
    B. 3.5
    C. 3.58
    D. 3.3
    E. 3.35

15. A teacher assessed the performance of her class of 15 students on a particular assignment and noted the following distribution of grades:

    {94, 71, 68, 83, 80, 86, 76, 86, 91, 97, 88, 77, 85, 70, 78}

    What is the median score on the assignment?
    A. 80
    B. 83
    C. 85
    D. 86
    E. 84

16. The expression below

    $$-342 + (-131) + 56$$

    is equivalent to which one of the following?
    A. −529
    B. −155
    C. 267
    D. −417
    E. 155

17. On a cold winter day, the low temperature was −6° and the high temperature was 11°. What was the average of the low and high temperatures?
    A. 2.5°
    B. 0.5°
    C. 1.5°
    D. −0.5°
    E. 0.25°

18. Each of 24 candies in a box is either chewy or hard. If 9 candies are chewy, how many hard candies alone must be removed from the box in order for it to contain the same number of hard candies and chewy candies?
    A. 9
    B. 12
    C. 6
    D. 15
    E. 7

19. The number 5 is what percent of 40?
    A. 8%
    B. 12.5%
    C. 80%
    D. 125%
    E. 1.25%

20. $4^{5}/_{6} - 2^{3}/_{4} =$
    A. $\dfrac{12}{25}$
    B. $\dfrac{25}{11}$
    C. $\dfrac{29}{6}$
    D. $\dfrac{11}{12}$
    E. $\dfrac{25}{12}$

21. If Andy receives 20% of the retail price on each of his published books, how much does he make on a book that retails for $35?
    A. $5
    B. $6
    C. $14
    D. $28
    E. $7

22. After surveying her fellow students in the teacher education program, Amber has found that five out of seven students are planning to become teachers and two out of seven want to become counselors or administrators. If the number of classmates who want to be teachers is 30, how many students want to become counselors or administrators?
    A. 10
    B. 12
    C. 15
    D. 18
    E. 16

23. At a 12% annual interest rate, how much interest is earned on $500 in one year?
    A. $60.00
    B. $12.00
    C. $4.00
    D. $9.00
    E. $14.00

GO ON TO THE NEXT PAGE.

2 ████████████████████████████████ **2**

24. A rectangular plot of land with a length of 150 feet has an area of 12,000 square feet. The width of the plot is
    A. 80 feet.
    B. 100 feet.
    C. 65 feet.
    D. 135 feet.
    E. 95 feet.

25. A train left Station A at 12:30 p.m. and arrived at Station B at 3:00 p.m. If the train's average speed was 40 miles per hour, how many miles did the train travel?
    A. 120
    B. 80
    C. 90
    D. 100
    E. 110

26. Dan and Stephanie are making cookies for a school bake sale. If they are making two thirds as many oatmeal raisin cookies as chocolate chip and they are making 60 oatmeal raisin cookies, how many cookies are they making in all?
    A. 80
    B. 90
    C. 150
    D. 180
    E. 130

27. If $3 + 4x = 23$, what is the value of x?
    A. 2
    B. 3
    C. 4
    D. 5
    E. 6

28. Theresa drove 3 miles to the grocery store, another 2 miles to the dry cleaner, and then returned home. How much time did her errands take her?

    Which piece of information is necessary to solve this problem?
    A. The amount of time it took for Theresa to drive from the dry cleaner to her home
    B. The gas mileage of Theresa's car
    C. Whether the route to the grocery store and the dry cleaner overlapped
    D. The amount of time it took for Theresa to drive from the grocery store to the dry cleaner
    E. How fast Theresa was driving

29. A deli refrigerator is filled with 86 sodas. There are 43 colas, 22 lemon-lime sodas, and 21 orange sodas. By the end of the day, 57 sodas have been sold.

    Which of the following facts can be determined from the information given above?
    A. The cost of a soda
    B. The number of colas sold
    C. The number of orange sodas sold

    D. The total number of sodas placed in the refrigerator when the deli opened at the beginning of the day
    E. The minimum number of colas sold

30. An engineer designed a car that runs on water instead of gasoline. If water costs $1.25 per gallon, how much will it cost to drive the car 50 miles?

    What information is required to solve this problem?
    A. The cost of water compared to the cost of gasoline and the car's water mileage
    B. The car's water mileage
    C. The number of gallons the car's tank can hold
    D. The car's water mileage and the number of gallons the car's tank can hold
    E. The car's gas mileage

31. If a soda costs S cents and a burger costs B dollars, which of the following represents the cost of one burger and one soda, in cents?
    A. $B + 100S$
    B. $100(S + B)$
    C. $100B + S$
    D. $S + B$
    E. $100S + B$

32. If the number of babies born in a certain maternity ward in January is five more than twice the number born in February, which of the following mathematical statements reflects this relationship?
    A. J = 2 + 5F
    B. J = (5 + 2)F
    C. J = 5 + 2F
    D. J = (2 + 5)F
    E. J = 5F + 2F

33. Melina's theater group is setting up chairs for a school production. They are expecting 120 people. Each row fits eight chairs and they want to add two rows of chairs in case more people show up than expected. Which expression below represents the number of rows they need to make in relation to the number of people if R stands for the number of rows and P for the number of people?
    A. R = P/8 + 2R
    B. R = (P + 2R) ÷ 8
    C. R = P/8 + 2
    D. R = P/8 + 2R/8
    E. R = P/8 + R

GO ON TO THE NEXT PAGE.

2 ████████████████████████████████ **2**

34. The chart below shows a relationship between a and b. Refer to the chart to find the answer to the question that follows.

a	b
4	10
5	12
6	
7	16

Given the relationship between a and b shown above, what would be the number that fits in the blank space in column b of the chart?

- **A.** 15
- **B.** 14
- **C.** 16
- **D.** 18
- **E.** 17

35. If Stacy drinks 25% of a 1-pint carton of milk and then later drinks 25% of the remaining milk, how many ounces of milk are left? (1 pint = 16 ounces)

- **A.** 11
- **B.** 9
- **C.** 8
- **D.** 10
- **E.** 12

36. Which of the statements below is correct?

- **A.** $14.2 > 14.18 > 14.111$
- **B.** $14.2 < 14.18 < 14.111$
- **C.** $14.111 > 14.18 > 14.2$
- **D.** $14.111 > 14.2 > 14.18$
- **E.** $14.111 > 14.2 > 14.15$

37. Which of the answer choices, when entered into the blank box below, makes the statement above a correct one?

$$\frac{2}{3} > \square > \frac{1}{4}$$

- **A.** $\frac{4}{6}$
- **B.** $\frac{1}{5}$
- **C.** $\frac{6}{18}$
- **D.** $\frac{3}{4}$
- **E.** $\frac{1}{3}$

38. If $a + 2b = b$, then $b =$

- **A.** $2ab + b$
- **B.** $4ab$
- **C.** $3a + 4b$
- **D.** $b + 2a$
- **E.** $3b + 4a$

39. Which of the numbers below is between $-1,892$ and -299?

- **A.** 0
- **B.** 28
- **C.** -28
- **D.** -1500
- **E.** -29

40. The value of y is represented by the following expression:

$$0.25 > y > 0.1$$

Which of the following could be a value of y?

- **A.** 0.3
- **B.** $\frac{1}{2}$
- **C.** $\frac{1}{4}$
- **D.** 0.11
- **E.** $\frac{1}{3}$

41. The population of a certain city is 2,355,002. Rounded to the nearest ten thousand, what is the city's population?

- **A.** 2,400,000
- **B.** 2,450,000
- **C.** 2,356,000
- **D.** 2,360,000
- **E.** 2,460,000

42. Mary Ellen thinks she can save $5.40 from her allowance each week to put toward a game console. The game console costs about $150. Rounding the amount she saves each week to the nearest dollar, how many weeks will it take her to save enough to buy the console? Assume there is no sales tax.

- **A.** 27.78 weeks
- **B.** 30 weeks
- **C.** About 32 weeks
- **D.** 25 weeks
- **E.** About 25 weeks

GO ON TO THE NEXT PAGE.

2 ▬▬▬▬▬▬▬▬▬▬▬▬▬▬ **2**

43. Miranda has soccer practice on Tuesday or Thursday with the following exceptions:
- There is no soccer practice on the last Thursday of the month.
- Soccer practice will be canceled if it rains.
- There is no soccer practice in the months of December, January, and February.

If it is Thursday and there is no soccer practice, then it must be true that

A. it is the last Thursday of the month, and it is raining, and it is December, January, or February.
B. it is raining or it is December, January, or February.
C. it is the last Thursday of the month and it is raining.
D. it is the last Thursday of the month or it is raining.
E. it is the last Thursday of the month, or it is raining, or it is December, January, or February.

44. Lucy works as an air traffic controller.
- If it is raining, Lucy will drive her car.
- If Lucy takes the train, she will be late.
- If the weather is cold, Lucy will not walk.

If Lucy is not late and she walked, what must be true?

A. It is raining and the weather is cold.
B. It is raining and Lucy took the train.
C. It is raining and Lucy did not take the train.
D. The weather is not cold and Lucy took the train.
E. The weather is not cold and Lucy did not take the train.

45.
- Samantha drove 3 miles from her home to the gas station.
- Samantha then drove 2 miles from the gas station to the farmer's market.
- Samantha then drove from the farmer's market back to her home.

Based on the information above, which of the following conclusions must be true?

A. The farmer's market is 5 miles from Samantha's home.
B. The farmer's market is at least 1 mile from Samantha's home.
C. The farmer's market is farther from Samantha's home than the gas station.
D. The gas station is closer to Samantha's home than the farmer's market.
E. The farmer's market is closer to Samantha's home than the gas station.

Refer to the menu below to answer the question that follows.

Pizzas (premium toppings 60¢ each)	Drinks	Sides and Dessert
Medium $14.99	Iced Tea $1.50	Salad $2.99
Large $18.99	Soda $1.75 (50¢ more for large)	Spumoni Ice Cream $1.99
Extra large $22.99	Coffee $1.25	Bread Sticks $2.75

46. Jorge and Sarah are going out to eat. They order a large pizza with three premium toppings and two large sodas and split an order of spumoni ice cream. How much is the total cost of their meal?

A. $27.28
B. $26.28
C. $30.37
D. $31.37
E. $28.28

Refer to the table below to answer the question that follows.

Parties	Votes	%	Seats
People's National Party	383,887	52.2	35
Jamaica Labor Party	346,860	47.2	25
Other	3,881	0.5	0
Total	734,628		60

47. Based on the table, how many more votes did the People's National Party receive than the combined vote of all other parties?

A. 37,027
B. 33,144
C. 40,908
D. 29,265
E. 32,146

GO ON TO THE NEXT PAGE.

2

Refer to the line graph below to answer the question that follows.

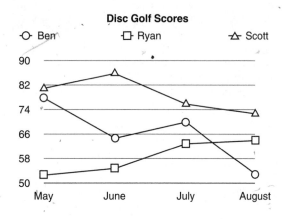

Disc Golf Scores

-O- Ben   -□- Ryan   -△- Scott

48. Ben, Ryan, and Scott tracked their scores in playing disc golf over the summer. Who showed the most improvement in his score from May to August? (In golf, lower scores are better.)

A. Ben
B. Bjorn
C. Ryan
D. Scott
E. Judy

Refer to the pie chart below to answer the question that follows.

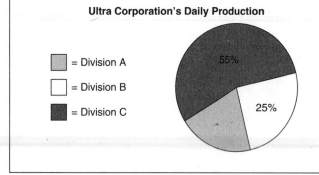

Ultra Corporation's Daily Production

■ = Division A
□ = Division B
■ = Division C

55%

25%

49. If the total production of the Ultra's three divisions is 7,500 units, how many units did Division A produce per day?

A. 1,875
B. 1,250
C. 1,500
D. 1,050
E. 1,025

Refer to the bar graph below to answer the question that follows.

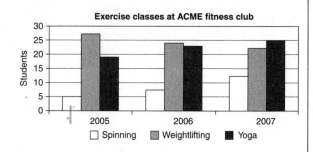

Exercise classes at ACME fitness club

□ Spinning   ■ Weightlifting   ■ Yoga

50. Which class or classes experienced an increase in participation during the time period shown in the graph?

A. Both spinning and yoga
B. Both spinning and weightlifting
C. Yoga only
D. Weightlifting only
E. Both weightlifting and yoga

3   **3**

WRITING TEST

TEST DIRECTIONS: The writing section of the CBEST includes two topics that assess your ability to write effectively. You must write essays responding to *both* topics.

Be sure to write about the given topics; essays on other topics will not be graded. Your answer must completely address all parts of the topic. Your response must be in your own words and not plagiarized from some other source. Write as legibly as possible; your answer can be scored only if it is legible.

Make sure you read each topic carefully. Before you begin to write, take several minutes to organize your thoughts. You may use any space provided in the test booklet to make notes or outline your response. Write your essay on the writing response sheets provided.

Topic 1

Former U.S. president General Dwight D. Eisenhower once said, "We succeed only as we identify in life...a single overriding objective and make all other considerations bend to that one objective." To what extent do you agree or disagree with this statement? Write an essay for an audience of educated adults, stating your position. Use logical arguments and specific examples to support your position.

RESPONSE SHEET FOR TOPIC 1

WRITING ESSAY

RESPONSE SHEET FOR TOPIC 1 (CONTINUED)

WRITING ESSAY

Topic 2

Most people have a much greater interest in either science or social studies; rarely do the two subjects interest someone equally. In an essay addressed to educated adults, discuss your own preference between science and social studies and how this preference developed. To what extent do you believe your own preference for either social studies or science is the result of the personality you were born with and to what extent is it the result of your life experience? Use logical arguments and specific examples to support your position.

RESPONSE SHEET FOR TOPIC 2

WRITING ESSAY

RESPONSE SHEET FOR TOPIC 2 (CONTINUED)

WRITING ESSAY

ANSWER KEY

PRACTICE TEST 1: DIAGNOSTIC

Reading		Mathematics	
1. E	26. C	1. A	26. C
2. C	27. B	2. D	27. D
3. A	28. D	3. D	28. E
4. D	29. C	4. C	29. E
5. B	30. B	5. A	30. D
6. A	31. A	6. E	31. C
7. E	32. A	7. D	32. C
8. E	33. B	8. B	33. C
9. E	34. D	9. C	34. B
10. A	35. D	10. C	35. B
11. D	36. C	11. A	36. A
12. A	37. A	12. E	37. E
13. E	38. E	13. B	38. C
14. A	39. A	14. A	39. D
15. A	40. D	15. B	40. D
16. B	41. E	16. D	41. D
17. C	42. C	17. A	42. B
18. D	43. A	18. C	43. E
19. C	44. D	19. B	44. E
20. B	45. B	20. E	45. B
21. B	46. A	21. E	46. A
22. A	47. A	22. B	47. E
23. E	48. B	23. A	48. A
24. C	49. A	24. A	49. C
25. C	50. C	25. D	50. A

Explanations for the Practice Test 1: Diagnostic

Reading Test

1. **Correct Choice: E.** "Now" correctly connects the content of the second sentence with the first sentence since a new, previously unpublicized danger is now being added to the list of well-known actions that may be hazardous to your health. "However" correctly connects the content of the final sentence with the preceding one since, in spite of the difficulty in studying the problem, there is sufficient evidence to document the risk.

2. **Correct Choice: C.** The main point of this passage is to show how exposure to toxins now can cause health problems later. The passage is not primarily about answer choices A and B, although both of these topics are mentioned to develop the main point. Answer choice D is good advice but unrelated to the central idea of this passage, other than as examples of other long-term health hazards. The passage does not state that lead is more dangerous than sun exposure, so choice E is incorrect.

3. **Correct Choice: A.** The reading passage is about the long-term health problems caused by exposure to lead and other toxic substances. From the information provided you can infer that people may be exposed to these substances more than they realize. Choice B is not a good answer because doctors are increasingly concerned about the effects of toxic substances on aging, not about the natural process of aging. There is not enough information to infer anything about the relative importance of various toxic substances such as lead (choice C) or about how to measure one's exposure to lead.

4. **Correct Choice: D.** Choice A is wrong because there is no information about the difficulty in tracing toxic substances in the body. Choice B contradicts the main idea of the passage; exposure to toxic substances such as lead, pesticides, and mercury is most likely a serious problem. Choice C is wrong because there is no information about how—of even if—these substances are discarded from the body. Choice E is wrong because the passage does not state anything about medical tests being unable to detect toxins in the body.

5. **Correct Choice: B.** Sentence 5 can be removed from the passage without any change to the development of the central purpose of the passage. Removal of any of the other sentences listed in the answer choices would affect the development of the author's points and the readability of the paragraph.

6. **Correct Choice: A.** In general the sentences of this passage are broad statements of widely accepted facts about apartment living and living in a house. However, the phrase "most important" makes sentence 2 a statement of the author's opinion. Since what is important to someone is usually very subjective and varies from person to person, statements of the relative importance of different factors are usually statements of opinion, not fact.

7. **Correct Choice: E.** The author compares the advantages and disadvantages of apartment living and living in a house. The author is not taking one side or the other, so choices A and C are incorrect. While he does list the main problems of living in an apartment, this is not the main point of the paragraph and the author provides no advice, making answer choice B incorrect. Answer choice D is incorrect because the author never mentions home ownership (only *living* in a home is addressed, which refers as much to tenants as owners) and does not seem to be addressing first-time home buyers at all.

8. **Correct Choice: E.** With 30% of the population, "Hispanic" comprises the second largest group on the pie after Caucasian, which accounts for 55% of the state's population. The question asks for an ethnic group, not a combination of ethnic groups (answer choices B and D).

9. **Correct Choice: E.** In the first paragraph, the author informs us that the length of a nanometer is about 10 times that of a hydrogen atom. Thus, a hydrogen atom is shorter than a nanometer, making answer choice E the correct one.

10. **Correct Choice: A.** The sentence's point is that the potential of nanotechnology is so great and far-reaching that we might soon look back on the Internet as comparatively insignificant—in other words, its importance will seem to "shrink." The other answer choices do not have the same meaning as *pale* and could not be substituted for *pale* without changing the meaning of the sentence.

11. **Correct Choice: D.** The author characterizes the development of fast-acting medicines for treating diseases as "more crucial"—in other words, more important—than other developments.

12. **Correct Choice: A.** The article mentions both wrinkle creams and sunblocks, both of which are types of cosmetics. None of the other answer choices are mentioned in the passage.

13. **Correct Choice: E.** The author devotes the entire third paragraph to expressing concern about nanotechnology's potential threat to public health.

14. **Correct Choice: A.** This short sentence connects the sentence before it with the one after it in a logical way. None of the other answer choices do this.

15. **Correct Choice: A.** The author is talking about how clear his memory is of events that happened long ago. The other answer choices are not words that can be substituted for *clarity* without changing the meaning of the sentence.

16. **Correct Choice: B.** A person's native land is the land in which they were born and grew up. His first years in America were not the first years of his life. But he implies that both the last years in his native land and his first years in America were a long time ago, suggesting that he immigrated to America when he was still quite young.

17. **Correct Choice: C.** The author states that although he is now an old man, he can vividly remember his early years as clearly as if they were only yesterday. Thus, his point is that older people can often clearly remember their youth.

18. **Correct Choice: D.** According to the passage, smallpox bacteria could be carried through the air for considerable distances.

19. **Correct Choice: C.** In the context of this paragraph, *inevitable* most closely means certain. The gist of the last two paragraphs is that almost no person could be sure to escape smallpox, which seemed to spread everywhere and affect nearly everybody. Within this context, it makes perfect sense that Europeans accepted a smallpox attack as certain or, as the passage states, "inevitable." The other answer choices do not have the same meaning as *inevitable* and could not be substituted for *inevitable* without changing the meaning of the sentence.

20. **Correct Choice: B.** In the final paragraph, the author gives some facts about the number of people who died or were disfigured from smallpox, answering the question of why people feared smallpox. The author doesn't address the questions in the other answer choices at all.

21. **Correct Choice: B.** In the second paragraph, the author tells us that the name "was given to the disease . . . to distinguish it from . . . the Great Pox, or syphilis...."

22. **Correct Choice: A.** The author devotes most of the passage to discussing the history of smallpox. Nevertheless, the first paragraph and the closing sentence together give us the clear impression that the author's larger purpose in this passage, rather than to simply recount historical events, is to alert, or *caution,* us about renewed dangers.

23. **Correct Choice: E.** The index would be the most efficient way for the reader to find all mentions of calcium in the book.

24. **Correct Choice: C.** Part Three is correct because it is the meat group. The table of contents even mentions the word poultry.

25. **Correct Choice: C.** The statement in answer choice A goes well beyond the study described in this passage. Choice B is not correct because the passage does not prescribe "hard" or intensive exercise as a remedy for fatigue. People who worked out more intensively reported higher levels of fatigue than those who exercised at a more leisurely pace. Choice D is not correct because, in this study, low-impact exercise was found to help reduce fatigue; the passage does not mention people with heart disease or cancer. Choice E is not correct because this statement is not the main idea of the passage.

26. **Correct Choice: C.** The group in choice A experienced no benefits, the group in choice B had more trouble with fatigue, and there was no group such as the one mentioned in choice D in this study. Choice E mentions two groups, one of which had some trouble with fatigue and exercise.

27. **Correct Choice: B.** Choice A is wrong because athletes were not involved in the study. Choice C is incorrect because the scientists were observers, not participants, in the study. Choice D is wrong because patients with life-threatening diseases were also not part of the study.

28. **Correct Choice: D.** In the context of the last sentence, *track* means a paved circular path used for running. Choices A, C, and E are other meanings of *track* but they do not apply in the context of the last paragraph. Choice B has nothing to do with the word.

29. **Correct Choice: C.** The author tells us that Hans had fooled his owner (as well as other people) into thinking that Hans could perform arithmetic.

30. **Correct Choice: B.** Nothing in the article suggests that Hans was ever punished for giving wrong answers to arithmetic questions, or for any other reason. Information in the article directly supports the statements that Hans was extremely intelligent (choice A), that he was very observant of the humans around him (choice C), that he was rewarded for his behavior (choice D), and that he liked treats (choice E).

31. **Correct Choice: A.** In the first paragraph, the author refers to people who claim that their pets can perform intellectual feats that are generally assumed to be things only humans can do. Then, in the second paragraph, the author tells us that these people can learn a lesson from Hans who, as we learn in the third paragraph, does not possess the sort of high-level, human-like intellectual ability that he appeared to demonstrate. The author does not seem skeptical of the intelligence of scientists who study animals (choice B), the claim that only humans can develop high-level language skills (choice C), the ability of animals to understand the body language of humans (choice D), or the ability of animals to respond consistently to rewards (choice E) like Hans apparently did.

32. **Correct Choice: A.** In all probability, Hans learned to stomp his hoof the appropriate number of times by watching his owner's body language very closely. This supports the statement in answer choice A.

33. **Correct Choice: B.** In the second paragraph, the author states that pet owners can learn a lesson from Hans, the horse. This statement, along with the general tone and focus of the article, strongly suggests it is directed to pet owners. Thus, the article would be most likely to appear in a magazine directed toward pet owners.

34. **Correct Choice: D.** This sentence connects the sentence before it with the one after it in a logical way. None of the other answer choices do this.

35. **Correct Choice: D.** The passage is about a trend in American culture and would thus appeal to people interested in trends in American society and culture (answer choice D). It just states facts and does not provide encouragement (answer choices A and E) or discuss pros and cons of cosmetic surgery for people considering it (answer choice B). Cosmetic surgeons (answer choice D) most likely already know the information the author is presenting, so it would be of little interest to them.

36. **Correct Choice: C.** In the first paragraph we are told that liposuction is the most common surgical cosmetic procedure.

37. **Correct Choice: A.** The first paragraph introduces the topic of cosmetic procedures, giving statistics on how widespread it is and identifying the two classes of cosmetic procedures. The second paragraph gives statistics and information on the growth of cosmetic surgery. Choice B, the most plausible of the other answer choices, is not the best answer because the first paragraph, while it does provide some statistics, is more focused on defining and explaining than simply providing statistics for their own sake. Furthermore, while the final sentence of the second paragraph does compare statistics for men and women, this is not the organizing theme of the paragraph. This sentence plays a supporting role to the main theme of the paragraph that the use of cosmetic procedures is growing rapidly.

38. **Correct Choice: E.** The trees are clearly organized by scientific period (i.e. Triassic Period).

39. **Correct Choice: A.** Growing trees in large quantities alludes to tree farms.

40. **Correct Choice: D.** The statement in choice D is a restatement of the second to the last sentence of the passage and thus something the author would definitely agree with. The author does not directly address the topics contained in answer choices A, C, and E. While he says most people now agree that environmental issues are important, he gives no indication that he would go so far as to say that "everyone" takes this position.

41. **Correct Choice: E.** *Espoused* most nearly means promoted. Answer choice C is a plausible answer, but to espouse a cause means taking a more active role than simply accepting it. The other answer choices have nothing to do with *espouse*.

42. **Correct Choice: C.** The overall tone of the passage is positive and speaks in a favorable tone about the growing attention and more serious consideration being given to environmental issues. Thus, the author seems glad that environmental concerns are being taken more seriously than before.

43. **Correct Choice: A.** The passage states that Napolean created the prize for a butter substitute so that the French armed forces and lower classes could have a less expensive option to butter; since the French navy is part of the French armed forces, this is the best answer. Clearly, royal classes, visiting dignitaries, and the upper classes would not fall into the categories of the French armed forces or the lower classes, making answer choices B, C, and E incorrect. There is nothing in the article to support the idea that margarine would be created for export to the United States (answer choice D).

44. **Correct Choice: D.** It is obvious that sales of margarine would cut into sales of butter, affecting dairy farmers and making this a group highly likely to oppose the widespread sale of margarine. In addition, the article states that the dairy industry fought to limit the distribution and sale of margarine. The groups listed in the other answer choices have no direct stake in the issue of margarine sales and distribution.

45. **Correct Choice: B.** The passage states that margarine is nearly white in color, which makes it unappealing to consumers; so much so that banning the production of yellow-colored margarine was the most effective way to slow its popularity.

46. **Correct Choice: A.** While we don't know who the author is, the content and the tone of the article allow us to exclude the other answer choices, leaving this as the only viable answer. The article's factual statements and historical approach are typical of a student research paper. The article does not get into the dangers of margarine (answer choice B) and it does not discuss cholesterol (answer choice C). Nor does it have any scientific analysis on the production of margarine (answer choice D). The author's voice is too objective to belong to a representative of the dairy industry (answer choice E).

47. **Correct Choice: A.** Answer choice A reflects that the passage is a history of margarine and also makes reference to "color," which was mentioned in the passage. Answer choices B and C are completely outside the scope of the passage. Answer choice D refers to only one piece of the history of margarine covered in this passage, not its main focus. Answer choice E is incorrect because the passage does not compare the advantages and disadvantages of margarine and butter.

48. **Correct Choice: B.** The article focuses on the risks of falling for older people. Choices A, C, and D all refer to secondary topics or details that support the main idea of the passage. The passage states that hip fractures are the most dreaded injury, not necessarily the most prevalent, so answer choice E is wrong.

49. **Correct Choice: A.** The author includes the quote to provide support for the basic idea presented in the passage. Choice B is incorrect because the quote does not contradict any of the author's ideas to create controversy. It does not provide statistics (answer choice C) or address the statement contained in choice D. The quote does not provide a differing opinion from that of the passage, so choice E is wrong.

50. **Correct Choice: C.** The article makes no claim about the effect of gentle exercise on weight, making this the correct answer choice. The article does mention all the other answer choices as positive results to be gained from gentle exercise by older people at risk of falling.

Mathematics

1. **Correct Choice: A.** The sum of the three scores must equal three times the average score. Set up an equation, letting x equal the third score, and then solve for x:

$$90 + 90 + x = 32 \times 3$$
$$180 + x = 276$$
$$x = 96$$

2. **Correct Choice: D.** To calculate 30% of $12, we would multiply 12 by 0.3, which equals $3.60. But be careful; that's how much to subtract from the original amount, so the answer is $12.00 − $3.60 = $8.40.

3. **Correct Choice: D.** You can determine the correct answer choice by making a common-sense estimate. Based on a mile-to-kilometer ratio of 1:1.6, 10 kilometers is significantly less than 10 miles, but a bit more than 5 miles. Or, to compute the precise answer, divide 10 by 1.6. Try converting 1.6 to the fraction $^8/_5$, then multiply 10 by its reciprocal:

$$10 \div \frac{8}{5} = 10 \times \frac{5}{8} = \frac{50}{8} = 6.25$$
$$\frac{1}{1.6} = \frac{x}{10}$$
$$1.6x = 10$$
$$x = \frac{10}{1.6}$$

4. **Correct Choice: C.** Cubic feet measures volume or the three dimensions of height, width, and depth. None of the other answer choices is a measure of volume.

5. **Correct Choice: A.** There are 16 ounces in a pound and, accordingly, 80 ounces in 5 pounds. Removing 30 ounces from 80 ounces leaves 50 ounces.

6. **Correct Choice: E.** Divide the figure into two rectangles, as shown below.

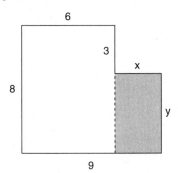

Then, find x and y in the figure. $x = 9 − 6 = 3$, and $y = 8 − 3 = 5$. The area of the shaded rectangle = $x \times y = 3 \times 5 = 15$. The area of the larger (unshaded) rectangle is $6 \times 8 = 48$. The total area of the figure is $15 + 48 = 63$.

7. **Correct Choice: D.** Assume each side of a certain square is 2 units in length. The area of this square is $2 \times 2 = 4$. Now, increase the length of each side by 50% to 3 units. The square's new area is $3 \times 3 = 9$. An increase from 4 to 9 is a 125% increase.

8. **Correct Choice: B.** If Jane has collected 132 stamps over 12 months, she has collected an average of $132 \div 12 = 11$ stamps per month.

9. **Correct Choice: C.** Set up a proportion, or two equal fractions, to compare these two scenarios. For example, *6 forms* might go in the numerator on the left and *15 minutes* in the denominator. Then *30 forms* would go in the numerator on the right, and x or another variable in the denominator. Cross-multiplying gives $6x = 450$, and dividing each side by 6 to solve for x gives 75.

10. **Correct Choice: C.** Of 10 cards, 4 are clubs. Thus, the probability of selecting a club is 4 in 10. You can express this probability as the fraction $^4/_{10}$, or $^2/_5$.

11. **Correct Choice: A.** Because 15 of 27 animals are monkeys, 12 are *not* monkeys. The ratio of monkeys to other animals is 15:12, or 5:4. You can express this ratio as the fraction $^5/_4$.

12. **Correct Choice: E.** To get the difference, subtract: $8{,}751 − 832$ is $7{,}919$.

13. **Correct Choice: B.** Ignoring the decimals, $398 \times 72 = 28{,}656$. There are four spaces to the right of the decimal (collectively) in 3.98 and 0.72, so move the decimal four spaces to the left and get 2.8656.

14. **Correct Choice: A.** Align the two numbers vertically at the decimal point and then subtract corresponding digits, borrowing a 1 from the "tenths" position for the "hundredths" position.

15. **Correct Choice: B.** The median is the middle or center value of the dataset when arranged in ascending numerical order, or 83.

16. **Correct Choice: D.** Negative 342 plus negative 131 is negative 473. Add a positive 56 and you get a negative 417.

17. **Correct Choice: A.** To find the average temperature, add the high and low and then divide the sum by 2:

$$\frac{(-6+11)}{2} = \frac{5}{2}, \text{or } 2.5°$$

18. **Correct Choice: C.** 15 of the 24 candies are hard. Eating 6 of the 15 hard candies leaves 9 of each type (hard and chewy).

19. **Correct Choice: B.** Let's translate: "5 is what percent of 40" becomes $5 = {}^x/_{100} \times 40$, or $5 = {}^{40x}/_{100}$. Multiply both sides by 100 and you get $500 = 40x$; divide each side by 40 and you get $12.5 = x$. Therefore, 5 is 12.5% of 40.

20. **Correct Choice: E.** To perform the subtraction $4^5/_6 - 2^3/_4$, first convert each of the fractions from a mixed number to its standard form and then find a common denominator to complete the subtraction process:

$$4\frac{5}{6} = \frac{4 \cdot 6 + 5}{6}$$
$$= \frac{24 + 5}{6}$$
$$= \frac{29}{6}$$

$$2\frac{3}{4} = \frac{2 \cdot 4 + 3}{4}$$
$$= \frac{8 + 3}{4}$$
$$= \frac{11}{4}$$

$$4\frac{5}{6} - 2\frac{3}{4} = \frac{29}{6}$$
$$= \frac{11}{4}$$
$$= \frac{58 - 33}{12}$$
$$= \frac{25}{12}$$

21. **Correct Choice: E.** Once you pare down the excess words, the problem is really asking what is 20% of 35, which is also $^1/_5$ of 35. $^1/_5 \times 35 = 7$.

22. **Correct Choice: B.** This is a basic proportion problem; set up 5 over 2 on one side and 30 over x on the other side. Cross-multiply and you get $5x = 60$, which solves to $x = 12$.

23. **Correct Choice: A.** To find 12% of $500, multiply: $0.12(\$500 = \$60$.

24. **Correct Choice: A.** A rectangular plot's area equals the product of its length and width ($A = lw$). Apply this equation, solving for w:

$$12,000 = 150w$$
$$\frac{12,000}{150} = w$$
$$80 = w$$

25. **Correct Choice: D.** The total trip time was 2.5 hours. Apply the *rate × time = distance* formula: 40 (m.p.h.) × 2.5 (hours) = 100 (miles).

26. **Correct Choice: C.** Dan and Stephanie are making two thirds as many oatmeal raisin cookies as chocolate chip cookies, and they're making 60 oatmeal raisin cookies. 60 is two thirds of 90, so they are making 60 + 90 = 150 cookies total.

27. **Correct Choice: D.** When you solve for x, you get:

$$3 - 3 + 4x = 23 - 3$$
$$4x = 20$$
$$\frac{4x}{4} = \frac{20}{4}$$
$$x = 5$$

28. **Correct Choice: E.** We need to know Theresa's speed in order to calculate how long she was driving. Choices A and D are wrong because they are not the complete duration of the entire trip. Choice B is wrong because gas mileage is irrelevant. Choice C is wrong because the question asks for the duration of time the errands took, not the distance.

29. **Correct Choice: E.** The total of lemon-lime and orange sodas is 43. This means that at least 14 colas must have been sold. The cost of a soda (choice A) is irrelevant. There is no way for us to know how many sodas were placed in the refrigerator at the beginning of the day (choice D), as the question does not tell us what moment of the day the 86 sodas sit in the refrigerator. We cannot know how many sodas of any type were sold (choices B and C).

30. **Correct Choice: D.** We need to know how many gallons of water the car's tank holds and how many miles to the gallon the car gets. Choice A is wrong because the cost of water versus gasoline is irrelevant here. Choices B and C are incomplete. Choice E is wrong because gas mileage doesn't matter here; we need water mileage.

31. **Correct Choice: C.** One burger costs B dollars. There are 100 cents to a dollar. Thus, the cost of a burger in *cents* is $100B$. The question asks for the *cent* cost of one burger ($100B$) *and* one soda (S).

32. **Correct Choice: C.** Simplify to make it easier to translate: J is five more than twice F. Now you can see the mathematical equivalent for each word, $J = 5 + 2F$.

33. **Correct Choice: C.** To get the number of rows needed for the 120 people, divide 120 by 8 since there are eight people per row. This number is 40. Then add 2 to get an answer of 42. The equation in answer choice C correctly states this operation. Don't be confused by the 2R in answer choice A. This indicates 2 times the total number of rows needed, not two additional rows.

34. **Correct Choice: B.** The chart shows the following relationship between a and b: $b = 2a + 2$. Therefore, when a is 6, b is 14.

35. **Correct Choice: B.** After Stacy drinks 25% of 16 ounces (which is 4 ounces), 12 ounces remain. After Stacy drinks 25% of 12 ounces (which is 3 ounces), 9 ounces remain.

36. **Correct Choice: A.** Remember that it's not the number of digits behind the decimal point that make a number large. You can add zeros after the decimal point if you need to visualize the numbers with an equal number of digits: $14.200 > 14.180 > 14.111$.

37. **Correct Choice: E.** $1/3$ is larger than $1/4$ but smaller than $2/3$. $4/6$ is equal to $2/3$, not smaller. $1/5$ is smaller than $1/4$. And $3/4$ is larger than $2/3$. If you need to, you can find the common denominator (60) and convert all the fractions to sixtieths to be able to directly compare all answer choices. For example, to convert $1/5$ to sixtieths, divide 5 into 50 and get 12 and then take 12 times the numerator (1) to get $\frac{1}{5} = \frac{12}{60}$.

38. **Correct Choice: C.** In the equation given, substitute $a + 2b$ for b, then simplify:

$$b = a + 2(a + 2b)$$
$$b = a + 2a + 4b$$
$$b = 3a + 4b$$

39. **Correct Choice: D.** −1500 is a number between −299 and −1892. All the other answer choice are larger than −299.

40. **Correct Choice: D.** 0.11 is larger than 0.1 but smaller than 0.25. One-fourth equals 0.25 and therefore can't be smaller than 0.25. One-half (0.5) and 0.3 are larger than 0.25 and therefore incorrect answer choices.

41. **Correct Choice: D.** You need consider only the right-most five digits. 55,002 is closer to 60,000 than to 50,000.

42. **Correct Choice: B.** $5.40 when rounded to the nearest dollar is $5.00. 150 divided by 5 is 30. It will take her about 30 weeks. In a problem such as this, it would not make sense to try to be too precise and figure out the exact number of weeks using $5.40 rather than $5.00 (this answer is 27.78 weeks). For one thing the $150 is a round number, not the exact price, and Mary Ellen is not even sure of the amount she can save each week. In a problem such as this, using precise numbers is inconsistent with the information (and the instructions) given.

43. **Correct Choice: E.** The key to this problem is to remember that *any* of the conditions above can be true, meaning that 1, 2, or even all 3 of the conditions might be true. We know that *at least 1* of them *must be true*. Choice A is wrong because it says that all of the conditions are true. Choice B is wrong because it does not mention the possibility that it is the last Thursday of the month. Choices C and D are wrong because they do not mention that it might be December, January, or February. Choice C states that two of the conditions must be true, and choice D states that either one of the two conditions must be true.

44. **Correct Choice: E.** Since Lucy is not late, we know that she did not take the train. Eliminate choices B and D. Since Lucy walked, we know that the weather is not cold. Eliminate choice A. Also note that since Lucy walked, she obviously did not drive her car. If she did not drive her car, then it was not raining. This eliminate choices A, B, and C.

45. **Correct Choice: B.** Samantha drove 3 miles to the gas station and then another 2 miles to the farmer's market. However, we do not know if these routes overlapped at all. Perhaps she drove in a straight line and then doubled back to the farmer's market on the way home. Perhaps the farmer's market is an additional 2 miles from the gas station in the opposite direction of her home. Therefore, eliminate choice A. In addition, we do not know which place is closer to her home. Eliminate choices C, D, and E. This leaves choice B.

46. **Correct Choice: A.** The pizza should be $18.99 + $1.80 for three premium toppings. Sodas come to $2.25 each. One order of spumoni ice cream is $1.99. Add $18.99 + $1.80 + $2.25 + $2.25 + $1.99 and you get $27.28.

47. **Correct Choice: E.** All other parties combined got 350,741 votes. Subtracting this number from 383,887, the answer is 33,146.

48. **Correct Choice: A.** Eyeballing the line chart shows that Ben's score improved the most from May to August. Scott's score improved more gradually, Ryan's score got worse, and Bjorn and Judy are not on the chart at all.

49. **Correct Choice: C.** Division A accounts for 20% (100% − 55% − 25%) of the total production (7,500). To find Division A's daily production, multiply: $0.2 \times 7,500 = 1,500$.

50. **Correct Choice: A.** Just looking at the height of the bars, we can see that both spinning and yoga saw increased participation over the previous years in both 2006 and 2007. Weightlifting saw a decline both years.

Writing Test

After you take the actual CBEST, two human scorers will read your essay and assign a number score from 1 to 4. The score they give will be based on the scoring standards described in the official CBEST Writing Score Scale. This scale can be viewed online at www.cbest.nesinc.com (go to the practice test and then the writing section). A summary of the writing score scale is provided below.

Use this summary to score your own essay. Better yet, ask someone else—a teacher, parent, friend, or colleague—to score your essay based on this summary of the CBEST writing score scale.

Scoring the CBEST Writing Test	
Score	**Summary of Scoring Guidelines**
4	**A Score of 4 indicates a well-written essay that effectively develops an idea for the specified audience.**
	The essay has a central idea or point of view and the writer maintains the focus on the idea in a well reasoned essay.
	Ideas or points the author presents are logically arranged and the essay is clear and well-organized.
	Assertions are supported with relevant information and specific examples.
	Words usage is careful and precise.
	Sentences and paragraphs are well constructed and coherent; however, the essay may contain minor flaws in grammar, spelling, punctuation, etc.
	The essay completely addresses the topic and is appropriate for the given audience.
3	**A Score of 3 indicates an essay that for the most part, is adequately written and develops an idea for the specified audience.**
	The essay has a central idea or point of view and the writer, for the most part, maintains the focus on this idea in a well reasoned essay.
	The presentation of ideas and points, for the most, is adequately organized and clear.
	Most assertions are supported with relevant information and specific examples.
	Word usage is adequate; there may be some errors in usage but they are not bad enough to make understanding difficult.
	Sentences and paragraphs are generally well contructed and coherent; errors in sentence structure and grammar are not serious enough to cause confusion and misunderstanding.
	The essay addresses the topic and is appropriate for the given audience.
2	**A Score of 2 indicates an essay that attempts to communicate an idea but the idea is only partially formed and sometimess difficult to understand.**
	The essay may state a central idea or point of view but the focus is not maintained throughout the essay and the central idea is underdeveloped or simplistically reasoned.
	The organization of ideas lacks clarity and is only partially effective.
	Assertions are not always supported and the essay may contain irrelevant or insufficient details.
	Word usage is not always clear and may cause confusion or even misunderstanding.
	Sentences and paragraphs are not always well constructed and can be difficult to understand due to errors in sentence structure and grammar.
	The essay may not completely address the topic or be appropriate in style and content for the given audience.
1	**A Score of 1 indicates an essay that is difficult to understand and fails to communicate an idea to the intended audience.**
	The central idea or point of view of the essay is unclear and the essay is simplistically reasoned or contains serious flaws in reasoning.
	The essay lacks organization and coherence, leaving the reader confused.
	Assertions are not supported or are seriously underdeveloped and the essay contains irrelevant and/or insufficient details.
	Word usage is often unclear and confusing, leading to confusion or misunderstanding on the part of the reader.
	Sentences and paragraphs are not well constructed with many errors in paragraphing, sentence structure, and grammar that make understanding difficult.
	The essay may not completely address the topic or be appropriate in style and content for the given audience.
U	**This score indicates the essay cannot be scored. Reasons for this can be the essay was illegible, completely off topic, or not written in English.**
B	**This score indicates the essay response sheet was left blank.**

CHAPTER 4

THE CBEST MATHEMATICS TEST: COMPUTATION AND PROBLEM SOLVING

The mathematics section of the California Basic Educational Skills Test (CBEST) requires an understanding of basic mathematics and the ability to apply this understanding to specific problems or situations. Most of the math questions on the CBEST are word problems, also known as story problems. They describe practical situations for teachers that involve some type of math problem. The math is basic and probably not that difficult for you; the difficult part for most people is figuring out how to apply the math they know to the situation described.

The CBEST requires an understanding of mathematics including basic algebra and geometry, statistics and probability, and tables and graphs. You have undoubtedly studied all of these topics at one time, but most people find a review of mathematics to be very helpful, especially if they haven't taken a math class in a while. This chapter and the three chapters that follow provide a review of the math you need to know for the CBEST.

Not only will you get a math review, you'll get practice questions that will help you check your understanding of the math you need to know. Pay special attention to the word problems in the practice sets; these problems require you to apply your understanding of math to practical situations. You may also want to review the strategies for taking multiple-choice tests described in Chapter 2.

Quite a few questions on the CBEST deal with percents. Teachers must understand and be able to compute percentages since so much of student testing and evaluation is expressed in terms of percents. Make sure you have mastered the skills of computing percentages (covered later in this chapter); these are an important part of the CBEST.

OK, let's begin!

INTEGERS

Most of the numbers on the CBEST are integers, which are also the ones that you deal with day to day. Integers are divisible by one, so they do not have anything after the decimal. You may round things to the nearest integer at the grocery store to keep track of how much you are spending without having to do a lot of mental math. They are the numbers you use to count things that are not divisible, such as cars, marbles, and children.

You may think of the term *whole number* when you hear or read *integer* if it is easier for you. (Technically, *whole numbers* do not include negative numbers, whereas *integers* do, but that is the only difference and it will not be tested on nursing school entrance exams.) We are going to use the word *integer* so that we do not get a lot of mail, but *whole number* is used more in everyday speech, so go ahead and substitute it if you wish.

The Number Line, Positive Numbers, Negative Numbers, and Zero

There may be questions on the test that deal with the concept of a number line, which is basically just a line with numbers on it, like this:

$$...-2\ -1\ \ 0\ \ 1\ \ 2...$$

Generally number lines are divided up in increments of 1, so they show you the integers close to and including 0. All numbers to the right of 0 are positive and all numbers to the left of 0 are negative. This means that anything greater than 0—even the fractions and decimals between 0 and 1—is positive. And the same is true for anything less than 0: even between 0 and –1, it is all negative.

So what does that make 0? It is neither positive nor negative. But it is an integer, and it does have a place on the number line.

Absolute Value

Whenever you see a number with vertical lines on either side of it, such as |–3|, you are being asked to figure out the *absolute value* of that number. Absolute values are positive numbers only, so the absolute value of –3 is 3. Or, to put it in math terms, |–3| = 3.

If there is a positive number inside the symbols, such as |2|, then the absolute value is just equal to that same number: |2| = 2. So when you see the absolute value signs, remember that everything goes on the right, or positive, side of the number line. (Yes, it really is that easy. We are going to trust that mathematicians had a very good reason for giving this simple concept a fancy name and unfamiliar symbols, but whatever that reason is, you are not going to need to know it for your entrance exams. You are going to be tested only on the basics.)

Another way to think of absolute value is *distance from 0*, and distances are always positive. For example, –5 is *five* tick marks from *0* on the number line, so |–5| = *5*.

Place Value

It's good to brush up on this terminology for your tests, and it will also help keep things straight when we review computation. The digit farthest to the right (unless there are digits after a decimal, but we will get to that later) is called the *ones* or *units* digit. Moving further to the left, you have the *tens, hundreds, thousands,* and *ten thousands* digits in order. So the number 36,827 has a 7 in the ones place, a 2 in the tens place, an 8 in the hundreds place, a 6 in the thousands place, and a 3 in the ten thousands place.

▓▓▓ COMPUTATION

On the CBEST, you'll find a number of problems that test your computation skills (addition, subtraction, multiplication, and division). You won't be able to use a calculator during the CBEST, and you will need to rely on your own skills and be very careful not to make a mistake. If you use a calculator to perform basic math in your daily life, you may need to brush up on your basic computational skills, such as the techniques of "borrowing" and "carrying," that you probably learned in school but may not have used recently.

Addition

Many addition problems simply line up two numbers and ask you to add them, like this:

$$
\begin{array}{r}
497 \\
+\,362 \\
\hline
\end{array}
$$

Other addition problems may present information in a word problem, which we will get to later. But word problems are really the same thing; you just need to write down the numbers yourself so that they look like the above problem. And remember—neatness counts!

So how to solve this problem? In bite-sized pieces. Make sure the numbers are lined up in neat columns, and start on the right:

$$
\begin{array}{r}
497 \\
+\,362 \\
\hline
9
\end{array}
$$

Now on to the middle column.

$$
\begin{array}{r}
497 \\
+\,362 \\
\hline
159
\end{array}
$$

Well, unfortunately you cannot fit both the 1 and the 5 in the same column, so you leave the 5 there and *carry* the 1 over to the left column. Now your left column looks like this:

$$
\begin{array}{r}
1 \\
497 \\
+\,362 \\
\hline
859
\end{array}
$$

So your total is 859.

Ready for another one? Try this one first, and the explanation will follow.

$$
\begin{array}{r}
2847 \\
+\,5463 \\
\hline
\end{array}
$$

Okay, here is how to do it, starting with the first column on the right. Adding up the far right column you get 10; leave the 0 there and carry the 1.

$$
\begin{array}{r}
1 \\
2847 \\
+\,5463 \\
\hline
0
\end{array}
$$

Adding up the second column you get 11; leave a 1 there and carry a 1.

$$
\begin{array}{r}
1 \\
2847 \\
+\ 5463 \\
\hline
10
\end{array}
$$

Adding up the third column you get 13; leave a 3 there and carry a 1.

$$
\begin{array}{r}
1 \\
2847 \\
+\ 5463 \\
\hline
310
\end{array}
$$

Adding up the fourth column you get 8, so your answer is 8,310.

Subtraction

Subtraction is very similar; you still line up the numbers in columns and deal with them one column at a time, starting with the right, even if the test writers do not line up the numbers for you. There is no carrying in subtraction; however, if the number you are subtracting in a column is larger than the number you are subtracting from, you may have to borrow from the column to the left.

For example:

$$
\begin{array}{r}
527 \\
-\ 335 \\
\hline
\end{array}
$$

Starting with the first column on the right, you can simply subtract 7 – 5.

$$
\begin{array}{r}
527 \\
-\ 335 \\
\hline
2
\end{array}
$$

In the next column over, you cannot really subtract 2 – 3, so you *borrow* from the column to the left. Borrowing lets you add 10 to the current number you are subtracting from, so now you can subtract 12 – 3 instead:

$$
\begin{array}{r}
41 \\
\cancel{5}27 \\
-\ 335 \\
\hline
92
\end{array}
$$

Now all you have left is the last column, the hundreds.

$$
\begin{array}{r}
41 \\
\cancel{5}27 \\
-\ 335 \\
\hline
192
\end{array}
$$

So your answer is 192.

Multiplication

In multiplication problems, you still want to be very aware of lining your numbers up properly. Multiplying several-digit numbers is always a matter of multiplying smaller numbers several times.

For example:

$$\begin{array}{r} 424 \\ \times\ 31 \\ \hline \end{array}$$

Because there are two digits in the number on the second line, you actually work two smaller multiplication problems. First, multiply everything in the first line by 1 (because you are starting from the right).

$$\begin{array}{r} \mathbf{424} \\ \mathbf{\times\ 31} \\ \hline \mathbf{424} \end{array}$$

Then move one column to the left and multiply everything in the top line by the 3. Notice how you shift over when writing your answer. Also, if you end up with a two-digit number, you can carry to the next column to the left, just like in addition. Then just add that carried number after you multiply the original first and second line.

$$\begin{array}{r} \mathbf{1} \\ \mathbf{424} \\ \mathbf{\times\ \ 31} \\ \hline 424 \\ \mathbf{1{,}272} \end{array}$$

Now you have two numbers, 424 and 1,272. Keeping them in their current columns, you add to get the final result:

$$\begin{array}{r} 424 \\ +\ 1272\ \ \\ \hline 13{,}144 \end{array}$$

And your final answer is 13,144.

Division

Division is a bit different. Division problems may be presented like this:

$$3\overline{)21}$$

. . . or like this:

$$21 \div 3$$

. . . or even like this:

$$\frac{21}{3}$$

All of these mean the same thing. You would say "21 divided by 3" or, as a question, "How many times does 3 go into 21?" We will talk about fractions later, but for now, let us focus on long division, which means if you are given a problem such as 21 ÷ 3, you will write it out as $3\overline{)21}$.

Unlike in addition, subtraction, and multiplication, you are going to start division problems on the left inside the division sign. But just as you did with the other operations, you are still going to keep things in neat columns.

Let us take $3\overline{)21}$. Starting at the left, ask: Is 2 divisible by 3? No, because 2 is smaller than 3. So then you include the next column to the right, as well: Is 21 divisible by 3? Yes, and the result is 7, so you put the 7 above the 1:

$$3\overline{)21}^{\,7}$$

. . . and that is your answer.

What if the problem were $3\overline{)210}$ instead? You just keep going; 21 is divisible by 3, and the result is 7, then 0 is divisible by 3, and the result is 0.

$$3\overline{)210}^{\,70}$$

Not all numbers divide evenly, however. Sometimes the *dividend* (the number inside the division sign) will have something left over when you divide it by the *divisor* (the number to the left of the division sign). Then you have a *quotient* (the result), and you also have a *remainder*. The remainder is the integer that is left over when you have divided out as many digits of the divisor as you can.

Whatif you are asked to divide $3\overline{)212}$? The first 2 is not divisible by 3, so you move on to $3\overline{)21}$. That gives you 7. The last 2 is not divisible by 3 either, so you put a 0 above the 2:

$$3\overline{)212}^{\,70}$$

However, that is not the whole story. You still have that 2 that is not represented in the answer, so it becomes your remainder, and you write that as 70r2. To check your math, you can multiply the quotient by the divisor, then add the remainder, and you should come up with the dividend: $70 \times 3 + 2 = 212$. The math works, so 70r2 is the correct answer.

Let us try one more problem with a remainder:

$$6\overline{)45} = ?$$

First, does 6 go into 4? No, so you include both columns in the divisor. Does 6 go into 45? Yes, 7 times.

$$6\overline{)45}^{\,7}$$

However, 7×6 is only 42, so you have a remainder of 3. Written out, $45 \div 6 = 7r3$.

Time for some practice on computation. Use scratch paper and remember to work carefully. Solutions are at the end of the chapter.

Practice Set 1: Addition, Subtraction, Multiplication, and Division

1. $1{,}473 + 582 =$
2. $5{,}391 + 6{,}729 =$
3. $12{,}843 + 5{,}928 =$
4. $3{,}609 - 1{,}727 =$
5. $2{,}381 - 963 =$
6. $768 - 529 =$
7. $408 \times 52 =$
8. $823 \times 7 =$
9. $521 \times 47 =$
10. $709 \div 4 =$
11. $341 \div 3 =$
12. $672 \div 16 =$

Order of Operations

When solving any equation or making any calculation that has more than one operation to perform, the order in which you perform the operations has an effect on what answer you will get. For example, in the expression $5 + 4 \times 2$, if you perform the addition first and then the multiplication, you get a result of 18. If you perform the multiplication first and then the addition, you get 13. So which is correct? Although many people just perform the operations from left to right, there is an order of operations that must be followed to get the math right. The order can be remembered with the acronym PEMDAS, which stands for:

- **P**arentheses
- **E**xponents
- **M**ultiplication and **D**ivision (from left to right)
- **A**ddition and **S**ubtraction (from left to right)

So anything that is in parentheses takes precedence and is calculated first, then exponents, and so on. That means that on the problem above, the multiplication should be done first and then the addition, giving you 13. Try the order of operations on the following drill; solutions are at the end of the chapter.

Practice Set 2: Order of Operations

1. $3 + 2 \times 4 =$
2. $(10 - 4) \div 3 =$
3. $4 \times 3 - 5 =$
4. $15 - 8 \div 2 =$
5. $(9 + 2) \times 2 =$
6. $3 \times 4 \div 2 + 5 =$

▨ DECIMALS

Decimals are one way to express parts of numbers. You have seen decimals all over the place—in price tags, paychecks, and digital scales. Everything after the decimal point is smaller than 1, and the place values have their own names: tenths, hundredths, thousandths, ten thousandths, and so on. So in the number 123.456, 4 is in the *tenths* place, 5 is in the *hundredths* place, and 6 is in the *thousandths* place.

Addition with decimals is exactly the same as it is with whole numbers; you just have to be sure to line up the decimals (remember—neatness counts!). So if a problem asks you to add 123.456 and 789.8099, you would line up the decimals with each other and get:

$$\begin{array}{r} 123.456 \\ + \underline{789.8099} \end{array}$$

Adding each column, you get 913.2659.

Subtracting with decimals is also exactly the same; just line up the decimals and subtract, borrowing as you need to.

$$\begin{array}{r} 25.64 \\ -\ 19.72 \\ \hline 5.92 \end{array}$$

You only get into new rules when you start multiplying and dividing with decimals. With multiplication, you do not really have to deal with the decimals and the multiplication at the same time—you just have to remember to add an extra step on the end. For example, if a problem asks you to multiply 14.6 and 2.1, you can ignore the decimals and treat it as a regular multiplication problem:

$$\begin{array}{r} 146 \\ \times\ \ \ 21 \\ \hline 3{,}066 \end{array}$$

Now it is time for the extra step. Go back to your original numbers, 14.6 and 2.1, and count the number of digits after the decimal. There is one in each number, or two total. That means your answer has to have two digits after the decimal. So 3,066 becomes 30.66. That is it. Having said that, you *must* be sure to include that last step, or you will definitely get the problem wrong (and the test writers may even include 3,066 in the answer choices so that you do not know you have made a mistake and therefore will not correct yourself). Tricky, but that is what the test creators like to do.

Let us try another one: 3.49×6.8. First, ignore the decimals and line them up like a regular multiplication problem:

$$\begin{array}{r} 349 \\ \times\ \ \ \ 68 \\ \hline 23{,}732 \end{array}$$

Then count the digits after the decimals: There are two in 3.49 and one in 6.8, giving you three total. So your answer also must have three digits after the decimal: 23.732. Done!

With division, the rules change a little bit, which is both good news and bad news. The good news is that you do not have to worry about remainders; remainders and decimals just do not mix. The better news is that dividing with decimals is usually kept pretty straightforward on these tests. Really, the only (kind of) bad news is that sometimes, you have to pay a little extra attention to what you are doing.

When dividing with decimals, you can ignore the decimals again, just like with multiplication. So if the problem says $4.8 \div 1.6$, you would put those numbers into our regular long division format: $1.6\overline{)4.8}$.

When you divide, you get 3. Here is the part where you have to pay attention to what you are doing: To determine how many digits are behind the decimal, you take the number of digits behind the decimal in the dividend (4.8) and subtract the number of digits behind the decimal in the divisor (1.6). Because there is one digit behind the decimal in each of these numbers, you have $1 - 1$, which equals 0. That means there are zero digits after the decimal in the answer (or we move the decimal zero places), so the answer remains 3.

Now try some problems with decimals. Solutions are at the end of the chapter.

Practice Set 3: Decimals

Answers for this practice set can be found at the end of this chapter.

1. $4.2 + 1.83 =$
2. $0.95 + 1.28 =$
3. $82.4 - 7.93 =$
4. $2.4 - 1.99 =$
5. $0.12 \times 0.27 =$
6. $6.23 \times 0.4 =$
7. $1.45 \div 0.5 =$
8. $2.06 \div 0.4 =$

Rounding Decimals

To round decimal numbers to the nearest place, follow these steps:

Consider the decimal number, 3.4925.

Step I: Identify the digit in the decimal number to be rounded.
• If asked to round to the nearest tenth, the digit is 4.
• If asked to round to the nearest hundredth, the digit is 9.
• If asked to round to the nearest thousandth, the digit is 2.

Step II: Then identify the digit immediately to the right of the number that is being rounded.
• The digit immediately to the right of the tenth position is 9.
• The digit immediately to the right of the hundredth position is 2.
• The digit immediately to the right of the thousandth position is 5.

Step III: Depending on the result of Step II, there are two possibilities.
• If the digit identified in Step II is 0 – 4 (0, 1, 2, 3, 4), then the digit being rounded remains the same.
• If the digit identified in Step II is 5 – 9 (5, 6, 7, 8, 9), then the digit being rounded increases by 1.

Step IV: Apply the result of Step III as follows.
• If asked to round 3.4925 to the nearest tenth, then the result is 3.5.
• If asked to round 3.4925 to the nearest hundredth, then the result is 3.49.
• If asked to round 3.4925 to the nearest thousandth, then the result is 3.493.

Practice Set 4: Rounding

Answers for this practice set can be found at the end of this chapter.

1. Round 8.7356 to the nearest hundredth.
2. Round 32.51 to the nearest whole number.
3. Round 99.99 to the nearest tenth.
4. Round 2.452 to the nearest tenth.
5. Round the same number in problem 4 above to the nearest hundredth.

▌▌▌ FRACTIONS

Fractions express the same kind of idea as decimals—basically, you are dealing with some parts smaller than one. The top of the fraction is called the *numerator* and the bottom is the *denominator*. The denominator tells you how many pieces the whole is being divided into, and the numerator tells you how many of those pieces you are dealing with. For example, if Scott has $\frac{2}{3}$ of a candy bar, the candy bar has been divided up into three pieces, and he has two of them. If Joanne counts 10 marbles in a bag and 7 of them are blue, $\frac{7}{10}$ of the marbles in the bag are blue.

Of course, sometimes fractions represent larger numbers than they seem to. Perhaps Heather tells you that $\frac{2}{5}$ of the employees in her office manage at least one other person. You know that Heather works in a large office, so she is probably talking about more than literally two people out of five in the whole office. The fraction is one way to present "two in every five." But how did she come up with that number? Perhaps there are 1,000 people who work in her office, and she heard a statistic that 400 of them are managers. That means the fraction was originally $\frac{400}{1,000}$. Those are pretty big numbers to manipulate, so we reduce fractions to make them more manageable. Also, on exams, you generally will have to reduce any fractions you work with because the correct answers are reduced as much as they can be, which means they have had as much as possible divided out of both the numerator and denominator— whatever you divide out of one of them, you must do with the other, as well.

Reducing Fractions

Let us reduce $\frac{400}{1,000}$. The first thing you should look for to reduce is whether there are 0s at the end of both the numerator and the denominator. In this case, there are two 0s in the numerator and three 0s in the denominator. Remember, you cannot do something to one part that you could not do to the other part, so in this case you can remove just two 0s from both parts. (It's actually not just removing 0s, of course; it's dividing by 100. This applies only to 0s; you could not just remove 3s on the end of both the numerator and denominator!)

Now your fraction is $\frac{4}{10}$. After removing 0s (i.e., dividing by 10 or 100 or 1,000), you look for other numbers to divide by. Remember the divisibility rules you reviewed in the Integers section? Those come in handy here. The number 2 is always a good one to check toward the beginning of the process; if both the numerator and the denominator are even, divide them both by 2 as many times as you can.

In this case, the numerator and the denominator are divisible by 2, so your fraction is now $\frac{2}{5}$. You cannot divide by 2 again because 5 is odd. You cannot divide by 3 either, because neither 2 nor 5 is divisible by 3. This is kind of similar to checking possible factors and trying to determine whether a number is prime; once you have reached halfway to the larger number, you can stop. The fraction $\frac{2}{5}$ is reduced as much as it can be. (One other way to tell that it is reduced is that both numbers are prime. Not *all* reduced fractions have two primes, but if you do have two primes, you know the fraction is reduced.) Let's try some more reducing.

What is the most reduced form of $\frac{96}{32}$? This problem does not let you divide by 10 or 100 because there are no 0s at the end, so let's go straight to 2. Both the numerator and the denominator are divisible by 2, giving you $\frac{48}{16}$.

Again, you can divide by 2, giving you $\frac{24}{8}$. Divide again by 2 to get $\frac{12}{4}$. And dividing *again* by 2 gives you $\frac{6}{2}$. Divide again and you have $\frac{3}{1}$ or just 3. One more.

What is the most reduced form of $\frac{15}{130}$? Again, you do not have 0s at the end, but this time you do not have two even numbers either. Checking divisibility for 3, you see that 15 is divisible but 130 is not. There is no reason to check for 4, because 15 is not even (and all numbers divisible by 4 are definitely even). Both are divisible by 5, so divide. Your new numerator is $15 \div 5 = 3$. Your new denominator is $130 \div 5 = 26$. The fraction must be reduced now because you know you cannot divide by 3 or anything smaller than 3. So your answer is $\frac{3}{26}$.

It's your turn to reduce some fractions. Solutions are at the end of the chapter.

Practice Set 5: Reducing Fractions

1. $\frac{40}{55} =$ 3. $\frac{64}{16} =$ 5. $\frac{12}{54} =$

2. $\frac{81}{45} =$ 4. $\frac{72}{28} =$ 6. $\frac{321}{243} =$

Adding and Subtracting Fractions

You may have learned in school that to add and subtract fractions, you need to find the least common multiple of the denominators or something to that effect. That is a good method, but we are going to use a shortcut method called the bowtie for our purposes. This method has three steps and it can be used on any two fractions, no matter whether you are adding or subtracting.

Let us try an example:

$$\frac{1}{2}$$

The first step of the bowtie is to multiply following the arrows below:

$$\frac{1}{2} \diagdown\!\!\!\!\diagup \frac{1}{3} = ?$$

So now you have $3 \times 1 = 3$ and $2 \times 1 = 2$. The second step is to add or subtract your new numbers, based on the operator in the problem. Here you have an addition sign, so you add: $3 + 2 = 5$. The result, 5, is the numerator of your answer. The third step is to multiply the denominators to get the denominator of your answer. In this case, $2 \times 3 = 6$, so your answer is $\frac{5}{6}$.

Let us try another:

$$\frac{5}{8}$$

Step 1 involves multiplying across in the direction of the arrows.

$$\frac{5}{8} \diagdown\!\!\!\!\diagup \frac{3}{5} = ?$$

$$5 \times 5 = 25 \text{ and } 8 \times 3 = 24$$

Step 2 involves adding or subtracting, according to the operation sign, to get the numerator of the correct answer.

$$25 - 24 = 1$$

Step 3 involves multiplying denominators to get the denominator of the correct answer.

$$8 \times 5 = 40$$

So the correct answer is $\dfrac{1}{40}$.

Now it is time to try a few on your own. The solutions to the drill are at the end of the chapter.

Practice Set 6: Adding and Subtracting Fractions

1. $\dfrac{4}{5} + \dfrac{3}{4} =$ 4. $\dfrac{5}{2} + \dfrac{6}{7} =$ 7. $\dfrac{8}{9} - \dfrac{2}{3} =$

2. $\dfrac{1}{3} + \dfrac{5}{7} =$ 5. $\dfrac{4}{5} - \dfrac{1}{2} =$ 8. $\dfrac{2}{3} - \dfrac{1}{5} =$

3. $\dfrac{2}{9} + \dfrac{3}{5} =$ 6. $\dfrac{7}{5} - \dfrac{3}{4} =$

Multiplying and Dividing Fractions

Multiplying fractions, by comparison, is pretty easy. All you have to do is multiply the numerators, then multiply the denominators. For example:

$$\frac{3}{2} \times \frac{2}{5} = ?$$

The calculation $3 \times 2 = 6$ makes 6 the numerator of the fraction. The calculation $2 \times 5 = 10$ makes 10 the denominator. So your new fraction is $\dfrac{6}{10}$, but that needs to be reduced to be a correct answer on most tests; you can reduce it to $\dfrac{3}{5}$.

Dividing fractions is almost the same, but there is one step to add at the beginning: You must flip the second fraction first, and then you can just multiply straight across as you did for multiplying fractions. So if you start with this problem:

$$\frac{3}{10} \div \frac{5}{4} = ?$$

You would just flip the second fraction so that your new problem looks like this:

$$\frac{3}{10} \times \frac{4}{5} = ?$$

Multiply straight across and you get $3 \times 4 = 12$ for the numerator and $10 \times 5 = 50$ for the denominator. $\dfrac{12}{50}$ reduces to $\dfrac{6}{25}$, so that is your answer.

One thing to note: Sometimes you may see fraction division problems expressed this way:

$$\frac{\frac{3}{10}}{\frac{5}{4}} = ?$$

A line separating a numerator from a denominator is essentially a division sign, so this is really the same as $\frac{3}{10} \div \frac{5}{4}$. Feel free to rewrite it that way first if it makes things easier to work!

Now it is your turn. Solutions are at the end of the chapter.

Practice Set 7: Multiplying and Dividing Fractions

1. $\frac{1}{5} \times \frac{3}{10} =$ 4. $\frac{4}{9} \times \frac{1}{7} =$ 7. $\frac{8}{3} \div \frac{5}{6} =$

2. $\frac{1}{2} \times \frac{4}{5} =$ 5. $\frac{3}{8} \div \frac{1}{2} =$ 8. $\frac{4}{5} \div \frac{3}{10} =$

3. $\frac{2}{3} \times \frac{5}{6} =$ 6. $\frac{6}{7} \div \frac{3}{1} =$

Comparing Fractions

You can use the bowtie method to compare two fractions as well, and the process is even shorter than for adding and subtracting. Given two fractions side-by-side, just multiply in the direction of the arrows again.

$$\frac{3}{8} \bowtie \frac{1}{4}$$

In this example, you end up with 12 on the left and 8 on the right, which means that the fraction on the left is larger than the fraction on the right.

Mixed Numbers

Occasionally, you will see numbers such as $1\frac{3}{8}$ or $3\frac{5}{6}$. These are called *mixed numbers*—numbers that are fractions but larger than 1. To add, subtract, or otherwise manipulate them, you must convert them to improper fractions, which are fractions that have a larger numerator than denominator. To convert a mixed number to an improper fraction requires two steps.

Let us take $3\frac{5}{6}$ as an example. Step 1 is to multiply the integer (in this case, 3) by the denominator (in this case, 6), which works out to $3 \times 6 = 18$. Step 2 is to add the result to the numerator, which is 5. So that looks like $\frac{18+5}{6}$, which solves as $\frac{23}{6}$. Done!

How about $1\frac{3}{4}$? Multiply the integer in front by the denominator ($1 \times 4 = 4$), then add it to the numerator $\frac{4+3}{4} = \frac{7}{4}$. And you are done; $1\frac{3}{4} = \frac{7}{4}$.

Once a mixed number is converted to an improper fraction, you can treat it exactly the same as a regular fraction; follow the same rules for adding, subtracting, multiplying, dividing, reducing, and anything else you can think of to do to a fraction.

Ready to try a few more? Solutions are at the end of the chapter.

Practice Set 8: Converting Mixed Numbers to Improper Fractions

1. $2\frac{2}{3} =$

2. $1\frac{5}{6} =$

3. $3\frac{3}{5} =$

4. $4\frac{1}{3} =$

5. $2\frac{3}{7} =$

6. $4\frac{5}{8} =$

▬▬▬ PERCENTAGES

You almost certainly deal with (or at least see) percentages every single day. If you think about it, there is a good chance that you have seen one or all of the following examples on a regular basis:

- Sales tax of 7% on your purchase
- Clearance sales offering 75% off the lowest marked price
- A 3% increase in inflation
- Annual interest of 19.99% on a credit card balance
- A 15% gratuity at a restaurant

So even if percentages were not a frequent topic on nursing school entrance exams (which they are), it would make your everyday life easier to know how to deal with them well.

First, you need to know that *percent* means *out of one hundred*. So if you are paying a 15% gratuity, you are paying 15 cents for every 100 cents (or one dollar) you have already paid. Have you ever heard the expression "pennies on the dollar"? Well, it is the same as saying *percent*—if you are paying only a few pennies on the dollar, you are paying only a few *percent* of the original price. (Of course, ads that say you are paying pennies on the dollar could well mean you will pay 80 pennies on the dollar, but the impression they want to give is that you are paying only a few percent.)

Converting Fractions, Decimals, and Percents

One of the most important things to know about percentages is how to convert fractions, decimals, and percents. In fact, some exams have sections dedicated to these conversions, but the lucky thing is that you can memorize the most common conversions, and learn a basic formula to calculate the rest. Ready with your index cards?

Percent	Fraction	Decimal
5%	$\frac{1}{20}$	0.05
10%	$\frac{1}{10}$	0.1 or 0.10
15%	$\frac{3}{20}$	0.15
20%	$\frac{1}{5}$	0.2 or 0.20
25%	$\frac{1}{4}$	0.25
30%	$\frac{3}{10}$	0.3 or 0.30
35%	$\frac{7}{20}$	0.35
40%	$\frac{2}{5}$	0.4 or 0.40
45%	$\frac{9}{20}$	0.45
50%	$\frac{1}{2}$	0.5 or 0.50
55%	$\frac{11}{20}$	0.55
60%	$\frac{3}{5}$	0.6 or 0.60
65%	$\frac{13}{20}$	0.65
70%	$\frac{7}{10}$	0.7 or .70
75%	$\frac{3}{4}$	0.75
80%	$\frac{4}{5}$	0.8 or 0.80
85%	$\frac{17}{20}$	0.85
90%	$\frac{9}{10}$	0.9 or 0.90
95%	$\frac{19}{20}$	0.95
100%	$\frac{1}{1}$ or 1	1 or 1.0 or 1.00
12.5%	$\frac{1}{8}$	0.125
37.5%	$\frac{3}{8}$	0.375
62.5%	$\frac{5}{8}$	0.625
87.5%	$\frac{7}{8}$	0.875

Should you come across a problem that is unfamiliar on one of your exams (or you blank out, as even the best test-takers do from time to time), remember that you can always follow these steps to convert from one system to another:

- **From percents to decimals.** Take off the percent sign and move the decimal two places to the left.
  75% becomes 0.75
  500% becomes 5.0

- **From decimals to percents.** Do the opposite; move the decimal two places to the right and add a percent sign.
  0.345 becomes 34.5%
  0.6 becomes 60%
  2.6 becomes 260%

- **From fractions to percents.** Treat the fraction as a division problem; actually move the numbers into a division sign and work the math. Then move the decimal two places to the right and add a percent sign at the end.

  $\frac{4}{5}$ becomes 0.8, or 80%

  $\frac{3}{8}$ becomes 0.375, or 37.5%

- **From percents to fractions.** Remove the percent sign and make the number the numerator of a fraction, with 100 on the bottom. Reduce, and you are done. (And if you need to brush up on reducing, see the section on fractions.)

  65% becomes $\frac{65}{100}$, which reduces to $\frac{13}{20}$

  120% becomes $\frac{120}{100}$, which reduces to $\frac{6}{5}$

- **From fractions to decimals.** Treat the fraction as a division problem; actually move the numbers into a division sign and work the math. This time you do not have to convert to percents, so you are done!

  $\frac{1}{4}$ becomes 0.25

  $\frac{11}{20}$ becomes 0.55

- **From decimals to fractions.** Move the decimal two places to the right and make the number the numerator of a fraction, with 100 on the bottom. Reduce and you are done.

  0.75 becomes $\frac{75}{100}$, which reduces to $\frac{3}{4}$

  0.60 becomes $\frac{60}{100}$, which reduces to $\frac{3}{5}$

Changing a percent or decimal to a fraction is less common than the other four types of conversions, but should you need to do it in the context of any problem type, there is your guide. One note on converting from fractions: If a problem asks you to convert from a ratio to a decimal or percent, it is the exact same as converting from a fraction; just take the ratio and change it into a fraction (for example, 3:2 becomes $\frac{3}{2}$).

Ready for some practice on your own? Solutions are at the end of the chapter.

Practice Set 9: Converting Fractions, Decimals, and Percents

1. What is 27.5% as a decimal?
2. What is 33% as a decimal?
3. What is 0.425 as a percent?
4. What is 3.9 as a percent?
5. What is $\dfrac{12}{15}$ as a decimal?
6. What is $\dfrac{8.75}{10}$ as a percent?

Calculating Percentages

As you may have noticed from the examples at the beginning of this section, you really never deal with percentages alone; a percent is only significant when it is a percent *of something else*. That means that you are always multiplying the percent times another number. So if you are calculating 7 percent sales tax on a $20 purchase, you multiply 7% × 20. You do that by converting the percentage to either a fraction or a decimal, whichever you prefer, and multiplying out:

$$0.07 \times 20 = 1.4$$

or

$$\frac{7}{100} \times 20 = \frac{140}{100} = 1.4$$

Either way, you end up with 1.4, or $1.40 in sales tax.

Let us take another example. You find a shirt on clearance and it is marked at 75% off the original price of $40. How do you find 75% of $40? With decimals, that is $0.75 \times 40 = 30$. With fractions, that is $\dfrac{75}{100} \times 40 = \dfrac{300}{100} = 30$.

So 75% of $40 is $30. But remember what you are calculating; the item is 75% *off*, which is the same as saying $30 off. The clearance price of the item is $40 – $30, or $10. A little ballparking will take you a long way toward the correct answer on these problems; if an item is 75% off, that is *more than half* off, so the final price should be *less than half* of the original.

One more: The bill at a restaurant is $80 and you want to leave a 15% gratuity. What is 15% of 80? With decimals, that is $0.15 \times 80 = 12$. With fractions, that is $\dfrac{15}{100} \times 80 = \dfrac{1,200}{100} = 12$. Either way, you are leaving a $12 tip.

By the way, what if the problem asked you to calculate the entire bill, including gratuity? You would just add $12 to the $80 you already had, giving you a $92 total.

Okay, now it is your turn for some practice. Solutions are at the end of the chapter.

Practice Set 10: Calculating Percentages

1. What is 75% of 120?
2. What is 40% of 75?
3. What is 80% of 90?
4. What is 45% of 80?
5. What is 25% of 30?
6. What is 65% of 160?

Word Problems Involving Percents

Some problems are set up as word problems and they appear as if you have to make up an equation to solve them. But actually, you do not have to make up that equation yourself. In fact, all it takes is some translation to take the problem directly from English into equation form. That is great news, because setting up the equation correctly is at least half the battle toward getting that question right.

For example, take the following question:

The number 5 is what percent of 4?

This type of question is extremely common, but do not worry—each word in the question has a direct correlation in math-speak (and the numbers stay the same). So here is the same sentence, translated into a mathematical equation:

$$5 = x\% \times 4$$

You know from your experience with percentages that *percent* means *out of one hundred* or *over one hundred*, so you can do a little bit of manipulating and get $5 = \dfrac{x}{100} \times 4$, which is the same as $5 = \dfrac{4x}{100}$. Now you can just solve the equation $5 = \dfrac{4x}{100}$.

Multiply each side by 100, which gives $500 = 4x$. Then divide each side by 4, which gives $\dfrac{500}{4} = \dfrac{4x}{4}$. And solve: $125 = x$.

If you do not remember how to manipulate the equation, do not worry. We will take it step by step and go into all of the "whys" in the algebra section.

Let us try another translation question:

80% of what number is 4?

First, you translate: $\dfrac{80}{100} \times x = 4$. That is the same as $\dfrac{80x}{100} = 4$. Multiply each side by 100 to get $80x = 400$. Divide each side by 80 to get $\dfrac{80x}{80} = \dfrac{400}{80}$. And solve: $x = 5$.

Ready to put these skills to the test? Translate and calculate percentages on the following drill. The solutions are at the end of the chapter.

Practice Set 11: Word Problems Involving Percents

1. 49 is what percent of 140?
2. 21 is what percent of 70?
3. 36 is what percent of 45?
4. 15% of what number is 12?
5. 80% of what number is 40?
6. 20% of what number is 12?

Shortcuts in Computing Percents

Now that you have learned how to approach most percent problems on your entrance exams, here are some other shortcuts to help out in a pinch (on tests and in real life). If you do not like multiplying by 15 or 12.5, you can use the hints to "brute force" your way through percentage problems when your math muscles just are not in shape.

- **You can calculate 10% of anything.** Calculating 10% is just moving the decimal one place to the left, so 10% of 50 is 5, 10% of 0.3 is 0.03, and 10% of 873 is 87.3. This alone can help you ballpark if, say, you are asked to take 12% of a number; just find 10% and pick the one that is a little bit more.
- **You can calculate 1% of anything.** Calculating 1% is just moving the decimal *two* places to the left, so 1% of 400 is 4, 1% of 62 is 0.62, and 1% of 0.4 is 0.004. Again, helpful for ballparking on its own, but when you combine it with your ability to take 10%, you are able to add or subtract 1% and zoom in on the correct answer with ease.
- **You can calculate 5% of anything.** Remember how you can calculate 10% of anything? Well, calculating 5% of that number is the same as calculating 10% of the same number, then dividing it by two. Between now and your test, practice calculating tips such as this: Take 10% of the bill (and write it down if you wish), then take half of that and add it to the 10% you wrote down. Voila—you have just calculated a 15% gratuity.

SOLVING WORD PROBLEMS

This section pertains to a skill that is probably tested more than any other on the CBEST—your ability to interpret a word problem and decide what to do. Many people know their math, but when they see a word problem, they freeze up and don't know what to do. However, even though most of the CBEST problems are word problems, there is no reason to panic. In this section, we'll go step-by-step through sample word problems. If you can break down word problems and approach them one step at a time, they're really not that hard.

Sample Word Problems Step-by-Step

You already know how to subtract fractions such as $6 - 2\frac{4}{5}$. Many problems on the CBEST test the same math but in a context that looks like this:

> A certain beaker can hold 6 ounces of fluid without running over. If there is $2\frac{4}{5}$ ounces already in the beaker, how much can be added without overflowing the beaker?

This kind of problem adds an extra step: You have to decide which operations to perform. The translation skills you have learned in the Percentages and Algebra sections will be helpful in this process, and this section will add a few helpful hints and lots of practice.

One of the best things you can do if you do not know where to begin on a word problem is to start drawing. If your mind is freezing up, it may be because it cannot deal concretely with the information it is given, and particularly if you are a visual learner, drawing a picture can help you start to deal with the information. Do not worry; you do not have to be an expert artist. Even the most basic shapes can represent the information you are given.

For example, for the beaker problem above, you might draw something that looks like this:

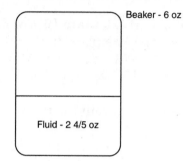

From there, you can even write out questions or emphasize areas that represent the amount you are trying to find. For example:

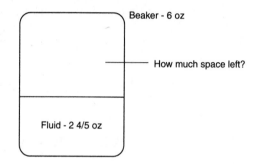

You can see that to find the missing quantity, you would have to subtract $2\frac{4}{5}$ from the whole. So set up the problem:

$$6 - 2\frac{4}{5}$$

$$= \frac{6}{1} - \frac{14}{5}$$

Multiplying across gives you $30 - 14$ for the numerator and 5 for the denominator, so that is a complete fraction of $\frac{16}{5}$ or, if the question has mixed numbers in the answers, $3\frac{1}{5}$.

Try another one.

Labels will be cut from a sheet of paper that measures 9 inches by 12 inches. If each label needs to be $2\frac{1}{4}$ inches by $1\frac{1}{3}$ inches, how many labels can be cut from that sheet of paper?

This is another good one to draw, just so that you do not have to deal with all of this in your head.

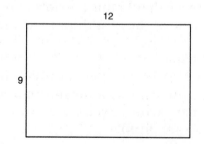

A problem like this does not require you to arrange each label; you just need to decide which side of the paper divides most neatly into sections of the size you need. Is 9 divisible by $2\frac{1}{4}$? Yes, but 12 is not, so it is a good bet that you are going to be dividing up the 9-inch side into $2\frac{1}{4}$-inch sections; $2\frac{1}{4}$ divides into 9 four times:

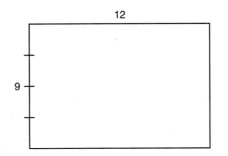

Now how many times does $1\frac{1}{3}$ go into 12? Some quick calculation tells you 9, so you will have 4×9 labels on the sheet of paper, which multiplies out to 36. Again, draw out as much as you need to help with the problem, label as much as you can, be neat, and do not waste time trying to make it perfect.

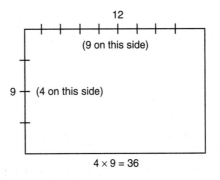

On the other hand, sometimes you will not have much to draw, but you still will have words in the problem that will give you clues of what to do.

Here is another example:

Mrs. Aziz walks two miles per day at the beginning of a fitness program. Exactly five months later, she is walking four miles per day. On average, how much per month has she increased her daily walk?

You can tell by the word "average" that this is an average/mean problem. Normally, you would be given a list of numbers to add up and divide, but does this problem have another way of telling you the total that you need to divide by? Well, you know that Mrs. Aziz's walk went from two to four miles, so that is an increase of two; that is your total. Because the increase happened over five months and you are being asked for a monthly average, you would divide by five. So she increased her daily walk an average of $\frac{2}{5}$ of a mile per month.

Try one more.

A certain hospital has 24 beds in the emergency room. If 25% of the beds are currently occupied, how many more patients can the emergency room accept before all beds are full?

Whether you draw this one is up to you; it might be a good idea just to remind you of what you're looking for.

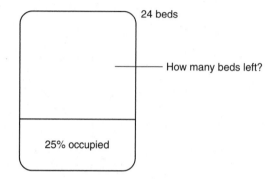

Now you need to do the math; 25% of 24 = 6. That means 6 beds are occupied, and 24 − 6 = 18 beds are available in the emergency room.

Be careful on problems like these to focus on what the problem is asking (how many beds are available) instead of the first calculation you need to do (how many beds are occupied). Drawing a quick picture can help keep you focused on the correct part of the problem.

Now it is your turn to try a few. Solutions are at the end of the chapter.

Practice Set 12: Applied Math

1. A patient is taking 150 mg of a certain prescription every day. How much of the prescription will the patient take during one week?
2. Marci is planning to sell all her shares of a certain stock if their value falls to $30 per share. If the value of the stock is now $45 per share, by what percent would they have to fall for Marci to sell?
3. A banquet room that measures 100 feet by 200 feet is being arranged for a party. If a space measuring 20 feet by 20 feet is needed for each table, what is the maximum number of tables that can be arranged in the room?
4. A certain barrel can hold 50 gallons of liquid. If Tom has to fill it using a one-quart container and he fills the container up completely each time, how many times will he have to pour the container into the barrel?
5. If Sara's current salary is $25,000 per year and she is due to get a 3% raise this year in addition to a 2% cost of living increase, how much will her salary be after these increases take effect?
6. If a family's total income is spent on the following expenses: one-fourth for the mortgage, one-eighth for car payments, one-eighth for groceries, two-fifths on other expenses, and the rest to savings, what fraction of the family's total income goes toward savings?

▉▉▉ NUMBER SEQUENCE QUESTIONS

There are a few number sequence questions in the mathematics section of the CBEST. These questions typically ask you to choose the correct sequence out of the answer choices or to select the number that is between two numbers provided in the question. These questions are relatively simple but must be read carefully so that you don't make a mistake. Usually, these questions include fractions, decimals, or lengthy numbers that are designed to trip up the careless reader.

Fractions: Problems involving fractions are not likely to involve comparable numbers (such as $\frac{2}{4}$ and $\frac{3}{4}$). One way to solve these problems is to convert the fractions to match each other. For example, you can covert $\frac{15}{20}$ to $\frac{3}{4}$. Many questions include fractions that are not easily converted or compared; for these questions, convert all of the fractions to decimals and solve.

Decimals: Remember the values of the places after the decimal point. Many questions provide numbers designed to confuse you. For example, compare the numbers 6.36, 6.24, 6.2, 6.3, and 6.12; 6.12 is the smallest number. Don't think of 6.12 as six point twelve; note that .12 is smaller than .2 because it has a lower quantity in the tenths place. In addition, a larger quantity of digits after the decimal point does not equal a larger value. Compare the values in the tenths place, then the hundredths, and so on.

Number order: Last, remember the values of the places to the left of the decimal point (tens, hundreds, thousands) and that negative numbers decrease in value as the number increases (–17 is a lower number than –16).

Practice Set 13: Number Sequences

1. Which is a number between 4,387,200 and 4,420,200?
   4,430,201   4,420,199   4,387,100   4,385,000   4,422,200
2. Which number is greater, $\frac{3}{5}$ or $\frac{4}{7}$?
3. List the numbers in order from least to greatest.
   0.737, 0.721, 0.73, 0.7888, 0.7
4. List the numbers in order from greatest to least.
   –55, –50, –53.3, –51, –46
5. List the numbers in order from greatest to least.

   $\frac{7}{13}, \frac{14}{37}, \frac{11}{33}, \frac{21}{31}, \frac{13}{17}$

6. List the numbers in order from least to greatest.

   $-\frac{3}{34}, 5.67, 7\frac{1}{8}, 10, -\frac{17}{13}$

▉ SOLUTIONS TO PRACTICE SETS

Congratulations! You've worked through content on computations, decimals, fractions, and percents that is on the CBEST mathematics test. Here are the answers to the practice sets.

Practice Set 1

1. $1,473 + 582 = 2,055$
2. $5,391 + 6,729 = 12,120$
3. $12,843 + 5,928 = 18,771$
4. $3,609 - 1,727 = 1,882$
5. $2,381 - 962 = 1,419$
6. $768 - 529 = 239$
7. $408 \times 52 = 21,216$
8. $823 \times 7 = 5,761$
9. $521 \times 47 = 24,487$
10. $709 \div 4 = 177$
11. $341 \div 3 = 114$
12. $672 \div 16 = 42$

Practice Set 2

1. $3 + 2 \times 4 = 11$. Multiply 2 and 4, and then add 3.
2. $(10 - 4) \div 3 = 2$. Subtract 4 from 10 first because these numbers are inside parentheses, and then divide by 3.
3. $4 \times 3 - 5 = 7$. Multiply 4 and 3, and then subtract 5.
4. $15 - 8 \div 2 = 11$. Divide 8 by 2, and then subtract the result from 15.
5. $(9 + 2) \times 2 = 22$. Add 9 and 2 first because these numbers are inside parentheses, and then multiply the result by 2.
6. $3 \times 4 \div 2 + 5 = 11$. Multiply 3 and 4, then divide by 2, and then add 5.

Practice Set 3

1. $4.2 + 1.83 = 6.03$
2. $0.95 + 1.28 = 2.23$
3. $82.4 - 7.93 = 74.47$
4. $2.4 - 1.99 = 0.41$
5. $0.12 \times 0.27 = 0.0324$
6. $6.23 \times 0.4 = 2.492$
7. $1.45 \div 0.5 = 2.9$
8. $2.06 \div 0.4 = 5.15$

Practice Set 4

1. 8.74
2. 33
3. 100.0
4. 2.5
5. 2.45

Practice Set 5

1. $\dfrac{40}{55} = \dfrac{8}{11}$

2. $\dfrac{81}{45} = \dfrac{9}{5}$

3. $\dfrac{64}{16} = 4$

4. $\dfrac{72}{28} = \dfrac{18}{7}$

5. $\dfrac{12}{54} = \dfrac{2}{9}$

6. $\dfrac{321}{243} = \dfrac{107}{81}$

Practice Set 6

1. $\dfrac{4}{5} + \dfrac{3}{4} = \dfrac{31}{20}$

   $16 + 15 = 31$ for the numerator and $5 \times 4 = 20$ for the denominator makes $\dfrac{31}{20}$.

2. $\dfrac{1}{3} + \dfrac{5}{7} = \dfrac{22}{21}$

   $7 + 15$ for the numerator and 3×7 for the denominator makes $\dfrac{22}{21}$.

3. $\dfrac{2}{9} + \dfrac{3}{5} = \dfrac{37}{45}$

   $10 + 27$ for the numerator and 9×5 for the denominator makes $\dfrac{37}{45}$.

4. $\dfrac{5}{2} + \dfrac{6}{7} = \dfrac{47}{14}$

   $35 + 12$ for the numerator and 2×7 for the denominator makes $\dfrac{47}{14}$.

5. $\dfrac{4}{5} - \dfrac{1}{2} = \dfrac{3}{10}$

    8 – 5 for the numerator and 5×2 for the denominator makes $\dfrac{3}{10}$.

6. $\dfrac{7}{5} - \dfrac{3}{4} = \dfrac{13}{20}$

    28 – 15 for the numerator and 5×4 for the denominator makes $\dfrac{13}{20}$.

7. $\dfrac{8}{9} - \dfrac{2}{3} = \dfrac{2}{9}$

    24 – 18 for the numerator and 9×3 for the denominator makes $\dfrac{6}{27}$, which reduces to $\dfrac{2}{9}$.

8. $\dfrac{2}{3} - \dfrac{1}{5} = \dfrac{7}{15}$

    10 – 3 for the numerator and 5×3 for the denominator makes $\dfrac{7}{15}$.

Practice Set 7

1. $\dfrac{1}{5} \times \dfrac{3}{10} = \dfrac{3}{50}$

2. $\dfrac{1}{2} \times \dfrac{4}{5} = \dfrac{4}{10} = \dfrac{2}{5}$

3. $\dfrac{2}{3} \times \dfrac{5}{6} = \dfrac{10}{18} = \dfrac{5}{9}$

4. $\dfrac{4}{9} \times \dfrac{1}{7} = \dfrac{4}{63}$

5. $\dfrac{3}{8} \div \dfrac{1}{2} = \dfrac{3}{8} \times \dfrac{2}{1} = \dfrac{6}{8} = \dfrac{3}{4}$

6. $\dfrac{6}{7} \div \dfrac{3}{1} = \dfrac{6}{7} \times \dfrac{1}{3} = \dfrac{6}{21} = \dfrac{2}{7}$

7. $\dfrac{8}{3} \div \dfrac{5}{6} = \dfrac{8}{3} \times \dfrac{6}{5} = \dfrac{48}{15} = \dfrac{16}{5}$

8. $\dfrac{4}{5} \div \dfrac{3}{10} = \dfrac{4}{5} \times \dfrac{10}{3} = \dfrac{40}{15} = \dfrac{8}{3}$

Practice Set 8

1. $2\dfrac{2}{3} = \dfrac{8}{3}$

2. $1\dfrac{5}{6} = \dfrac{11}{6}$

3. $3\dfrac{3}{5} = \dfrac{18}{5}$

4. $4\dfrac{1}{3} = \dfrac{13}{3}$

5. $2\frac{3}{7} = \frac{17}{7}$

6. $4\frac{5}{8} = \frac{37}{8}$

Practice Set 9

1. 27.5% as a decimal = 0.275
2. 33% as a decimal = 0.33
3. 0.425 as a percent = 42.5%
4. 3.9 as a percent = 390%
5. $\frac{12}{15}$ as a decimal = 0.8
6. $\frac{8.75}{10}$ as a percent = 87.5%

Practice Set 10

1. 90
   0.75×120
   $75 \times 120 = 9,000$, then move the decimal two places to the left.
2. 30
   0.40×75
   $40 \times 75 = 3,000$, then move the decimal two places to the left.
3. 72
   0.80×90
   $80 \times 90 = 7,200$, then move the decimal two places to the left. (Or you can start with 0.8×90, calculate $8 \times 90 = 720$, and move the decimal 1 place to the left. You end up in the same place, and the same is true for question 2 above.)
4. 36
   0.45×80
   $45 \times 80 = 3,600$, then move the decimal two places to the left.
5. 7.5
   0.25×30
   $25 \times 30 = 750$, then move the decimal two places to the left.
6. 104
   0.65×160
   $65 \times 160 = 10,400$, then move the decimal two places to the left.

Practice Set 11

1. 35
   Translation: $49 = \frac{x}{100} \times 140$

   $$49 = 49 = \frac{140x}{100}$$
   $$4900 = 140x$$
   $$\frac{4900}{140} = \frac{140x}{140}$$
   $$35 = x$$

2. 30

Translation: $21 = \dfrac{x}{100} \times 70$

$$21 = \dfrac{x}{100}$$

$$2{,}100 = 70x$$

$$\dfrac{2{,}100}{70} = \dfrac{70x}{70}$$

$$30 = x$$

3. 80

Translation: $36 = \dfrac{x}{100} \times 45$

$$36 = \dfrac{45x}{100}$$

$$3{,}600 = 45x$$

$$\dfrac{3{,}600}{45} = \dfrac{45x}{45}$$

$$80 = x$$

4. 80

Translation: $\dfrac{15}{100} \times x = 12$

$$\dfrac{15x}{100} = 12$$

$$15x = 1{,}200$$

$$\dfrac{15x}{15} = \dfrac{1200}{15}$$

$$x = 80$$

5. 50

Translation: $\dfrac{80}{100} \times x = 40$

$$\dfrac{80x}{100} = 40$$

$$80x = 4{,}000$$

$$\dfrac{80x}{80} = \dfrac{4000}{80}$$

$$x = 50$$

6. 60

Translation: $\dfrac{20}{100} \times x = 12$

$$\dfrac{20x}{100} = 12$$

$$20x = 1{,}200$$

$$\dfrac{20x}{20} = \dfrac{1200}{20}$$

$$x = 60$$

Practice Set 12

1. 1,050

   The patient is taking 150 mg per day over 7 days, so you need to multiply to get the total amount taken during that period; $150 \times 7 = 1,050$.

2. $33\frac{1}{3}\%$.

   Because the problem asks "by what percent" a change is made, you are dealing with percent change. The original is 45, and a drop to 30 would represent a difference of 15; this would make the fraction $\frac{15}{45}$, which reduces to $\frac{1}{3}$, or $33\frac{1}{3}\%$.

3. 50

   It may help to draw this one out if you are having trouble visualizing it. Twenty can fit into the 100-ft side five times and into the 200-ft side ten times. When you multiply 5×10, you get 50.

4. 200

   This is essentially a proportions problem. There are four quarts in a gallon, and the question is asking how many quarts there are in 50 gallons. The fraction on the left should have 4 (quarts) on the top and 1 (gallon) on the bottom, and the fraction on the right should have 50 (gallons) on the bottom and x on top. Cross-multiply and solve, and you get 200.

5. $26,250

   This problem is asking you to calculate a certain percentage of 25,000. The two percentages total up to 5%, and 5% of 25,000 is 1,250. Add this to 25,000 and you get 26,250.

6. $\frac{1}{10}$

   To complete this problem, you need to add up the fractions. You can do this by using the bowtie method on individual fractions or by combining fractions using any shortcuts you can find. For example, $\frac{1}{8} + \frac{1}{8} = \frac{2}{8}$, which reduces to $\frac{1}{4}$. Then, $\frac{1}{4} + \frac{1}{4} = \frac{2}{4}$, which you can bowtie with $\frac{2}{5}$ to get $\frac{9}{10}$. If $\frac{9}{10}$ is spent on other expenses and the rest is saved, then $\frac{1}{10}$ is saved.

Practice Set 13

1. 4,420,199

2. $\frac{3}{5}$

3. 0.7, 0.721, 0.73, 0.737, 0.7888

4. −46, −50, −51, −53.3, −55

5. $\frac{13}{17}, \frac{21}{31}, \frac{7}{13}, \frac{14}{37}, \frac{11}{33}$

6. $-\frac{17}{13}, -\frac{3}{34}, 5.67, 7\frac{1}{8}, 10$

CHAPTER 5

THE CBEST MATHEMATICS TEST: BASIC GEOMETRY AND ALGEBRA

Don't worry, you won't find difficult algebra or geometry on the CBEST. But you might need to review some of the basics. You need to be able to compute perimeters and areas of simple geometric figures. You also need to be able to solve equations with one variable (usually an x). And you need to be able to write algebraic expressions to represent word problem solutions.

Since most of the problems on the CBEST mathematics test are word problems, pay special attention to sections of this chapter dealing with these types of problems. Let's get started!

BASIC GEOMETRY

Geometry is one of the most dreaded subject areas for people who have not taken a math class in a long time. But there is good news. First, there are very few geometry problems on the CBEST. Second, there are no proofs or theorems. Do you remember those from high school math classes? Third, you will only be tested on basic geometry concepts and applications, such as finding the perimeter of a simple shape.

Angles

Okay, angles are not shapes, but they are important. Any time two lines or line segments connect, they form an angle, and that angle can be measured in degrees. Some of the important degree measurements to know are:

- 180 degrees: This is really a straight line.
- 90 degrees: This is probably the most common angle measurement that you will see. Lines that cross each other at a 90-degree angle are *perpendicular* lines. You will see 90-degree angles in right triangles and rectangles (including squares). When you see an angle with a little box where the lines meet, that means it is a 90-degree angle.

Rectangles

Rectangles are four-sided figures and, by definition, they have to have four right angles. In fact, "rectangle" is Latin for right angle. Because all four of the angles are "right" angles (meaning they are 90 degrees each), the total degree measure is 360 degrees.

To obtain the *perimeter* of a rectangle (which is the measurement around the outside), you add up the lengths of all of the sides. Hint: There are always two pairs of sides, so if you know the length of one side, you know the length of the side directly opposite. To obtain the *area* of a rectangle, you multiply one side by another side that is *adjacent* to (or right beside) it. The sides are known as *l* and *w* for length and width, but it really doesn't matter which is which. Here are the formulas:

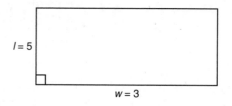

Perimeter: $P = 2l + 2w$

Area: $A = lw$

What is the perimeter of the rectangle above? _____ (all answers to the questions in this section are at the end of the shapes review, before the drill.)

What is the area of the rectangle above? _____

The word *rectangle* is usually used to mean the kind of shape shown above, where the height is different from the length. But technically, rectangles include squares.

Squares

Squares follow all the same rules that rectangles do, but they have one additional requirement: All sides have to be the same length. So a square is just a rectangle (a four-sided, 360-degree, all–right-angle shape) with all sides the same length.

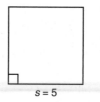

Because all sides are the same length, there are some shortcuts you can use once you know one of the sides (abbreviated as *s*): You can multiply by four to get the perimeter or square one side (raise it to an exponent of two) to get the area. Here are the formulas:

Perimeter: $P = 4s$

Area: $A = s^2$

What is the perimeter of the square above? _____

What is the area of the square above? _____

Triangles

Triangles are three-sided figures with angles that add up to 180 degrees. That does not necessarily mean that each angle is 60 degrees; the angles can have any combination of measurements. The triangles that you will deal with most on your exam are *right triangles*, which are triangles that have one right angle. Right triangles look like this:

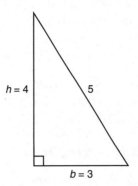

You will see mostly right triangles on your exam, because you can figure out the perimeter and area of these triangles much more easily than with other kinds of triangles. Here are the formulas for area and perimeter of a triangle:

Perimeter: $P = s_1 + s_2 + s_3$ (just add up all the sides)

Area: $A = \frac{1}{2}bh$

What is the perimeter of the triangle above? _____

What is the area of the triangle above? _____

(In a later section, we will review a couple ways to calculate the third side of a triangle, because you will usually need to calculate it—it will not be given to you.)

Circles

Circles have no sides, but they do have some measurements you need to review. First, they have 360 degrees total, just like a rectangle or square. They have a center, and the measurement from the center to any part of the outside edge is called the *radius*. Any radius within one circle is equal to all others. The radius is the most important measurement because if you have it, you can find many other measurements. Double the radius and you get the *diameter*, the longest measurement across the circle. Multiply the radius by 2π and you get the *circumference*, which is similar to the perimeter; it is the measurement around the outside of the circle. Square the radius and multiply it by π (pi), and you get the area of the circle.

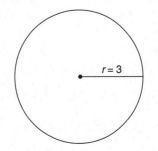

Here are the formulas for diameter, circumference, and area of a circle.

Diameter of a circle: $d = 2r$
Circumference of a circle: $C = 2\pi r$
Area of a circle: $A = \pi r^2$

What is π again? It is a Greek letter that stands in for $\frac{22}{7}$, or 3.14. It turns out that this measurement figures into both the circumference and the area of circles, no matter how big or small the circle is. Don't worry, you won't have to deal with π much. You can think of it like any other variable because it follows the same rules.

What is the diameter of this circle? _____
What is the circumference of this circle? _____
What is the area of this circle? _____

Geometric Shapes Quick Facts

Let's take a few minutes to review the following quick facts about basic geometric shapes. If you're having trouble remembering any of this information, it's time to make flash cards, because you don't want to waste time trying to recall it during the test. Also, if you had trouble figuring out any of the above measurements, the solutions provide the answers step-by-step.

- Angle measure of a straight line: 180 degrees
- Angle measure of a right angle: 90 degrees
- A word that describes two lines that meet at a right angle: *perpendicular*
- A word that describes two lines on the same plane that never touch: *parallel*
- Total degree measure in a rectangle: 360 degrees
- Formula for perimeter of a rectangle: $P = 2l + 2w$
- Formula for area of a rectangle: $A = lw$
- Total degree measure in a square: 360 degrees
- Formula for perimeter of a square: $P = 4s$
- Formula for area of a square: $A = s^2$
- Only difference between rectangles and squares: *All sides are equal in a square.*
- Total degree measure in a triangle: 180 degrees
- Formula for perimeter of a triangle: $P = s_1 + s_2 + s_3$
- Formula for area of a triangle: $A = \frac{1}{2}bh$
- Total degree measure in a circle: 360 degrees
- Formula for diameter of a circle: $d = 2r$
- Formula for circumference of a circle: $C = 2\pi r$
- Formula for area of a circle: $A = \pi r^2$

Ready for the answers to the questions in this section? Here they are:

Rectangle:	**Triangle:**
perimeter:	16 perimeter: 12
area:	15 area: 6
Square:	**Circle:**
perimeter: 20	diameter = 6
area: 25	circumference = 6π
	area = 9π

Now it's time for some practice. Solutions are at the end of the chapter.

Practice Set 1: Angles, Rectangles, Squares, Triangles, Circles, and Geometric Shapes

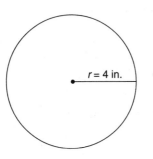

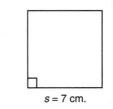

1. What is the circumference of the above circle?

    A. 8 in.
    B. 16 in.
    C. 8π in.
    D. 16π in.

3. What is the area of the above triangle?

    A. 11 in.²
    B. 15 in.²
    C. 17 in.²
    D. 30 in.²

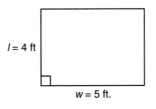

2. What is the perimeter of the above rectangle?

    A. 9 ft.
    B. 18 ft.
    C. 20 ft.
    D. 22 ft.

4. What is the area of the above square?

    A. 7 cm.²
    B. 14 cm.²
    C. 28 cm.²
    D. 49 cm.²

Now that you have covered the basic geometric shapes, let's review a few other geometry topics that are likely to come up on the exam.

▬▬▬ BASIC ALGEBRA

Algebra is another dreaded subject area for people who have not taken a math class in a long time. It's easy to freeze up when you see letters instead of the numbers that you are used to working with. If x and y make you freeze up, rewrite any algebra problem so that it uses blanks or symbols that are more friendly to you.

Let's look at a traditional math problem and see how it relates to algebra.

$$2 + 4 = \underline{\hspace{2cm}}$$

In this problem, there is an unknown. It is represented by a ____. What is the value of the ____? If you answered 6, you are correct.

Algebra problems are just a little different. Algebra problems essentially say this instead:

$$2 + \underline{\quad} = 6.$$

What is the value of the blank now? If you said 4, you are correct. But how did you know that? You probably have this sum memorized, or you may not have even noticed that you quickly and automatically performed an operation in your head. If you didn't get it, that's okay, too. To figure out the value of the blank, you need to figure out how many are between 2 and 6, which is just another way to say the *difference* between 2 and 6. So you would subtract 2 from 6 to get 4.

Solving for *x*

Most algebra test questions have to do with solving for the unknown, usually called *x*, and there are very straightforward rules to follow to do this. Basically, they go like this:

1. Get *x* alone. The main goal is to get *x* on one side of the equal sign and everything else on the other. That's because you want to end up with a statement that says, *x equals this*. When you get that, you have solved for *x*.
2. Don't play favorites. In the process of getting *x* alone, whatever you do to one side of the equation, you have to do the same thing to the other side. Think of it this way: When you see an equation, it's like seeing this:

The scales are perfectly balanced right now, because the two sides are equal. If you were to add something to one side but not the other, the scales would tip and you would no longer have an equation, and that is not good.

Let's see how those rules work out in the above example, $2 + \underline{\quad} = 6$, which can be rewritten as $2 + x = 6$. The *x* is the variable, (also called an unknown), which could also be represented as a blank space, question mark, smiley face, or any symbol you want to use. According to rule 1, you need to get *x* alone, which means you need to get rid of that 2 that is being added to it. The rules for this are also very straightforward:

1. If a variable has a number *added* to it, *subtract* to get rid of the number.
2. If a variable is being *multiplied* by a number, *divide* to get rid of the number.

The other two rules are exactly the same, just reversed:

3. If a variable has a number *subtracted* from it, *add* to get rid of the number.
4. If a variable is being *divided* by a number, *multiply* to get rid of the number.

In $2 + x = 6$, the variable has a 2 added to it. So you would subtract the 2 to get the x alone. But you can't just subtract it from the right side of the equation; that would be playing favorites. You must also subtract it from the left side. So your equation looks like this:

$$2 - 2 + x = 6 - 2$$

Now you have $0 + x = 4$, or just $x = 4$. You have solved for x.

Let's solve another problem together, and then you can solve a few problems on your own.

$$4x = 12$$

In case you don't remember from algebra class, $4x$ is another way of saying 4 times x. You could also see it written as $4(x)$, but it all means the same thing: 4 multiplied by x. When a number is multiplied by a variable, you divide by that number to get the variable alone. Dividing by 4 on both sides gives you: $\frac{4x}{4} = \frac{12}{4}$. So $x = \frac{12}{4}$, which means $x = 3$.

Ready to try some on your own? Here's a short drill. Solutions can be found at the end of the chapter.

Practice Set 2: Solving for *x*

1. $3 + 2x = 7$
2. $3x - 10 = 5$
3. $5 + \frac{x}{2} = 12$
4. $4x + 3 = 15$
5. $2x + 8 = 4$
6. $\frac{4x}{5} + 7 = 15$

Combining Terms

Some algebra problems will not ask you to solve for x at all; in fact, solving for x will not even be possible. These problems just ask you to simplify as much as possible. For example, you could see a problem that asks

$4x - 2x + 3x =$

A. $9x$
B. $5x$
C. $3x$
D. $-x$

See how all of the answer choices include x? That is a giveaway that the correct answer includes x (makes sense, right?), so you will not actually solve for x and get rid of it. All you have to do is combine terms that are alike. The $4x$, $2x$, and $3x$ are alike, because they all include the x. That means you can add and subtract them as if they were regular numbers. So $4x - 2x + 3x = 5x$, just like $4 - 2 + 3 = 5$. Remember that if the test-makers had thrown in a term that was not multiplied by x, you could not have combined that term with the others. So $4x - 2x + 3x + 6$, for example, would equal $5x + 6$.

Even when a problem requires solving for x, you may still need to combine terms to do it. For example:

If $2x + 3x = 15$, what is the value of x?

A. $\dfrac{5}{2}$

B. 3

C. 5

D. $\dfrac{2}{5}$

Clearly, you are going to be solving for x because the problem asks for the value of x. But you can't get x alone on one side until the terms have been combined. Both terms are alike, so you can simply add $2x$ and $3x$ to get $5x$. Now you have $5x = 15$. What else do you need to do to get x alone? Because it is multiplied by 5, you need to divide each side by 5:

$$\frac{5x}{5} = \frac{15}{5}$$

Once you reduce, $x = 3$ (choice B).

Combining Terms

Some algebra problems simply involve translating from English into math, as you did with percentages. For example, if $10x$ is equal to 42 more than $28x$, what is the value of x?

Although you are unlikely to see percents in algebra translation, you still have a few translations that you have seen before:

- "Of" translates to × (multiplication).
- "Is" (as well as *has, have, do, does, equals*, and some other words) translates to = (equal sign).
- "Number" translates to x or any variable of your choosing.

You are also more likely to see these words:

- "More than" means you need to add.
- "Less than" means you need to subtract the number *before* the "less than."
- "Divided by" or "multiplied by" means you need to divide or multiply.

Let's try a couple.

If 8 more than a certain number is the same as three times that number, what is the number?

Translation:

$$8 + x = 3x$$

And then solve. The most direct way to get x alone is to remove the x from the left side.

$$8 + x - x = 3x - x$$
$$8 = 2x$$
$$\frac{8}{2} = \frac{2x}{2}$$
$$4 = x$$

And you're done! Try another.

If 2 less than 3 times a certain number is 13, what is the value of that number?

Translation: $3x - 2 = 13$. And then solve:

$$3x - 2 + 2 = 13 + 2$$
$$3x = 15$$
$$\frac{3x}{3} = \frac{15}{3}$$
$$x = 5$$

Ready to try a few on your own? Solutions are at the end of the chapter.

Practice Set 3: Combining Terms

1. If 10 more than a certain number is the same as 3 times that number, what is the number?
2. When a certain number is multiplied by 5, that's the same as increasing its value by 8. What is the value of that number?
3. A certain number is 4 less than 5 multiplied by 10. What is the value of that number?
4. A certain number divided by $\frac{3}{4}$ is equal to 40. What is the value of that number?

EXPONENTS

There aren't many CBEST problems that involve exponents. If you encounter an exponent in a CBEST problem, be assured that a complete understanding of exponents is not required; you only need to know the basics. Here is a quick review of the basics of exponents.

What are Exponents?

Exponents are very easy to recognize: Whenever you see a superscript number (like this: 3^2), you are working with exponents. For the sake of simplicity in this section, we are going to give some terminology; *exponents* themselves are the numbers in superscript, whereas the number being raised to an exponent is called a *base*. So in 5^2, 5 is the base and 2 is the exponent.

Exponents are like shorthand for multiplication; they tell you how many times the same number is being multiplied together. For example, if you see 2^4, that is the same as $2 \times 2 \times 2 \times 2$, or 2 multiplied four times.

$$2 = 2^1$$
$$2 \times 2 = 2^2$$
$$2 \times 2 \times 2 = 2^3$$
$$2 \times 2 \times 2 \times 2 = 2^4$$

. . . and so on.

To solidify your familiarity with exponents, let's do a short drill. If you see the exponent (with a superscript number, such as 2^4), write out the multiplication (such as $2 \times 2 \times 2 \times 2$). If you see the multiplication, write the exponent. Solutions are at the end of the chapter.

Practice Set 4: What are Exponents?

1. $3^5 =$
2. $4^3 =$
3. $2^3 =$
4. $6 \times 6 \times 6 \times 6 =$
5. $3 \times 3 =$
6. $8 \times 8 \times 8 \times 8 =$

Multiplying and Dividing Exponents

Now that you have refamiliarized yourself with the concept of exponents, let's review how to work with them. Whenever you have exponents that are being multiplied, divided, or raised to other exponents, there are a few rules to follow. Let's look at some examples.

- **Multiplication:** If a problem has exponents of the same base being multiplied, such as $3^2 \times 3^5$, you combine or *add* the exponents to get 3^7.
- **Division:** If a problem has exponents of the same base being divided, such as $4^7 \div 4^5$, you *subtract* the exponents to get 4^2.
- **Exponents:** If an exponent is raised to another exponent, such as $(3^2)^4$, you *multiply* the exponents to get 3^8.

Warning: It's *really* easy to confuse multiplication of exponents and raising exponents to exponents, so be careful! Also, be aware that if you are dealing with two different bases, you cannot combine the exponents in any way—by adding, subtracting, multiplying, or dividing. For example, 4^3 and 3^2 cannot be combined, because their bases (4 and 3) are not the same. (And yes, technically there is an exception to this, and that is when one base can be raised to an exponent to equal the other base. But you are extremely unlikely to see that on the exam, so we are not going to spend time on it here.)

Now it's time for some more practice. In each of the following, combine the exponents using the above rules, or write "cannot be combined" if the bases are unequal. You do not need to actually calculate the result. Solutions are at the end of the chapter.

Practice Set 5: Multiplying and Dividing Exponents

1. $3^2 \times 3^3 =$
2. $4^5 \times 5^5 =$
3. $2^7 \div 2^3 =$
4. $x^8 \div x^3 =$
5. $(2^5)4 =$
6. $(y^2)3 =$

▨▨ PROPORTIONS AND RATIOS

Proportions and ratios are the same type of problem; they just use different terminology. Several questions on the CBEST mathematics test deal with proportions or ratios, so be sure you understand these concepts and can solve word problems that involve proportions and ratios.

Proportions

Proportions compare two parts, such as miles and gallons or cents and oranges. They are usually presented like this:

>   If Ben can type 5 pages in 12 minutes, how long will it take him to type 15 pages?
>
>   If apples cost 50 cents for 3, how many apples can you buy with $2?
>
>   If it takes 2 cans of paint to cover a wall, how many walls can be covered with 8 cans of paint?

Essentially, proportions ask you to convert one pair of numbers. They are easy to miss if you are not being careful or if you are making up a method on the spot, but there are very predictable ways to set them up properly. Once you realize you are working with a proportion problem, draw two blank fractions, like this:

$$\underline{\hspace{2cm}} = \underline{\hspace{2cm}}$$

Be sure to remember the equal sign, because they *will* actually be equal fractions. Now it's time to fill in the information that you know.

For example, let's take the first problem above:

>   If Ben can type 5 pages in 12 minutes, how long will it take him to type 15 pages?

The first part of the problem tells you that Ben can type 5 pages in 12 minutes. So fill that information into your first blank fraction, making sure that you label both the numerator and the denominator.

$$\frac{5 \text{ pgs}}{12 \text{ mins}} = \underline{\hspace{1.5cm}}$$

The second part of the problem asks how long it will take to type 15 pages. Because "pages" is in the numerator of the first fraction, you are going to put it in the numerator of the second fraction—that's why it's important to label. You don't know what the time is in the second fraction—that's what you are trying to figure out—so you will put an x there.

$$\frac{5 \text{ pgs}}{12 \text{ mins}} = \frac{15 \text{ pgs}}{x}$$

Now there are two ways to solve. First, you can cross-multiply, which will work in any situation. Cross-multiplication is a lot like comparing fractions using the bowtie method; just multiply diagonally and upward. Cross-multiply here:

$$5x = 15 \times 12$$
$$5x = 180$$
$$x = \frac{180}{5}$$
$$x = 36$$

So 36 is your answer; it takes Ben 36 minutes to type 15 pages.

There is another way to do the math, and it does not work in every situation, but when it does, it can save you some calculation. Starting by filling in the fractions:

$$\frac{5 \text{ pgs}}{12 \text{ mins}} = \frac{15 \text{ pgs}}{x}$$

If you notice that a number in one fraction is easily divisible by a number directly across from it, for example, 15 and 5, you can use that as a shortcut. The number 5 multiplied by 3 is 15, so you would also multiply 12 by 3 to get the value of x. It is just like finding the multiplier in a ratio problem. Because $12 \times 3 = 36$, again, Ben can type 15 pages in 36 minutes.

Try another:

If apples cost 50 cents for 3, how many apples can you buy with $2?

First, fill in your fractions:

$$\frac{50 \text{ cents}}{3 \text{ apples}} = \frac{\$2}{x}$$

Now, you may notice that when you fill in 50 cents and $2, they are not in the same units and therefore, the math really is not going to be accurate. The easiest way to deal with this is to convert dollars to cents, or change the $2 to 200 cents.

$$\frac{50 \text{ cents}}{3 \text{ apples}} = \frac{200 \text{ cents}}{x}$$

That's better. Now you can either cross-multiply or find the multiplier. If you cross-multiply:

$$3 \times 200 = 50x$$
$$600 = 50x$$
$$\frac{600}{50} = x$$
$$12 = x$$

You can buy 12 apples for $2. Or, you may recognize a multiplier; $50 \times 4 = 200$. Therefore you can multiply 3 by 4 to get 12, the number of apples that can be bought for $2.

One more:

> If it takes 2 cans of paint to cover a wall, how many walls can be covered with 8 cans of paint?

The only trick in this problem is that it doesn't appear to give you two numbers to put into the first fraction, but it does: *2* cans of paint and *1* wall. You may see the same situation if the problem tells you something can be done *per* minute, *per* gallon, or *per* mile. Just think of that as *per 1* minute, *1* gallon, *1* mile, and so on. So your fractions look like this:

$$\frac{2 \text{ cans}}{1 \text{ wall}} = \frac{8 \text{ cans}}{x}$$

Cross-multiplying, you get:

$$8 \times 1 = 2x$$
$$8 = 2x$$
$$\frac{8}{2} = x$$
$$4 = x$$

It takes 4 cans of paint to cover 8 walls. Or you may see that 2 and 8 have a multiplier of 4, and $4 \times 1 = 4$ cans of paint.

Ratios

Ratios are also comparisons of numbers, and if you have ever doubled or halved a recipe, you have worked with ratios. The best news about ratios is that they are pretty easy to spot; they usually have the word "ratio" right there in the problem. Ratio problems do not tend to be very complex; you will usually have two parts to deal with. For example:

> The ratio of minivans to sedans in the parking lot is 3:2. If there are 69 minivans in the parking lot, how many sedans are there?

So start by setting up two equal fractions, this time with the parts of the ratio (3 and 2) making up one fraction:

$$\frac{3 \text{ minivans}}{2 \text{ sedans}} = \frac{69 \text{ minivans}}{x}$$

Then cross-multiply:

$$3x = 2 \times 69$$

And solve:

$$3x = 138$$
$$\frac{3x}{3} = \frac{138}{3}$$
$$x = 46$$

Another way ratios can be expressed is even closer to proportions.

> The ratio of the base to height of two triangles is equal. If one triangle has a base of 4 and a height of 7, and the second triangle has a base of 6, what is the height of the second triangle?

Set up fractions:

$$\frac{4 \text{ base}}{7 \text{ height}} = \frac{6 \text{ base}}{x}$$

Cross-multiply:

$$4x = 42$$

And solve:

$$\frac{4x}{4} = \frac{42}{4}$$
$$x = 10.5$$

And now it is time for you to attack a few ratio and proportion problems on your own. Solutions are at the end of the chapter.

Practice Set 6: Proportions and Ratios

1. If long-distance telephone calls are billed at a rate of $0.13 per minute, how many minutes can Jorge talk for $6.50?
2. Sally's lemonade stand charges $0.15 for a glass of lemonade. How many glasses can Charlie buy for $1.80?
3. Ferdinand paid $0.25 for 3 marbles. How much would it cost him to buy 15 marbles?
4. If the ratio of women to men in the debate club is 5:4 and there are 40 women in the club, how many men are in the club?

▬▬▬ MISSING-DATA QUESTIONS

The mathematics section of the CBEST includes a few questions that test your ability to find the missing data necessary to solve a problem. Missing-data problems usually ask questions such as, What information is necessary to solve this problem? or Which of the following statements can be determined from the information provided above?

To find the information that is missing from a problem, look at the question asked at the end of the data provided. Here is an example:\.

Required Information

A shoe store has 336 pairs of shoes in stock. Half of them were sold. There are 87 pairs of boots, 91 pairs of sandals, 72 pairs of athletic shoes, 52 pairs of dress shoes, and 26 pairs of flip-flops. Of these, 55 pairs of boots, 61 pairs of athletic shoes, and 27 pairs of dress shoes were sold. How many pairs of sandals were sold?

What information is required to solve this problem?

    A. Whether any pairs of flip-flops were sold
    B. Whether more pairs of flip-flops were sold than sandals
    C. The number of pairs of boots sold
    D. Whether the number of pairs of flip-flops sold exceeded the number of pairs of sandals sold
    E. The number of pairs of flip-flops sold

Missing-data problems often throw a lot of numbers at you in an attempt to confuse you. Don't panic! Take a look at the information provided in the problem and jot down any rudimentary calculations that you need to perform.

In the problem above, you know that the shoe store had 336 pairs of shoes and that half of them were sold. Solve $336 \div 2$.

$$336 \div 2 = 168$$

You now know that 168 pairs of shoes were sold. It may be tempting to keep adding and subtracting many of the other numbers in the problem. However, stop for a minute and look at the question. You need to know how many pairs of sandals were sold. What information do you need to answer that question? Put aside the numbers for a minute and just think about the data you need.

You need to know the number of pairs sold of each of the other kinds of shoes:

The number of pairs of boots sold
The number of pairs of athletic shoes sold
The number of pairs of dress shoes sold
The number of pairs of flip-flops sold

Now, add together the number of shoes that were sold.

$$55 \text{ (boots)} + 61 \text{ (athletic shoes)} + 27 \text{ (dress shoes)} = 143$$

How many pairs of an unknown type of shoe were sold?

$$168 - 143 = 25$$

The number 25 tells you that any combination of pairs of sandals and flip-flops, or even only one of those types, was sold.

Now, look at your answer choices. Answer choice A will not solve the problem. Whether any pairs of flip-flops were sold does not tell you how many sandals were sold. Eliminate it. It doesn't matter whether more pairs of flip-flops were sold than sandals. Eliminate answer choice B. Answer choice C repeats information already provided in the problem. Answer choice D is incorrect because whether the number of pairs of flip-flops sold exceeds the number of sandals sold does not tell you how many pairs of flip-flops were sold. There could be 24 pairs of flip-flops and 1 pair of sandals, or the other way around. Eliminate it.

Answer choice E is the correct choice because you need to know the number of pairs of flip-flops sold in order to figure out the number of pairs of sandals sold.

For some problems, you might have been able to figure out the answer without completing any calculations. This question didn't really require you to complete any math. Other problems might require some computation.

Let's move on to the other type of missing-data question you might encounter on the text.

Determining a Conclusion

Juana has $50 to spend on clothing. Shirts costs $22, skirts cost $31, scarves cost $13, and shoes cost $36.

Which of the following statements can be determined from the information given?

A. Juana was able to buy shoes and a skirt.
B. Juana was able to buy a shirt, skirt, and scarf.
C. Juana was able to buy a shirt and skirt.
D. Juana was able to buy a scarf and shoes.
R. Juana was able to buy shoes and a shirt.

This type of problem can be solved using the process of elimination. Examine each answer choice and see if it works.

A. $36 (shoes) + $31 (skirt) = $67.   Eliminate.
B. $22 (shirt) + $31 (skirt) + $13 (scarf) = $66.   Eliminate.
C. $22 (shirt) + $31 (skirt) = $53.   Eliminate.
D. $13 (scarf) + $36 (shoes) = $49.   This is our correct answer.
E. $36 (shoes) + $22 (shirt) = $58.   Eliminate.

This example enabled you to use computation to find the correct answer. Some questions may also involve information that is extraneous to the problem. In this problem, such an answer choice would be one that mentions the cost of an irrelevant item, such as a radio. Since Juana is only buying clothing, that answer choice would not be a conclusion that one could draw from the information in the problem.

Practice Set 7: Missing-Data Questions

1. A flower garden has 26 carnations, 31 daffodils, 19 roses, and 24 lilies. By the end of the day, 72 flowers have been picked and made into bouquets.

Which of the following facts can be deduced from the information provided above?

A. More roses were picked than lilies.
B. More carnations were picked than daffodils.
C. At least 1 daffodil was picked.
D. At least 1 carnation was picked.
E. At least 1 lily was picked.

> 2. Jamal sailed his boat 6 miles to the island in the center of the lake, sailed around the small island two times, and then sailed back to the dock, arriving at 4:15 p.m. He had sailed 18 miles total. What was Jamal's average speed?

What information is necessary to solve the problem above?

A. The time Jamal left the dock
B. The amount of time it took for him to sail from the island in the middle of the lake back to the dock
C. The amount of time it took for him to sail to the island in the middle of the lake
D. The weight of his boat
E. The total distance around the island in the center of the lake

▇▇▇ SOLUTIONS TO PRACTICE SETS

Congratulations! You've worked through content on basic geometry, algebra, and missing-data questions. Here are the answers to the practice sets.

Practice Set 1

1. C

The radius of the circle is 4 in. When you plug that into the formula for circumference, you get $C = 2 \times 4\pi$, or $C = 8\pi$.

2. B

The formula for perimeter of a rectangle is $P = 2l + 2w$. When you plug in the values from the picture, you get $P = 2 \times 4 + 2 \times 5$, which equals 18. Be careful to calculate perimeter, not area!

3. B

The formula for area of a triangle is $A = \frac{1}{2}bh$, and when you plug in the base of 5, and the height of 6, you get $A = \frac{1}{2} \times 5 \times 6$ which equals 15.

4. D

Each side of the square is 7 cm, so you just need to square that to get a value of 49 cm^2.

Practice Set 2

1. $x = 2$
Translation: $3 + 2x = 7$
$3 - 3 + 2x = 7 - 3$
$2x = 4$
$\frac{2x}{2} = \frac{4}{2}$
$x = 2$

2. $x = 5$
Translation: $3x - 10 = 5$
$3x - 10 + 10 = 5 + 10$
$3x = 15$
$\frac{3x}{3} = \frac{15}{3}$
$x = 5$

3. $x = 14$
Translation: $5 + \frac{x}{2} = 12$
$5 - 5 + \frac{x}{2} = 12 - 5$
$\frac{x}{2} = 7$
$\frac{x}{2} \times 2 = 7 \times 2$
$x = 14$

4. $x = 3$
Translation: $4x + 3 = 15$
$4x + 3 - 3 = 15 - 3$
$4x = 12$
$\frac{4x}{4} = \frac{12}{4}$
$x = 3$

5. $x = -2$

Translation: $2x + 8 = 4$

$$2x + 8 - 8 = 4 - 8$$
$$2x = -4$$
$$\frac{2x}{2} = \frac{-4}{2}$$
$$x = -2$$

6. $x = 10$

Translation: $\frac{4x}{5} + 7 = 15$

$$\frac{4x}{5} + 7 - 7 = 15 - 7$$
$$\frac{4x}{5} = 8$$
$$\frac{4x}{5} \times 5 = 8 \times 5$$
$$4x = 40$$
$$\frac{4x}{4} = \frac{40}{4}$$
$$x = 10$$

Practice Set 3

1. $x = 5$

Translation: $10 + x = 3x$

$$10 + x - x = 3x - x$$
$$10 = 2x$$
$$\frac{10}{2} = \frac{2x}{2}$$
$$5 = x$$

2. $x = 2$

Translation: $5x = x + 8$

$$5x - x = x - x + 8$$
$$4x = 8$$
$$\frac{4x}{4} = \frac{8}{4}$$
$$x = 2$$

3. $x = 46$

Translation: $x = 5 \times 10 - 4$

$$x = 50 - 4$$
$$x = 46$$

4. $x = 30$

Translation: $x \div \frac{3}{4} = 40$

$$x \times \frac{4}{3} = 40$$
$$\frac{4x}{3} = 40$$
$$\frac{4x}{3} \times 3 = 40 \times 3$$
$$4x = 120$$
$$\frac{4x}{4} = \frac{120}{4}$$
$$x = 30$$

Practice Set 4

1. $3^5 = 3 \times 3 \times 3 \times 3 \times 3$
2. $4^3 = 4 \times 4 \times 4$
3. $2^3 = 2 \times 2 \times 2$
4. $6 \times 6 \times 6 \times 6 = 6^4$
5. $3 \times 3 = 3^2$
6. $8 \times 8 \times 8 \times 8 = 8^4$

Practice Set 5

1. $3^2 \times 3^3 = 3^5$
2. $4^5 \times 5^5$ cannot be combined.
3. $2^7 \div 2^3 = 2^4$
4. $x^8 \div x^3 = x^5$
5. $(2^5)^4 = 2^{20}$
6. $(y^2)^3 = y^6$

Practice Set 6

1. 50
2. 12
3. $1.25
4. 32

Practice Set 7

1. **Correct Choice: C.** At least 1 daffodil was picked.

Add all of the numbers to obtain the total number of flowers.

$$26 \text{ (carnations)} + 31 \text{ (daffodils)} + 19 \text{ (roses)} + 24 \text{ (lilies)} = 100 \text{ flowers}$$

Next, subtract the number of flowers picked to make bouquets from the total number of flowers.

$$100 - 72 = 28$$

This number shows that at least 1 daffodil must have been picked because there are 31 daffodils and only 28 flowers remaining in the garden.

2. **Correct Choice: A.** The time Jamal left the dock.

You have Jamal's end time but also need his start time to calculate his average speed. Answer choices B and C are incorrect because each of them only provides part of the time of Jamal's complete trip. The length of the distance around the island and the weight of his boat are irrelevant (answer choices D and E).

CHAPTER 6

THE CBEST MATHEMATICS TEST: STATISTICS AND PROBABILITY

The California Basic Educational Skills Test (CBEST) has a special focus on terminology and mathematics relating to standardized testing, which has become part of the American education system. An understanding of the terms and statistical processes associated with testing has become a necessary part of teaching. In addition to a knowledge of how to compute percentages, you're expected to understand averages, medians, percentiles, modes, ranges, and stanines. This chapter covers all of this plus the basics of probability—a topic closely related to statistics.

■ STATISTICS

An understanding of the meaning of scores on standardized tests requires a basic understanding of statistics. Among the statistical measures you'll be expected to understand and compute on the CBEST are the mean, median, and mode. These are all ways of interpreting a related set of numbers. Expect to see several questions on this topic on the CBEST. You'll be expected to know the difference between mean, median, and mode and be able to compute these based on a given set of scores.

Mean

Mean is basically another word for average. When you are calculating a grade based on several tests, or a batting average based on many at-bats, you are calculating a mean. Calculating a mean involves adding and dividing. You are generally given a list of numbers—such as 8, 11, 4, 17, and 5—and asked to find their mean.

To do this, add up the list of numbers: $8 + 11 + 4 + 17 + 5 = 45$. Then divide by the number of numbers in the original list, which in this case is 5. The expression $\frac{45}{5} = 9$. And you're done! The average of 8, 11, 4, 17, and 5 is 9. Now it's your turn to find the means of the following number sets. Solutions are at the end of the chapter.

Practice Set 1: Mean

1. 2, 6, 9, 4, 14
2. 9, 2, 5, 11, 18
3. 7, 21, –5, 8, 4
4. –2, 9, –5, 6

Median

A *median* is simply the number in the middle in an ordered list. Calculating a median involves less math—it simply involves putting numbers in order and eliminating some of them.

For example, if you're asked to find the median of the list 8, 11, 4, 17, and 5, you would start by putting them in numerical order: 4, 5, 8, 11, 17. And then choose the number in the middle. For a short list such as this one, you can probably see that 8 is in the middle; however, to check yourself or to find the middle of a longer list, start eliminating the pairs on the ends. That means the 4 and the 17 are first—just cross them out. Then the 5 and 11.

When you are left with only one number, that is your median (in this case, 8). Another good reason to eliminate end pairs is to make sure that you don't actually have two numbers left in the middle. If that happens, you just take the mean of those two numbers, and that is your median.

Ready to try finding medians by yourself? Solutions are at the end of the chapter.

Practice Set 2: Median

1. 3, 5, 2, 7, −2   3. −3, 5, 1, 9
2. 4, 8, 2, 7, 3   4. −5, 3, 2, 10, 2

Mode

The *mode* is the number that appears most frequently in the list. As with medians, it is a good idea to put the list of numbers in order first, because that makes the repeated numbers to stand out.

Let us take this list: 11, 8, −4, 11, 4, 17, and 5. First, you would carefully put the numbers in order. (It is a good idea to cross out numbers as you go, and remember, a negative number never has the same value as a positive—so it is not the same number!) Your ordered list looks like this: −4, 4, 5, 8, 11, 11, 17.

If you want, feel free to cross off numbers that only appear once after you have made your list. So you would cross off −4, 4 (remember, they are not the same), 5, 8, and 17. That just leaves two 11s, so 11 is your mode.

You are unlikely to run into this scenario, but in case you do find two different values that appear the most, both of them are modes. You do not "average" them by finding their mean; they stay as they are. For example, in the list −4, 4, 5, 5, 8, 11, 11, and 17, 5 and 11 are the modes.

It is your turn to find the modes. Solutions are at the end of this chapter.

Practice Set 3: Mode

1. 2, 10, −2, 3, 8, 2   3. 4, −2, 2, −3, 5, −3
2. 3, 5, 3, −5, 0   4. 5, 12, 11, 11, 9, 12, 11

■ STATISTICAL INTERPRETATION OF STANDARDIZED TESTING SCORES

In addition to the mean, median, and mode, you'll be expected to understand the meaning of several other terms and concepts used in evaluating standardized testing. You should understand all the terms listed below, especially the term *percentile*. It's almost guaranteed that you'll find a question relating to percentiles on the CBEST.

Percentile

The concept of percentile refers to how a test score relates to the scores of the other people taking the test. It tells where a person stands relative to all other test takers. For example, if a person's score is in the 60th percentile, it means that the person scored as high as or higher than 60% of the people who took the test. The higher the percentile associated with a score, the better the person did relative to all other test takers.

The percentile associated with a person's score does not tell you anything about how many questions the person got right or wrong. On a very difficult test, for example, it would be theoretically possible for a person to miss more than half the questions and still be in the 99th percentile if she/he got more right than anyone else taking the test. Remember, a score associated with the 80th percentile does *not* mean the person got 80% of the questions right. It means only that the person did as well as or better than 80% of the test takers.

In standardized testing, the percentile is derived by comparing a person's score to the scores of thousands of other people who took the test. However, using the concept of percentile, a test score can also be compared to a smaller group, like the other students in a school. For example, it would be possible for a student's score to be in the 80th percentile in his/her school but in the 90th percentile in the nation. That would mean that the person's score was as good as or better than 80% of the student in her/his school and as good as or better than 90% of the students in the nation.

Stanine

Stanine, like percentile, is a way of ranking students' test scores relative to those of other test takers. There are nine stanines, or score ranges; in fact, the word comes from "standard nine." Nine is the highest stanine and includes the top scorers; one is the lowest stanine and includes the lowest scorers. Each stanine represents an interval on a normal bell-shaped curve, with the largest number of scores assigned to the middle stanine (5) in the middle of the curve.

To compute the stanines for a set of test takers, you assign a stanine of 1 to the lowest 4% of test scores, a stanine of 2 for the next 7% of test scores, and so forth, according to the following table.

Stanine Distribution

Stanine = 1	lowest 4% of test scores
Stanine = 2	next 7% of test scores
Stanine = 3	next 12% of test scores
Stanine = 4	next 17% of test scores
Stanine = 5	middle 20% of test scores
Stanine = 6	next 17% of test scores
Stanine = 7	next 12% of test scores
Stanine = 8	next 7% of test scores
Stanine = 9	highest 4% of test scores

Range

In a series of related numbers, the range is the difference between the largest number and the smallest number. For test scores, the range is the difference between the highest score and the lowest score.

For example, below are the scores a group of students got on a standardized test.

$$\{65, 67, 60, 72, 79, 81, 83, 86, 95, 97\}$$

The highest score is 97 and the lowest score is 65. To find the range, subtract 65 from 97: 32.

PROBABILITY

A flip of a coin, a roll of the dice, or a card picked from a deck are three examples of probability. The probability of an event is a numerical measure of the likelihood that the given event will occur. Probability can get complicated when multiple events are involved. Fortunately, the probability problems on the CBEST are relatively easy, but they must be carefully thought through.

Single-Event Probability

To find the probability of a single event occurring, you need to know the number of possible outcomes and the number of "successful" outcomes. For example, if you want to know the probability of getting heads when flipping a coin, you need to know the following:

the number of "successful" outcomes: 1 (heads)

the number of possible outcomes: 2 (heads or tails)

Then the probability is measured by dividing the number of successful outcomes by the number of possible outcomes.

$$\frac{\text{Number of successful outcomes}}{\text{Number of possible outcomes}}$$

For the example above, the probability of getting heads on a single coin toss is $\frac{1}{2}$. Probabilities can be expressed mathematically as a fraction ($\frac{1}{2}$) or as a percent (50%).

Let's try a slightly more difficult example. A standard playing card deck has 52 cards. So the number of possible outcomes if you were to draw one card from the deck is 52. There is only one ace of hearts in the deck, so the probability of drawing the ace of hearts is 1/52.

Now, what is the probability of *not* drawing the ace of hearts? There are 51 "successful" outcomes that would not be the ace of hearts. So the probability of not drawing the ace of hearts is 51/52.

What is the probability of drawing a 4? There are four "successful" outcomes: the 4 of diamonds, 4 of hearts, 4 of spades, and 4 of clubs. The probability of drawing a 4 from a deck of cards is 4/52, or 1/13.

One more example: What is the probability of drawing a red card? Half the deck is red cards, so the number of "successful" outcomes is 26. The number of possible outcomes remains 52. The probability of drawing a red card from the deck is 26/52, or ½, or 50%.

Now try this: Sally has a bag of marbles. There are 10 red marbles, 9 green ones, and 6 white ones. What is the probability of randomly drawing a red marble out of the bag? There are 25 possible outcomes and 10 "successful" outcomes. The probability of drawing a red marble is 10/25, or 2/5, or 40%.

Multiple-Event Probability

Multiple-event probability is only a little more difficult as long as the events are independent (the result of the first event doesn't have an influence on the result of the second event). What is the probability that if you toss a coin twice you will get heads both times? The probability of getting heads the first time is ½ and the probability of getting heads the second time is also ½. The probability of getting heads *both* times is ½ × ½.

$$\tfrac{1}{2} \times \tfrac{1}{2} = \tfrac{1}{4}$$

The probability of getting heads on two consecutive flips of a coin is ¼, or 25%.

Now let's go back to the bag of marbles. Again, there are 10 red marbles, 9 green ones, and 6 white ones. What is the probability of randomly drawing two red marbles in a row? If, after drawing the first marble, it is returned to the bag, the probability of drawing two red marbles in a row is:

$$2/5 \times 2/5 = 4/25, \text{ or } 16\%$$

If the first marble is not returned to the bag after being drawn, then the problem becomes more complex.

$$2/5 \times 9/24 \text{ (or } 3/8) = 6/40 = 3/20, \text{ or } 15\%$$

Practice Set 4: Multiple-Event Probability

1. What is the probability of randomly drawing either a queen or a king from a standard deck of cards?
2. What is the probability of getting heads on three consecutive tosses of a coin?
3. A bag has 20 marbles, 8 of them are red. If a marble is drawn from the bag at random, what is the probability of *not* getting a red marble?
4. Abby is taking a multiple-choice test. There are five answer choices for each question. If she guesses randomly, what is the probability of getting two questions right in a row?

■■■ LOGICAL REASONING QUESTIONS

Logical reasoning questions are different from any other question type on the mathematics section of the CBEST. These questions don't involve any computation at all, but rather list a few rules in a given situation and then ask you to answer a question about it.

These problems ask you questions such as:

- Which of the following must be true?
- Which of the following could be true?
- Which of the following must be false?
- Which of the following conclusions could be drawn based on the information above?

Take special care to remain aware of what the question is asking you.

- *Must be true* means that all other answer choices are false.
- *Could be true* means that the answer choice could be true but could also be false. All other answer choices either must be true or must be false.
- *Must be false* means that all other answer choices must be true or could be true.
- *Which of the following conclusions could be drawn* means that the correct answer choice must be true and the other answer choices must be false.

Once you have read the question, look at the answer choices and use the process of elimination. The incorrect answer choices will violate the rules of the scenario. For example,

---

Joaquin has five books to read for school: one biography, one novel, one book about the Revolutionary War, one play, and one collection of essays.

- Joaquin must read the play last.
- If Joaquin reads the book about the Revolutionary War fourth, then he reads the biography second.
- Joaquin cannot read the collection of essays before the novel.

If Joaquin reads the novel third, then it must be true that

A. Joaquin reads the collection of essays first.
B. Joaquin reads the book about the Revolutionary War last.
C. Joaquin reads the biography first.
D. Joaquin reads the biography second.
E. Joaquin reads the collection of essays fourth.

This question may look confusing, but if you take each rule one at a time, it is actually quite simple. Write down what you know about this scenario.

Joaquin reads the novel third.

What else do you know from the rules? Look at the easiest rule first.

Joaquin must read the play last.

You already know the placements of two of the books! Can you figure out anything else from the rules? If you examine rule 2, you can see that there is nothing that rule 2 will tell you in this scenario. You don't know the placement of the book about the Revolutionary War.

Let's look at rule 3. Can you figure out anything from it?

Joaquin must read the collection of essays fourth.

Since Joaquin cannot read the collection of essays before the novel (which is third) and the play must be read last (fifth), he must read the collection of essays fourth.

1.
2.
3. Novel
4. Collection of essays
5. Play

Since you cannot figure out the placement of the other two books, you should move on to the answer choices. Remember that the question is asking what *must be* true.

Answer choices A and B are incorrect. Eliminate. You don't know if answer choices C and D must be true. Answer choice E must be true. This is your answer.

Sometimes logical reasoning questions attempt to trip you up by creating a scenario in which you might make assumptions. This is particularly true with scenarios involving the distance between multiple locations. Let's try an example.

> • The juice bar is 16 kilometers from the bagel shop.
> • The bagel shop is 13 kilometers from the diner.

Based on the information above, which of the following conclusions can be made?

A. The juice bar is 29 kilometers from the diner.
B. The diner is exactly 3 kilometers from the juice bar.
C. The juice bar is exactly 3 kilometers from the diner.
D. The juice bar is exactly 3 kilometers from the diner.
E. The diner is not more than 29 kilometers from the juice bar.

This question has an obvious trap. Don't assume that these three locations are in a straight line. Answer choice A is designed to trip you up. You don't know if the juice bar is 29 kilometers from the diner. Eliminate.

Beware of answer choices that use words such as "exactly." The number 3 is designed to trap you because 16 – 3 = 3. Don't look for arbitrary relationships between numbers and assume that they mean something. Since you don't know the layout of the 3 locations in relation to each other, you can eliminate answer choices B, C, and D.

This leaves answer choice E, which is correct. The straight line scenario is the farthest distance that the diner can be from the juice bar.

Practice Set 5: Logical Reasoning Questions

> 1. Deniqua joined multiple sports teams. A sports team member can only participate in two sports per day.
>
>   • Field hockey practice is held on Tuesday and Thursday.
>   • Track and field practice only on Thursday.
>   • Basketball practice on Monday and Tuesday.
>   • Softball practice is on Tuesday.
>   • Thursday and Friday are the only days that the swim team has practice.

Which of the following sets of teams could Deniqua *not* have joined?

A. Field hockey, basketball, swimming
B. Field hockey, track and field, softball
C. Field hockey, track and field, swimming
D. Track and field, swimming, basketball
E. Softball, swimming, basketball

> 2. Kwame chooses his type of exercise based on the weather. Kwame always runs, with the following exceptions:
>
> Kwame rides the exercise bike only if it is raining.
>
> If it is really hot outside, Kwame rollerblades.

If it is not raining, which of the following conclusions can be made?

A. Kwame runs
B. Kwame runs or rollerblades
C. Kwame rollerblades or rides the exercise bike
D. Kwame rollerblades
E. Kwame runs or rides the exercise bike

▬▬ SOLUTIONS TO PRACTICE SETS

Congratulations! You've worked through content on testing and statistics. Here are the answers to the practice sets you encountered.

Practice Set 1

1. $(2 + 6 + 9 + 4 + 14) \div 5 = 7$
2. $(9 + 2 + 5 + 11 + 18) \div 5 = 9$
3. $(7 + 21 + -5 + 8 + 4) \div 5 = 7$
4. $(-2 + 9 + -5 + 6) \div 4 = 2$

Practice Set 2

1. The median of ordered list −2, 2, 3, 5, and 7 is 3.
2. The median of ordered list 2, 3, 4, 7, and 8 is 4.
3. The median of ordered list −3, 1, 5, and 9 is 3 (the mean of 1 and 5).
4. The median of ordered list −5, 2, 2, 3, and 10 is 2.

Practice Set 3

1. The mode of ordered list −2, 2, 2, 3, 8, and 10 is 2.
2. The mode of ordered list −5, 0, 3, 3, and 5 is 3.
3. The mode of ordered list −3, −3, −2, 2, 4, and 5 is −3.
4. The mode of ordered list 5, 11, 11, 9, 11, 12, and 12 is 11.

Practice Set 4

1. There are 8 "successful" outcomes and 52 possible outcomes. The probability of getting either a queen or a king on one random draw is 8/52, or 2/13.
2. For each toss there is one "successful" outcome and two possible outcomes for each flip of the coin.

$$1/2 \times 1/2 \times 1/2 = 1/8$$

The probability of getting three heads in a row is 1/8, or 12.5%.
3. There are 12 "successful" outcomes (20 – 8) and 20 possible outcomes. The probability of not getting a red marble is 12/20, or 3/5, or 60%.
4. For each question there is one "successful" outcome and five possible outcomes.

$$1/5 \times 1/5 = 1/25$$

Thus, the probability of randomly guessing two questions in a row right is 1/25. or 4%. By the way, the probability of randomly guessing *three* questions in a row right is $1/5 \times 1/5 \times 1/5$. or only 1/125 (less than 1%).

Practice Set 5

1. **Correct Choice: C.** Field hockey, track and field, swimming
   A table is the simplest way to solve this problem. These three sports take place on Thursday, and Deniqua cannot participate in more than two sports on one day.

	Field Hockey	Basketball	Softball	Track and Field	Swimming
Monday		X			
Tuesday	X	X	X		
Wednesday					
Thursday	X			X	X
Friday					X

2. **Correct Choice: B.** Kwame runs or rollerblades.
   Since it is not raining, you know that Kwame does not ride the exercise bike. Eliminate answer choices C and E. You don't know whether it is really hot outside. Therefore, you can't conclude if Kwame runs or rollerblades.

CHAPTER 7

THE CBEST MATHEMATICS AND READING TESTS: TABLES, CHARTS, AND GRAPHS

Both the California Basic Educational Skills Test (CBEST) reading and mathematics tests require an understanding of tables and graphs. Most questions regarding tables and graphs are on the mathematics test. You're likely to find four or six questions on the math test that require you to understand and interpret tables and graphs and then do basic calculations to arrive at a conclusion. On the reading test, there is likely to be only one or two questions on tables and graphs; you will only have to "read" the table or graph, not do any calculations.

You won't need to memorize or review information; all the information you need to answer the questions regarding graphs and charts will be right there on the test. To do your best on these questions, review how information is presented in pie graphs, line graphs, and bar graphs so that you won't be confused by the graphs on the test.

TABLES, CHARTS, AND GRAPHS

Fortunately, tables, charts, and graphs tend to be fairly straightforward once you know what to look for. They tend to fall into very predictable types: bar graphs, line graphs, pie charts, and tables. In this section, we will review each type of chart or graph that you are likely to encounter on the CBEST.

Bar Graphs

A column chart generally compares categories of information, such as a car model's sales revenue in different regions, numbers of adoptions of different dog breeds, or the number of people who went to see a particular movie by age range. The "columns" in column charts make it easy to compare amounts, because the taller the column, the larger the amount. Here's an example:

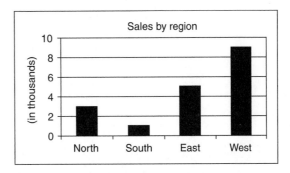

Notice the lines on the bottom and left of the chart. Those are called *axes*. Each axis contains a different kind of information. Generally in a column chart, the *x-axis* (or the line across the bottom) is labeled according to the categories of information (regions where a car was sold, breeds of dog that were adopted, age ranges of people going to see a movie). The axis on the left side of the columns generally displays numbers that represent how many cars were sold, dogs were adopted, or people went to see the movie. This is called the *y-axis*. Sometimes, the *y-axis* displays very large numbers, so to save space, the makers of the chart tell you that every unit or "1" on the chart actually represents tens, hundreds, thousands, or even millions. The above chart does that, using the label (*in thousands*).

Occasionally, you could see a column chart that looks like this:

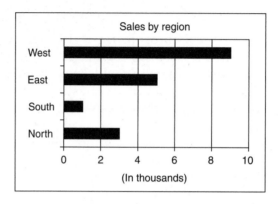

But it's really the same chart, just on its side. The numbers are going to run along the length of the columns to show you "how many" each column represents, so don't be thrown off by a chart being on its side.

Line Graphs

Line graphs are very similar to column charts, but they tend to be used to track progress over time. For example, a line chart may track the closing value of a stock day by day, a patient's temperature hour by hour, or a country's gross domestic product from year to year. Again, the labels across the bottom tell you which categories or units of time you are viewing, and the numbers on the left tell you the values at each point, which may be expressed in larger units. Line graphs look like this:

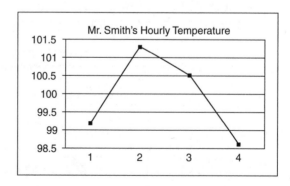

Pie Charts

Pie charts are different from column charts and line graphs in two major ways: First, they have no axes. Second, they do not necessarily have any real values. Instead, pie charts make it easy for you to see percents of a whole. For example, you may see a pie chart that shows the percentage of males versus females in a certain science class, the percentage of students who make As, Bs, Cs, Ds, and Fs in a freshman-level class, or the percentage of cars sold that are economy, mid-size, or luxury. For example, take this pie chart:

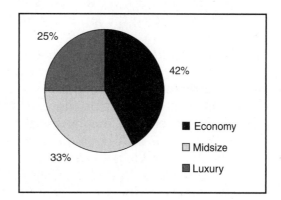

You can easily tell that more economy cars were sold than mid-size, and more mid-size than luxury, but you can't tell the actual numbers of cars sold in any particular category or in total.

Pie charts are usually labeled with the percentage that each "slice" represents, and the category that is being measured by each slice may be labeled on the pie as well, or the labels might be in a legend (also called a key) near the chart.

Tables

Finally, there are tables that organize numeric data. They are not as visual as charts and graphs, but they can make it easier to display large amounts of data in a small amount of space. They also make it possible to see exact numbers for calculations, whereas using charts and graphs often just allows you to ballpark and compare. Tables look like this:

Movie Ticket Sales			
	Big Blockbuster	Romantic Comedy II	Animated Flick
Kids	973	287	3,492
Adults	4,729	2,841	1,134
Seniors	582	1,397	1,052

■■■■ TEST-TAKING TIPS FOR READING CHARTS AND GRAPHS

Be careful when you come to a chart or graph on the CBEST. Generally, these questions are not hard, but it you don't carefully read the chart of graph, you can run into trouble. Here are test-taking steps that will help you when you see charts or graphs on the test.

1. *Read the labels.* It may sound obvious, but most of the mistakes people make on questions regarding charts and graphs result from not reading the labels carefully. Before you even look at the question, look at the graph. Be sure to read the title, if there is one, the categories, and the values (numbers). Read the legend, if there is one, and any other statements or notes.
2. *Check the values.* The numbers, which usually appear on the vertical axis of a line or bar graph, are sometimes simply the values relating to the points on the line. In other cases, these numbers may be in tens, hundreds, thousands, millions, or more. If there is a notation "in millions," for example, then a "1" means one million and a "2" means two million.
3. *Look at the data.* Take a quick look at the graph and see what appears to be displayed in the graph. Many line graphs show a growth or decline over time. Don't do any math at this stage; just take a second to see what data are being presented. Now you're ready to move to the question(s).

Once you're done with these three steps, read the question that follows the chart or graph. Practice these steps as you work through the problems in the practice set below.

■■■ PRACTICE SET

Use the bar graph below to answer questions 1 and 2.

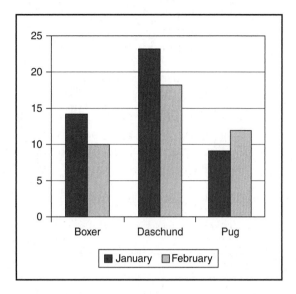

1. Which breed of dog was adopted more often in February than January?
   A. Boxer
   B. Dachshund
   C. Pug
   D. Not enough information to tell

2. Combining the numbers for January and February, which breed of dog was adopted most often?
   A. Boxer
   B. Dachshund
   C. Pug
   D. Not enough information to tell

Use the line graph below to answer questions 3 and 4.

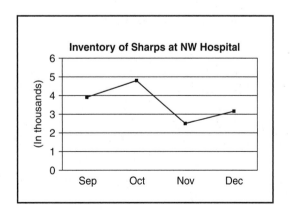

3. According to the graph, in which month was there the greatest decrease in the inventory of sharps over the previous month?

   A. September
   B. October
   C. November
   D. December

4. Which of the following is the best approximation of the change in the inventory of sharps from September to December?

   A. The inventory declined from 4 sharps to 3 sharps.
   B. The inventory increased by approximately 1,000 sharps.
   C. The inventory increased by approximately 200 sharps.
   D. The inventory declined by approximately 1,000 sharps.

Use the chart below to answer questions 5 and 6.

The Endocrine System			
Gland	**Location**	**Hormone**	**Effect on the Body**
Anterior pituitary	Hypothalamus	Growth hormone/ Thyroid-stimulating hormone	• Controls growth • Controls thyroxine release
Posterior pituitary	Hypothalamus	Oxytocin/ Vasopressin	• Affects uterine contractions • Affects water reabsorption in nephrons
Thyroid gland	Below larynx, in front of trachea	Thyroxine	• Regulates rate of metabolic activities
Parathyroid	Behind the thyroid gland	Parathormone	• Regulates calcium and phosphate metabolism

5. According to the chart above, which of the following hormones is created by the posterior pituitary gland?

   A. Hypothalamus
   B. Oxytocin
   C. Thyroxine
   D. Growth hormone

6. Which gland regulates the rate of metabolic activities?

   A. Thyroxine
   B. Larynx
   C. Parathyroid
   D. Thyroid

Answers and Explanations for the Practice Set

1. **Correct Choice: C.** Use the key to determine which columns stand for January and February. More pugs were adopted in February than January. For boxers and dachshunds, the opposite was true; they were adopted more times in January than in February.

2. **Correct Choice: B.** To get the correct answer to this question, you do not need to actually add or combine numbers for January and February. You can see at a glance that the daschund led the other two breeds in both January and February and was thus the breed that was adopted most often for the two-month time period.

3. **Correct Choice: C.** There is no need to do math or figure out numbers. Just look at the rise or fall of the line. The only decline shown in the graph is from October to November, making November the correct answer.

4. **Correct Choice: D.** To respond to this question, you need to compare the beginning of the line (September) with the end of the line (December). There was a decline since the mark for December is below the mark for September. There were approximately 4,000 sharps in inventory in September and 3,000 sharps in inventory in December, so the decline was approximately 1,000 sharps.

5. **Correct Choice: B.** To get this answer, you find the posterior pituitary gland in the gland column and look across the hormone column.

6. **Correct Choice: D.** To get this answer, find "regulates the rate of metabolic activities" under "Effect on the Body" and then look across that row to see which gland is listed in the "Gland" column.

CHAPTER 8

THE CBEST READING TEST: READING COMPREHENSION

The reading section of the California Basic Educational Skills Test (CBEST) does not test specific knowledge. You won't be required to remember any facts or other content that you've learned. Instead, the CBEST reading test measures your ability to comprehend, analyze, and evaluate information from written passages, charts and graphs, and indexes and tables of contents. All the information you need to answer the questions will be right there on the test.

Because a reading comprehension exam does not test specific knowledge, it is not possible to *study* for it. However, there are some things you can do to *prepare*.

In this chapter, we'll focus on preparing you for the reading comprehension questions, which account for the bulk of the questions in the CBEST reading test. In the next chapter, you'll review charts and graphs as well as tables of contents and indexes. Reading and understanding this type of material is also part of the CBEST reading test.

PREPARING FOR THE READING COMPREHENSION QUESTIONS

The format of the reading comprehension questions will likely be familiar to you. You have probably taken many reading comprehension tests similar to the CBEST during your years in school. You'll be given a passage to read and then be asked several multiple-choice questions about the passage. These questions will test your comprehension of the passage that you've read.

By this stage in your educational career, you should have a pretty good sense of your reading skills. If you have achieved solid scores on reading comprehension tests in the past, the reading comprehension questions of the CBEST should be no problem at all. But if your comprehension skills are below par, if you freeze when faced with difficult reading passages, if you read very slowly, or if English is not your first language, take the time to work through this section of the book.

Read

The best way to learn to read *better* is to read *more*. If reading is not something that you do frequently, you are limiting yourself in a way that may show up on your test score. Reading broadly in subject areas that do not, at first glance, hold much appeal for you will train you to focus your attention on what you are reading. Pick up a magazine that is not familiar. Read a short article.

Summarize the key ideas. Consider the author's purpose. Decide whether the author's argument makes sense to you. Think about where the author might go next with his or her argument. Think about the author's tone.

All of this sounds like a chore, but it is the key to reading actively. An active reader is interacting with a text rather than just reading the words. Success on reading comprehension tests requires active reading.

You can use any of the strategies below to focus your attention on your reading. You may use many of them already, quite automatically. Others may be just what you need to shift your reading comprehension into high gear.

Active Reading Strategies

- **Monitor your understanding.** When faced with a difficult text, it is all too easy to zone out and skip through challenging passages. Pay attention to how you are feeling about a text. Are you understanding the author's main points? Is there something that makes little or no sense? Are there words that you do not know? Figuring out what makes a passage hard for you is the first step toward correcting the problem. Once you figure it out, you can use one of the following strategies to improve your connection to the text.
- **Predict.** Your ability to make predictions is surprisingly important to your ability to read well. If a passage is well organized, you should be able to read the first few sentences and have a pretty good sense of where the author is going with the text. Practice this with newspaper articles, where the main ideas are supposed to appear in the first paragraph. Move on to more difficult reading. See whether your expectation of a text holds up through the reading of the text. Making predictions about what you are about to read is an immediate way to engage with the text and keep you engaged throughout your reading.
- **Ask questions.** Keep a running dialogue with yourself as you read. You do not have to stop reading; just pause to consider, What does this mean? Why did the author use this word? Where is he or she going with this argument? Why is this important? This will become second nature after a while. When you become acclimated to asking yourself questions as you read a test passage, you may discover that some of the questions you asked appear in different forms on the test itself.
- **Summarize.** You summarize when you take notes in class or when you prepare an outline when studying for an exam. Try doing it as you read unfamiliar materials, but do it in your head. At the end of a particularly dense paragraph, try to reduce the author's verbiage to a single, cogent sentence that states the main idea. At the end of a longer passage, see whether you can restate the theme or message in a phrase or two.
- **Connect.** Every piece of writing is a communication between the author and the reader. You connect to a text first by bringing your prior knowledge to that text and last by applying what you learn from the text to some area of your life. Even if you know nothing at all about architecture or archaeology, your lifetime of experience in the world carries a lot of weight as you read an article about these topics. Connecting to a text can lead to "Aha!" moments as you say to yourself, I knew that! or even I never knew that! If you are barreling through a text passively, you will not give yourself time to connect with it. You might as well tape the passage and play it under your pillow as you sleep.

Speed-Reading Strategies

You do not need to speed-read to perform well on the Reading Comprehension section, but you might benefit from some pointers that speed-readers use.

- **Avoid subvocalizing.** It is unlikely that you move your lips while you read, but you may find yourself "saying" the text in your head. This slows you down significantly, because you are slowing down to speech speed instead of revving up to reading speed. You do not need to "say" the words; the connection between your eyes and your brain is perfectly able to bypass that step.
- **Do not regress.** If you do not understand something, you may run your eyes back and forth and back and forth over it. Speed-readers know this as "regression," and it is a big drag on reading speed. It is better to read once all the way through and then reread a confusing section.
- **Bundle ideas.** Read phrases rather than words. Remember, you are being tested on overall meaning, which is not derived from single words but rather from phrases, sentences, and paragraphs. If you read word by word, your eyes stop constantly, and that slows you down. Read bundles of meaning, and your eyes will flow over the page, improving both reading speed and comprehension.

▆▆▆ TYPES OF READING COMPREHENSION QUESTIONS ON THE CBEST

When it comes to taking reading comprehension tests, knowing what to expect is half the battle. On the CBEST you will be given a series of short passages. Each passage is followed by several questions based on its content. The questions are in the multiple-choice format.

The questions assess a variety of reading skills, from basic comprehension skills to higher-level analysis and evaluation skills. Here is a list of the skills that are usually tested in reading comprehension.

Find the Main Idea

This type of question asks you to identify the main idea of the passage as a whole. With this type of question, you need to be very careful to select the answer choice that reflects the main idea of the entire passage and not just a part of it. Don't pick choices that focus on supporting details or minor ideas in the passage. Here are some sample question stems for this type of question:

- The main point of the passage is...
- The central thesis of the passage is...
- The best title for this selection is...

Recall a Fact

This type of question asks you to identify a fact or a detail that was stated somewhere in the passage. If you have read carefully, you should either be able to remember the fact or have a good idea of where it is located. Before selecting an answer choice, it is a good idea to look back at the passage and be sure that your memory of details is correct. Here are some sample question stems for this type of question:

- According to the passage...
- The passage suggests that...

Draw a Conclusion

This type of question asks you to think about ideas or facts given in the passage and to put them together to draw some kind of logical conclusion. In questions of this kind, it is very important to choose an answer that is directly supported by the facts in the passage. Incorrect answer choices will be statements that are not supported by anything in the passage. Here are some sample question stems for this type of question:

- The purpose of the process described in the passage is to...
- Why were the scientists studying...

Infer Information

This type of question asks you to look closely at ideas or facts stated in the passage and deduce something about them that the author has left unsaid. As with questions asking you to draw a conclusion, it is very important to choose an answer that is directly supported by some fact or idea in the passage. Incorrect answer choices will be statements that are not supported by anything in the passage. Here are some sample question stems for this type of question:

- Based on the passage, you can tell that...
- The passage implies that...
- The reason that the author suggests X is...

Identify the Author's Purpose

This type of question asks you to tell why the author of the passage presents a certain fact or idea or what that author is trying to do when he or she describes a given item or process. Or it may ask you to identify the author's purpose for the entire passage. Here are some sample question stems for this type of question:

- The author's purpose in the third paragraph is . . .
- The author includes X to show . . .
- The author's purpose in writing the passage was . . .

Identify the Meaning of a Word in Context

This type of question asks you to identify the correct meaning of a word used in the passage. Sometimes the word selected can have many different meanings, but only one will make sense within the context of the passage. Your task is to select that meaning. Here is how such questions are usually stated:

- What does the word x mean as used in this passage?
- As used in this passage, the word x can best be defined as . . .

Index Questions

This type of question shows you a page of a book index. It may ask you on what pages to find a particular topic or asks you about the way a topic is organized in the index. Here are some question stems for this type of question:

- On which pages should one look to find information about ...?
- Which of the following best describes the organizational pattern used in the section of the book dealing with ...?

Table of Contents Questions

This type of question shows you the table of contents of a book. It may ask you where information on a specific topic would most likely be found or what is the best location to find that information most efficiently? Here are examples of how these questions are usually stated:

- In which part of the book would information about ... most likely be found?
- A reader is looking for .... This information could most easily be found in which of the following sections of the book?

■ TEST-TAKING TIPS FOR READING COMPREHENSION

Here is a step-by-step method for attacking the reading comprehension questions. Practice using this method on the passages in this chapter. This method is based on common sense and helps most people to focus their thoughts and use their time more efficiently.

1. *Preview* the passage. Read the first sentence. Skim the passage.
2. *Skim* the question stems (the part of each question that does not include the answer choices). This will give you a quick idea of what to look for as you read.
3. *Read* the passage, using your active reading strategies.
4. *Answer* the questions. Read all the answer choices before choosing the best one. Sometimes an answer may seem right at first glance but it is not. Always see if there is a better answer choice further down the list.

If you don't know an answer, don't panic or get bogged down. Here is what you should do:

- If a question stumps you, skip ahead and come back to it at the end of the question set.
- If you still don't know the answer, take a guess. There is no guessing penalty and you have a one-in-five chance of getting it right. Try to eliminate as many answer choices as possible. The more answer choices you can eliminate, the better your odds become.
- Mark those questions you want to come back to, if you have time, after you have finished the test. Mark the question in the test booklet or on scratch paper, never on the answer sheet, because stray pencil marks on the answer sheet can affect your score.

Finally, if you are stressing out and find that you are unable to think clearly—your mind is racing and you're unable to focus—pause for a moment, take several deep breaths, and try to relax. Think positive thoughts and imagine yourself succeeding. Don't try to race through the test, keep calm and try to maintain a steady pace.

▆▆ PRACTICE SETS

Each of the following passages is followed by questions based on its content. Select the choice that best answers the question. Answers and explanations are given at the end of each question set.

Remember that on the actual test you will be timed, so keep an eye on the clock and see how long it takes you to complete each question set. That will give you an idea of your average time, and you will know if you have to speed up before you take the actual test.

Passage 1

The food pyramid is a visual representation of how the different food groups can be combined to form a healthy diet. Although it has been a vital part of dietary guidelines for years, the pyramid is constantly undergoing analysis and revision as additional studying is done in nutritional fields. Recently, the pyramid underwent another change regarding the unique dietary needs of seniors.

Recent modifications in the pyramid for older adults include an emphasis on fiber and calcium, as well as on vitamins D and B_{12}. By incorporating these changes, the pyramid now indicates that the nutrients found in a person's routine daily consumption typically are not enough for seniors. Seniors need supplementation.

As people age, they tend to move less and thus need fewer calories to maintain their weight. Because seniors tend to eat a more limited amount, dietitians urge them to choose wisely. They are urged to eat nutrient-rich meals featuring such food as fruits, vegetables, low-fat dairy products, and high-fiber whole grains.

The newly designed pyramid also focuses on the importance for older people of ingesting adequate amounts of fluids on a daily basis. This helps to ensure proper digestion and prevent any possibility of dehydration.

Finally, the revised pyramid includes information on incorporating exercise and other physical activities into the lives of older adults. Suggestions include swimming, walking, or simple yard work. Because recent reports have stated that obesity levels for people older than 70 years of age are climbing, performing some type of regular exercise is more essential than ever.

1. The best title for this selection is
   A. America's Seniors Need Exercise
   B. A New Food Pyramid for Seniors
   C. Finding Supplementation for Aging
   D. Dietary Changes in Older Americans
   E. Weight Control Methods for Seniors

2. The purpose of updating the food pyramid as described in the passage is to
   A. change how seniors eat.
   B. increase food supplement sales.
   C. encourage people to eat more fruit.
   D. encourage people to eat more fiber.
   E. convince older people to start swimming.

3. The passage says that seniors should support their digestion by
   A. taking vitamin D.
   B. eating fewer calories.
   C. eating more fiber.
   D. incorporating some exercise into their regular routine.
   E. drinking adequate fluids.

4. The reason that the author of the passage suggests exercise such as swimming, walking, and yard work is because those activities are
   A. ways to interact with other people.
   B. things that can be done alone.
   C. low-impact in nature and relatively safe.
   D. useless for burning up calories.
   E. convenient everyday activities for most people.

5. The author's purpose in writing this passage was primarily to
   A. alert people to the different dietary needs of seniors.
   B. encourage students to study the pyramid's requirements.
   C. inform nurses about what supplements are most essential.
   D. educate physicians on the differences between dried and fresh fruit.
   E. reinforce the recommendations of the National Health Institute to dieticians.

GO ON TO THE NEXT PAGE.

Passage 1: Answers and Explanations

1. **Correct Choice: B.**

   This is a question that asks you to identify the main idea of the passage. The key is to ask yourself if each choice is too broad or too specific. You do not want to confuse details with the main idea. For example, choice A is too specific; the need for exercise was only one small detail at the end of the passage. Choices C and E are also too detailed; supplementation and weight control are only details from the passage. Choice D, however, is too broad; it does not focus on the pyramid's changes as the correct answer does.

2. **Correct Choice: A.**

   This is a question that asks you to draw a conclusion from the information you read. You are to think about the changes made to the food pyramid and determine their overall, general purpose. Those changes might have resulted in more sales of food supplements (choice B), more fruit or fiber being consumed (choices C and D), but neither of those was the purpose of the changes. It is said that older people are being encouraged to swim (choice E), but that too was not the purpose of the changes to the food pyramid. The purpose was to get older people to change their eating habits.

3. **Correct Choice: E.**

   The question asks you to recall a fact stated in the article to make sure you understood an important point made in the passage. Although all five choices are mentioned in the passage as something seniors should do, only one is actually associated with helping proper digestion.

4. **Correct Choice: C.**

   This question is asking you to infer information based on what is provided in the passage. None of these statements is directly stated, but by combining details from the passage, you can determine which is the correct answer. Choice A does not make sense because the activities listed are designed to promote health; there is nothing to indicate that they are supposed to improve seniors' social lives. Choice B does not make sense because the point is not to find activities that seniors can do alone. Choice D is not correct because burning up calories is important for seniors. Choice E is wrong because the author does not reference everyday convenience. But the author is deliberately suggesting forms of exercise that would not be risky for older adults.

5. **Correct Choice: A.**

   This question asks you to identify the author's purpose. Choices B, C, D, and E are not correct because there is nothing to indicate that the passage was written specifically for students, nurses, physicians, or dieticians. The purpose of the passage is to alert readers to the fact that according to modern research, seniors have special dietary needs.

Passage 2

Elk were once found in the eastern United States, from Georgia north to New York and Connecticut. By the time of the Civil War, hunting and habitat destruction had caused their extinction in most eastern states. By the beginning of the twentieth century, all eastern subspecies of elk were extinct. Elk County, Pennsylvania, for example, was without an elk for over a century.

In 1913 the federal government decided to try to reestablish elk herds in the eastern states. Fifty elk were gathered up from Yellowstone National Park and shipped to Pennsylvania, and two years later, 95 more elk were moved from Yellowstone to Pennsylvania. However, at that time, there was little understanding of the kind of acclimatization required when moving animals from one habitat to another. The elk were simply released from cattle cars and chased into the wild to fend for themselves.

The elk did not do well. Little effort was made to restore their habitat, and many were killed illegally by farmers who found them in their fields harming their crops. By 1971, an extensive study found only 65 elk in Pennsylvania. However, intensive work by the Bureau of Forestry to improve elk habitat, especially through the reclamation of old strip mines, brought the number up to 135 by the early 1980s. By the year 2000, there were over 500 elk in Pennsylvania, including many in Elk County.

1. According to this passage, a major early threat to elk populations was

   A. wolves and cougars.
   B. vehicular traffic.
   C. disease.
   D. hunting.
   E. land taken up by farming.

2. Based on information in this passage, how many elk were moved from Yellowstone to Pennsylvania?

   A. 50
   B. 95
   C. 135
   D. 145
   E. 155

3. The passage implies that

   A. reclamation of land is a bad idea.
   B. hunters have ulterior motives for reintroducing elk.
   C. species reintroduction is a good idea where feasible.
   D. elk reintroduction may be doomed to failure.
   E. farmers must use nonviolent means to keep animals out of their crops.

4. Which of the following statements from the passage expresses a personal opinion, rather than a fact?

   A. "Elk County, Pennsylvania, for example, was without an elk for over a century."
   B. "The elk did not do well."
   C. "By the time of the Civil War, hunting and habitat destruction had caused their extinction in most eastern states."
   D. ". . . at that time, there was little understanding of the kind of acclimatization required when moving animals from one habitat to another."
   E. "Little effort was made to restore their habitat, and many were killed illegally by farmers who found them in their fields harming their crops."

GO ON TO THE NEXT PAGE.

5. The author would most likely agree with which of the following statements?

   A. Habitat restoration is key to the effectiveness of species reintroductions.
   B. Animals should not be moved from their native regions.
   C. We shouldn't worry about species extinction because we can always reintroduce a similar species later.
   D. Elk numbers in the eastern United States have increased enough to allow some limited hunting.
   E. Hunting should be banned.

6. What is the best title for this article?

   A. No Elk in Elk County
   B. The Growth of Elk Herds in Pennsylvania
   C. The Elk Are Back in Elk County
   D. Programs to Reintroduce Species to Their Native Lands
   E. The Rise and Fall of Elk Populations

Passage 2: Answers and Explanations

1. **Correct Choice: D.**

   The question asks you to recall a fact stated in the article. In the second sentence of the first paragraph, the author states that hunting and habitat destruction were the reasons for the extinction of elk in the eastern United States.

2. **Correct Choice: D.**

   This question requires you to recall facts stated in the article. Did you read carefully enough to understand that there were two releases of elk mentioned in the article? The article states that 50 elk from Yellowstone were released in Pennsylvania and then two years later, 95 more elk were released. That brings the total to 145 based on the information mentioned in this article.

3. **Correct Choice: C.**

   This question asks you to make an inference based on what is stated in the passage. Although the author never says explicitly that the reintroduction of species to their native lands is a good idea, the statements he makes and the tone he takes clearly indicates that he thinks the reintroduction of elk into Pennsylvania has been a good thing, especially when the reintroduction is accompanied by the restoration of habitat. Therefore, we can infer that the author supports this type of program.

4. **Correct Choice: B.**

   The question asks you to distinguish between statements of opinion and statements of fact. The words "good" or "well" often indicate that a personal opinion is being expressed. Doing well is open to interpretation. What is the criteria for doing well—survival or growth? Someone could argue that they did quite well to just survive all those years given the difficult situation in which they found themselves. If the author had said the elk herd did not grow or that it barely survived, that would be a statement of fact. But as the author stated it, it represents his opinion and is based on his definition of doing well.

5. **Correct Choice: A.**

   This question asks you to make an inference based on what is stated in the passage. Although the author never states it explicitly, it is clear from the importance he places on habitat restoration in making the reintroduction of elk successful,

that he would agree in general that habitat restoration is key to the success of efforts to reintroduce species.

6. **Correct Choice: C.**

   This is a question that asks you to identify the main idea of the passage. Although the passage is about Pennsylvania, not just Elk County, answer choice C correctly captures the central idea of the passage—the story of how the elk have returned to land they once roamed. Focusing the title on Elk County makes it more catchy without distorting the main idea. Answer choice A is contrary to the main theme that the elk are back. Answer choice B ignores the main subject—reintroduction of vanished species—and would seem to be an article about how elk herds grow. Answer choice D captures the main topic of the article but misstates what's in the article; there are no different species or programs. The story is only about elk. Answer choice E reverses the decline and increase of the elk population and also fails to mention Pennsylvania or Elk County.

Passage 3

Years of research have proven that Alzheimer's disease, along with other types of dementia, elevates the risk of dying early in the majority of patients. In a recent study, scientists set out to determine exactly how long people were likely to survive following the onset of dementia.

Currently, approximately 24 million people throughout the world suffer from the memory loss and orientation confusion that comes with Alzheimer's disease and other forms of dementia. That number appears to double every 20 years, and experts predict that by the year 2040, there will be 81 million people living with some level of the condition. The more the researchers and doctors can learn about what causes the problem, as well as how to treat it, the better prepared they will be to handle these millions of future patients.

To determine how people's life spans are affected by this medical condition, the scientists studied 13,000 seniors for a period of 14 years. During that time, 438 people developed dementia, the vast majority of whom died. The factors of age, disability, and gender were analyzed to see how they affected longevity as well.

Conclusions from the study showed that women tended to live slightly longer than men, averaging 4.6 years from the onset of dementia, as opposed to 4.1 years for men. The patients who were already weak or frail at the onset of the dementia died first, regardless of age. Marital status, living environment, and the degree of mental decline were not shown to be influential on life spans.

Researchers hope that this new information will help patients, clinicians, care providers, service providers, policy makers, and others who deal with dementia. The more they know, the better they will be able to respond to this heart-breaking condition.

1. The best title for this selection is

   A. Alzheimer's Disease on the Rise.
   B. Women's Life Spans Are Longer.
   C. Average Time of Survival with Dementia.
   D. The Effect of Marital Status on Longevity.
   E. Learning Better Ways to Treat Alzheimer's Disease.

GO ON TO THE NEXT PAGE.

2. What fact did researchers already know before beginning this new study?

A. Women with Alzheimer's disease tend to live slightly longer than their male counterparts.

B. A patient's overall condition before dementia onset was a key factor in survival.

C. Age was not a large factor in survival.

D. The living environment had a small influence on the overall life span of a patient with dementia.

E. People diagnosed with some kind of dementia usually have a higher risk of dying early.

3. The author mentions the number of patients with Alzheimer's disease to

A. point out the rarity of the disease.

B. emphasize the average age at which onset occurs.

C. clarify why the disease strikes one sex more than another.

D. explain why knowing more about the condition is so essential.

E. compare the rates of the disease with the rates of death for people with the disease.

4. Why did the researchers undertake this new study on dementia?

A. To better understand the effects of the disease

B. To educate families on how to cope with the condition

C. To show physicians and other professionals a new kind of treatment

D. To prove that degree of mental decline is not the most important factor

E. To demonstrate that women with the disease live longer than men with the disease

5. According to the passage, the factor that affects dementia survival rate the most is

A. marital status.

B. health at onset.

C. living environment.

D. degree of mental decline.

E. gender.

6. Ironically, the one group of people mentioned in the passage that will be unable to make use of the conclusions of the study are

A. physicians.

B. nurses.

C. patients.

D. policy makers.

E. physician assistants.

Passage 3: Answers and Explanations

1. Correct Choice: C.

This is a main-idea question. By picking out the best title, you are pinpointing the focus of the passage. Choice A is not correct because the rise of Alzheimer's disease is a supporting detail rather than the main idea. Choice B highlights a relatively minor detail in the passage, and choice D does as well. Answer choice E references a topic that the article briefly touches upon, but better treatments aren't actually discussed. The focus of the entire passage is best stated in choice C.

2. Correct Choice: E.

This question asks you to infer information. If you look at how the passage was written, the only fact that the researchers knew before embarking on this experiment was that dementia patients had shorter life spans, which is stated in choice E. Choices A, B, C, and D were factors that researchers learned through their study.

3. Correct Choice: D.

This question asks you to identify the author's purpose from details given in the passage. Choice A does not make sense with the information provided about the prevalence of the disease. The number of cases has no connection to the average age at onset as in choice B. Nothing in the passage discusses how the genders are affected differently (choice C) or compares the rates of the disease with the rates of death of people with the disease (choice E). The reason that the author mentions the large number of patients with Alzheimer's disease is to support his or her claim that knowing about the condition is increasingly essential.

4. Correct Choice: A.

This question asks you to draw a conclusion. The last paragraph is your best clue as to the right answer. Choice B is not true because there are no coping tips in this passage; choice C is wrong because there is nothing about treatment methods; and choices D and E are based on a fact discovered in the study, but that fact is not the reason why the research was done.

5. Correct Choice: B.

The question asks you to recall a fact to make sure you comprehend what you read. All four answer choices are factors mentioned in the passage, but only choice B is pinpointed as an influential one. The rest are considered either not influential or not as relevant.

6. Correct Choice: C.

This is another question that asks you to infer information based on what is in the passage. Physicians, nurses, policy makers, and physician assistants can all make use of the information provided by this study, but the patients themselves cannot do so and in fact would not even be aware of it.

Passage 4

In recent years, there have been frightening headlines about harmful ingredients such as mercury and lead in ordinary cosmetics. However, these are hardly the first examples of people paying a heavy price to conform to cultural ideals of beauty. That is a tradition that has been around for centuries.

Ancient Egyptians decorated their eyes with malachite (a green ore of copper), galena (a lead sulfide), and kohl (a paste made from soot, fat, and metals such as lead). This may have made them look more beautiful but it also led to health problems such as insomnia and mental confusion.

GO ON TO THE NEXT PAGE.

The ancient Greeks went even further. They applied lead to their entire faces, supposedly to clear their complexions of any blemishes and improve the coloration of the skin. Health problems that resulted ranged from infertility to insanity. The lead ointment whitened their faces—a sure sign of beauty—so they then added some red lead to the cheeks for that rosy glow. As if that toxic mess was not enough, they also used hair dyes that contained lead. Some historians suspect that lead poisoning was part of what later led to the fall of the Roman Empire.

Lead played a huge role in cosmetics for centuries, but it was not until the mid-nineteenth century that the American Medical Association (AMA) published a paper about the connection between lead in cosmetics and health concerns. Despite the availability of this information, sellers still offered powders and potions that contained harmful chemicals and other materials. These products had innocuous names such as Snow White Enamel, Milk of Roses, and Berry's Freckle Ointment.

The Pure Food and Drug Act (1906) and the creation of the Food and Drug Administration (FDA) helped put an end to some of the most dangerous cosmetics, although products such as a lotion containing rat poison and a mascara that caused blindness still made it onto the market. In 1938 cosmetics came under the control of the FDA, and in 1977 a law was passed requiring cosmetic manufacturers to list all ingredients on their products.

Although these steps have helped ensure product safety, problems still exist. As recently as 2007, lipsticks for sale were found to contain lead and mascara was found to contain mercury. An additional concern is phthalates, industrial chemicals that can cause birth defects and infertility. They are found in personal care products such as shampoos, lotions, perfume, and deodorants.

An old saying states that beauty has a price. Sometimes it just may be much higher than consumers realize.

1. Which of these topics is the main focus of the passage?

   A. Frightening news stories from the past
   B. Ancient Egyptian and Greek cultures
   C. The dangers of cosmetics throughout history
   D. The control of makeup by the FDA
   E. Historical standards of beauty

2. Why did the ancient Greeks put white lead ointment on their faces?

   A. To make themselves look younger
   B. To clear up their complexions
   C. To keep from getting seriously ill
   D. To achieve an overall rosy glow
   E. To make their eyes stand out

3. One might infer from this passage that

   A. lead is no longer used in cosmetics.
   B. manufacturers of cosmetics will continue to ignore FDA rulings.
   C. the AMA regulates cosmetic ingredients.
   D. phthalates are not nearly as dangerous as ingredients used in the past.
   E. beauty is more important than health.

4. Which of the following is identified in the passage as a health hazard resulting from lead?

   A. Cancer
   B. Paralysis
   C. Infertility
   D. Deafness
   E. Numbness

5. Which of the following type of cosmetics was not mentioned as containing toxic materials?

   A. Lipstick
   B. Deodorant
   C. Mascara
   D. Blush
   E. Lotion

6. What conclusion can be drawn from the fact that as recently as 2007, cosmetics were being pulled from store shelves?

   A. The FDA is no longer performing its job properly.
   B. The AMA believes that all cosmetics are completely safe now.
   C. Manufacturers are still using harmful ingredients in their products.
   D. Personal care products that contain phthalates are also being removed from stores.
   E. Only products that contain lead were removed from store shelves.

Passage 4: Answers and Explanations

1. **Correct Choice: C.**

   This is a find-the-main-idea question. Although the passage starts out by referring to frightening headlines (choice A), that reference is merely an introduction and not the focus of the passage. Ancient Egyptian and Greek cultures (choice B) are mentioned as supporting details, but once again, they are not the main focus. Choices D and E are additional supporting details but not the main idea.

2. **Correct Choice: B.**

   The question asks you to recall a fact. Choice A is not correct because the idea of looking younger is never mentioned in the passage. Choice C is ironically wrong; the Greeks did not use lead ointment to stay healthy, and it actually made them sick. Choice D is not correct because a different kind of lead was used to provide the pink color. Choice E references the Egyptians outlining their eyes, which is a different example altogether.

3. **Correct Choice: E.**

   This question asks that you infer information. The passage provides information that contradicts answer choice A(lipsticks as recently as 2007 were found to contain lead. Choice B is not true because there is nothing in the passage to support this idea. Choice C is not true because the FDA regulates cosmetic ingredients, not the AMA. Choice D is not true because phthalates are just as dangerous as ingredients used in the past and even more prevalent.

GO ON TO THE NEXT PAGE.

4. Correct Choice: C.

The question asks you to recall a fact. Choices A, B, D, and E are not mentioned in the passage. Only choice C is listed as one of the potential risks of lead.

5. Correct Choice: D.

This is another question that asks you to recall a fact. Choices A, B, C, and E were all mentioned as, at one time or another, containing toxic materials. Only choice D was not discussed.

6. Correct Choice: C.

This question asks you to draw a conclusion from the information in the passage. Choice A is not correct because there is not enough information in the passage to support it. Choice B has no foundation in the passage and goes against the correct conclusion. Choice D is also wrong because these products are not being removed from the shelves. There is no information in the passage to support answer choice E.

Passage 5

Most people get a little grumpy when they do not get enough sleep, but when it comes to children, the problem may be more than just some extra irritation. Lack of sleep may also affect their weight, as well as their overall behavior.

A study published in the medical journal *Sleep* followed almost 600 children from infancy through seven years of age. Researchers observed the children's sleep patterns and found that generally they slept less on the weekends than during the week and even less during the summer months.

According to the findings, the children who tended to sleep the least were at greater risk for being overweight and/or experiencing behavioral problems. In fact, those who regularly slept less than 9 hours a night were three times more likely than longer sleepers to be obese and to show signs of attention deficit disorder (ADD) and attention deficit hyperactivity disorder (ADHD). These results were based on questionnaires handed out to the children's parents and teachers.

How does sleep affect weight? The answer to that is still not clear, but experts suspect that chronic sleep deprivation somehow alters the hormones involved in appetite control and metabolism. This is a connection that still needs to be explored to be better understood.

How much sleep is enough for a child? Experts recommend that preschoolers get 11 to 13 hours of sleep each night, whereas school-age children should get between 10 and 11 hours per night. Many children average only 8 hours.

The study concluded that sleep duration is one risk factor that can be fairly easily altered to prevent future health problems for today's young people.

1. What would be the best title for this passage?
   A. Preventing ADHD in Your Child
   B. The Cure for Childhood Obesity
   C. Hormones and Appetite Control
   D. Children and the Need for Sleep
   E. Preventing Behavior Problems in Your Child

2. This passage suggests that children sleep the most during the
   A. cold weather months.
   B. weekend.
   C. summer.
   D. holidays.
   E. week.

3. This study was conducted primarily through
   A. lab experiments.
   B. questionnaires.
   C. brief research.
   D. years of interviews.
   E. observations.

4. According to the passage, inadequate sleep can result in all of the following EXCEPT
   A. hyperactivity.
   B. obesity.
   C. irritability.
   D. behavior problems.
   E. anxiety.

5. What conclusion can you draw about the connection between sleep and young children?
   A. Lack of sleep causes children to fail in school.
   B. Inadequate rest raises the risk of behavioral and physical problems.
   C. Sleeping less than 10 hours a night is guaranteed to result in obesity.
   D. Eight hours of sleep each night meets the requirements of most children.
   E. Too little sleep causes the attention spans of children to decrease.

6. According to the passage, which of the following ideas needs further exploration?
   A. The amount of sleep children actually need at each age
   B. How children's sleep patterns change during the seasons
   C. How sleep affects children's appetite and overall metabolism
   D. How teachers and physicians determine a diagnosis of ADD or ADHD
   E. How sleep affects children's weight

Passage 5: Answers and Explanations

1. Correct Choice: D.

This is a find-the-main-idea question. To pick out the best title, you have to grasp the focus of the entire article rather than just one or more supporting details. In this case, choice A is just one of the details in the passage. The passage does mention ADHD in children, but that is not the main idea. Obesity (choice B) is another detail mentioned in the passage, but nothing is said about a cure. Choice C implies that the whole article is about the link between hormones and appetite control, when in actuality, that is just one theory that is mentioned. The passage as a whole

GO ON TO THE NEXT PAGE.

is about the importance of enough sleep for children. Choice E was also mentioned in the passage, but it is only a detail.

2. Correct Choice: E.

The question asks you to recall a fact. The passage states in the second paragraph that children sleep less in the summer and on weekends. Cold weather months and holidays are not mentioned. This means that the only correct answer is choice E.

3. Correct Choice: B.

The question asks you to recall a fact. It requires you to identify details that you did and did not find in the passage. Choice A is wrong because no lab experiments are mentioned in the passage. Choice C is wrong because this study took place over a period of seven years, so the word *brief* is incorrect. Choice D is also wrong because there is no mention of interviews. Choice E is wrong because the passage never mentions observations.

4. Correct Choice: E.

The question asks you to recall a fact. Looking back through the passage, you can see that choices A, B, C, and D are all mentioned in the passage as possible results of inadequate sleep. Only choice E is not found anywhere in the passage.

5. Correct Choice: B.

This question asks you to draw a conclusion from the information presented in the passage. Based on the passage, choice A is not correct because it draws an unwarranted conclusion. Not enough sleep does not necessarily mean that a child will fail in school. Choice C is also incorrect because it is an unwarranted conclusion: obesity is a risk, not something guaranteed to occur. Choice D is also incorrect and goes against the evidence presented throughout the passage. Choice E is another unwarranted conclusion; lack of sleep does not necessarily cause a decrease in a child's attention span.

6. Correct Choice: C.

This question requires you to infer information. You have to read the passage carefully to be sure of the correct answer to this question. Choice A is not up for further study; the numbers are made clear within the passage. Choices B and E are not considered issues that need to be further clarified. Choice D is beyond the scope of this passage.

Passage 6

Is there a foolproof way to detect a lie? Most of us have heard of the polygraph test, more commonly known as a lie-detector test. In this test, a pair of plates that can sense and measure *subtle* increases in sweating is attached to a person's fingers, while at the same time other devices monitor increases in blood pressure and pulse rate as well as breathing depth. However, factors such as hunger or alcohol use can cause misleading polygraph results. Minor self-inflicted pain during the test can also result in false positives, and so can the truthful statements of pathological liars.

Another technology, the electroencephalograph (ECG), is also used to detect lies, but in quite a different way. As

it turns out, one particular brain wave, which researchers have isolated and can graph, surges whenever we see something we recognize. It's impossible for any person to voluntarily suppress this surge. So, when a crime suspect wearing a special headband hooked up to an ECG machine is shown images or words connected with the crime and the brain wave suddenly spikes, the suspect's brain is essentially shouting, I'm guilty!

A newer form of lie detector is far simpler than any other technology, aside from simply observing body language. People cannot help hesitating ever so briefly just before telling a lie. With modern computer technology, we can now detect and measure the briefest such pauses, which tell us when someone is lying.

1. According to the passage, when people lie they often
   A. speak more softly.
   B. hold their breath.
   C. stare unnaturally.
   D. avert their eyes.
   E. sweat more.

2. According to the passage, pathological liars
   A. are more likely than other people to commit crimes.
   B. can fool polygraph examiners.
   C. are often used to test polygraph equipment.
   D. rarely volunteer for polygraph tests.
   E. lie for every single response in a polygraph test.

3. As used in the passage, the word *subtle* most nearly means
   A. sweaty.
   B. irregular.
   C. normal.
   D. sudden.
   E. slight.

4. During an electroencephalograph (ECG) test, the test taker
   A. answers questions.
   B. wears finger plates.
   C. wears a special headband.
   D. repeats words after the examiner.
   E. has plates attached to his/her fingers.

5. The electroencephalograph (ECG) test might detect
   A. a lie before it is told.
   B. subtle body language.
   C. brief pauses in speech.
   D. changes in blood pressure.
   E. increases in sweating.

6. A good title for the passage is
   A. How to Cheat on a Lie Detector Test
   B. Do Polygraph Tests Always Reveal Lies?
   C. In Search of the Perfect Lie Detector
   D. The Technology of Crime Investigation
   E. Pathology Tests vs. ECG Tests

GO ON TO THE NEXT PAGE.

Passage 6: Answers and Explanations

1. **Correct Choice: E.**

   The question asks you to recall a fact. The first paragraph describes the polygraph test, in which plates are attached to the fingers in order to detect any increase in sweating.

2. **Correct Choice: B.**

   The question also asks you to recall a fact. At the end of the first paragraph, the author tells us that truthful statements of pathological liars can result in false positives, which mislead a polygraph examiner to believe that such statements are actually lies.

3. **Correct Choice: E.**

   This question requires you to identify the meaning of a word in context. A special device would not be needed to detect large, obvious changes in sweating. Thus, if you substitute the word *slight,* which means "very small," for *subtle,* the sentence makes perfect sense.

4. **Correct Choice: C.**

   The question asks you to recall a fact. This type of test measures brain waves detected by sensors attached to a special headband.

5. **Correct Choice: A.**

   The question also asks you to recall a fact. An ECG test detects brain wave surges that occur whenever a person sees something recognizable. If a crime suspect views images from the crime scene and the brain wave spikes, an investigator could then question the suspect about the crime and detect whether the suspect is lying.

6. **Correct Choice: C.**

   This question asks you to identify the main idea of the passage. The passage begins by asking, Is there a foolproof way to detect a lie? Then, the passage's author proceeds to trace the development of lie-detection technology, from the less reliable polygraph to newer, more reliable tests. The title suggestion in choice C conveys the main point of the article in a succinct and clever way. Answer choice B is plausible, but the article doesn't ever discuss how accurate each technology is; the focus is on the technology and how it is used. The passage isn't a direct comparison of the two technologies discussed, so answer choice E is incorrect.

Passage 7

The health risks of coffee have long been debated, but a recent study has added another argument against too much coffee consumption. This study looked at the effect of drinking coffee on pregnant women and explored the connection between caffeine and the risk of miscarriage.

The connection is one that has been studied before, but this study took a different approach. It took morning sickness into account, whereas other studies did not. The findings were significant: 200 milligrams of caffeine a day—about the amount found in two cups of coffee—is enough to increase the risk of having a miscarriage. The source of the caffeine, whether coffee, tea, or soda, was irrelevant; the amount was the key.

This study followed more than 1,000 women who became pregnant within a two-year period. The amount of caffeine they drank was logged, as well as which women experienced a miscarriage. The results showed that the risk of miscarriage more than doubled in women who consumed 200 mg or more of caffeine per day.

Why does caffeine carry this risk? Researchers are not sure, but they theorize that the caffeine restricts blood flow to the placenta. This, in turn, can harm the developing fetus.

Does this mean the physicians will start advising women to quit drinking coffee while pregnant? Yes and no. Some doctors will certainly take this report to heart and encourage their patients to stay away from more than one cup of coffee a day, just as they recommend not drinking alcohol or smoking cigarettes. Others are not so convinced and doubt that this single study is enough to *overturn* the established guidelines of the American College of Obstetricians and Gynecologists. Instead, they believe that a lot more research needs to be done.

1. What is the main idea of this passage?

   A. Coffee carries some obvious health risks for people.
   B. Two cups of coffee a day may be enough to raise the risk of miscarriage.
   C. There is a link between miscarriages and morning sickness.
   D. Miscarriage rates are on the rise internationally.
   E. Pregnant women should never drink coffee.

2. Based on the study, which aspect of caffeine consumption seemed to be the key to the risk of miscarriage?

   A. The source of the caffeine
   B. The time at which the caffeine is ingested
   C. The amount of caffeine ingested
   D. The time between doses of caffeine
   E. The combination of caffeine with certain other food additives

3. What do some researchers believe is the link between caffeine and miscarriages?

   A. They believe that caffeine is a toxin.
   B. They believe that caffeine makes the heart beat too rapidly.
   C. They suspect that caffeine interferes with the immune system.
   D. They theorize that caffeine prevents some nutrients from crossing the placenta.
   E. They think that caffeine inhibits placental blood flow.

4. The word *overturn* as used in the last paragraph of the passage can best be defined as

   A. justify.
   B. strengthen.
   C. support.
   D. review.
   E. invalidate.

GO ON TO THE NEXT PAGE.

5. Based on this passage, what conclusion can best be drawn about the advice physicians will give their pregnant patients about coffee consumption?

   A. The majority will recommend an increase in caffeine intake.
   B. The majority will ignore the study altogether and continue to advise caffeine in moderation as before.
   C. All of them will demand additional research to be done before they change what they tell their patients.
   D. Some will continue to make their normal recommendations about caffeine, while others will be more cautious than before.
   E. Almost all of them will advise women to stop drinking any caffeine until after the baby is born.

6. Based on this passage, what conclusion can best be drawn about the potential effects of drinking coffee?

   A. It is completely safe for anyone.
   B. There are absolutely no concerns unless you are pregnant.
   C. It can be extremely dangerous for everyone.
   D. It may pose health risks for some people.
   E. It is dangerous unless you are pregnant.

Passage 7: Answers and Explanations

1. **Correct Choice: B.**

   Clearly, this question requires you to identify the main idea. Choice A is too broad and goes beyond the scope of the passage, choice C is a side detail briefly mentioned, and choice D is not stated anywhere in the passage. Although the passage discusses miscarriages, it does not mention statistics. Choice E makes a conclusion; the article remains ambivalent.

2. **Correct Choice: C.**

   The question asks you to recall a fact. If you read the passage carefully, you know that the answer is choice C. Where the caffeine came from and when it was ingested are irrelevant according to the passage. The passage never mentions combining caffeine with other food additives.

3. **Correct Choice: E.**

   The question also asks you to recall a fact. The answer is found in paragraph 4. Choice E is correct and is the only theory presented anywhere within the passage, making choices A, B, C, and D all incorrect.

4. **Correct Choice: E.**

   This question requires that you identify the meaning of a word in context. The findings of the study run counter to the established guidelines of the American College of Obstetricians and Gynecologists, so if accepted, the findings would invalidate those guidelines. None of the other choices fit the meaning in context.

5. **Correct Choice: D.**

   This is a draw-a-conclusion question. If you look at the last paragraph again, you see that the only correct answer is choice D. Some physicians will regard this study as conclusive and change their recommendations, whereas others will wait for more research.

6. **Correct Choice: D.**

   This is another draw-a-conclusion question. Choices A and C are sweeping conclusions that are not supported by the passage. There is also no reason to think that coffee is completely safe for anyone who is not pregnant, so choice B is incorrect. Choice E is the opposite of the information it the passage. Choice D is the only conclusion that is supported by the passage.

Passage 8

In some schools around the country, physical education classes look a lot different than they did a generation or two ago. Kids are still in motion, stretching, running, lifting, and sweating. But instead of everyone doing the same activity at the same time as a team, they are exercising independently. They are being taught movements and activities that their teachers hope they will incorporate into their lives rather than just perform long enough to get a good grade.

By teaching kids the pleasure of exercise, gym teachers hope to *instill* important lessons about maintaining good health, staying fit, and keeping weight under control. By getting the chance to work out at their own pace, rather than being forced to keep up with other classmates, students are often more willing to try new things and stick with them. They can also participate in low-impact sports like yoga, martial arts, and weightlifting. Instead of playing basketball or baseball, they can focus on more general skills like passing the ball.

A growing number of physical education (PE) teachers are also putting more of an emphasis on general nutrition and health. According to Craig Buschner, president of the National Association for Sport and Physical Education, "This field has to make changes." With the continual increase in the number of children who are obese, there is greater pressure to teach students about how to stay fit. To do this, PE teachers have to look at new ways to introduce exercise to their students that will not intimidate or overwhelm them but instead intrigue and engage them.

One other difference found in some modern gym classes is the grading system. Instead of being graded on the ability to run laps in a set time or make a certain number of baskets, the students are graded simply on the effort they make in the class. Some even get extra credit if they are sweatiest student in the room!

1. What would be the best title for this passage?

   A. Being a Team in PE
   B. A New Kind of Grade
   C. Nutrition and PE
   D. PE for School and Life
   E. Learning Martial Arts

2. The term *instill* as used in the second paragraph of the passage can best be defined as

   A. encourage.
   B. indoctrinate.
   C. demand.
   D. create.
   E. reinforce.

GO ON TO THE NEXT PAGE.

3. What can you conclude is the primary difference between traditional PE and how some PE classes are being taught today?

   A. For the first time, low-impact sports have been introduced.
   B. Today's students are stretching, running, and lifting.
   C. There is a greater emphasis on lifelong fitness.
   D. PE teachers are grading more harshly.
   E. PE is about teaching good health.

4. What can be inferred about the "sweatiest student" referred to in the last sentence in the passage?

   A. This student is more overweight than anyone else.
   B. This student is more out of shape than anyone else.
   C. This student does not need extra credit.
   D. This student is behind all of his/her classmates.
   E. This student has worked hardest during class.

5. According to the passage, PE teachers are trying to teach students lessons about all of the following EXCEPT

   A. the importance of good nutrition for health.
   B. staying generally physically fit.
   C. ways to avoid contracting contagious diseases.
   D. keeping weight under control.
   E. the pleasure of exercise.

6. Why does the author quote Craig Buschner in the passage?

   A. To make an entirely new point about physical education
   B. To lend authority to ideas presented in the passage
   C. To demonstrate that not all PE teachers are in agreement
   D. To debunk the idea that childhood obesity is a growing problem
   E. To demonstrate that PE teachers are following a new national curriculum

Passage 8: Answers and Explanations

1. **Correct Choice: D.**

   This is a find-the-main-idea question. Choice A is incorrect because this article is about how PE classes are focusing less on team activities and more on the individual. Choice B is not true because although grades are mentioned, they are not the focus of the passage. Choice C is wrong because there is no mention of nutrition in the passage. Choice E is incorrect because it focuses on a very minor detail. Choice D is correct because the focus of the passage is on teaching PE in such a way that the lessons last a lifetime.

2. **Correct Choice: A.**

   This question requires that you identify the meaning of a word in context. If you look at the context clues in the sentence, the answer becomes clear. *Indoctrinate* (choice B) is much too harsh because it means "teach against one's will." *Demand* (choice C), *create* (choice D), and *reinforce* (choice E) do not make sense in the sentence. Only choice A makes sense with the rest of the sentence.

3. **Correct Choice: C.**

   This is a draw-a-conclusion question. Choice A does not make sense because low-impact sports are not necessarily brand new. Choice B is wrong because students have been stretching, running, and lifting in PE class for years. Choice D is also false because there is nothing in the passage to indicate harsher grading, just different parameters. Choice E is wrong because PE classes have included a health component for years. The correct answer is choice C because the emphasis in classes now is to teach physical exercise in a way that students will be encouraged to continue it for the rest of their lives.

4. **Correct Choice: E.**

   This question is an inference question requiring you to infer information. In this case, the clue to the answer comes in the sentence before the last one. It says that students are graded for the effort they put forth. This makes it clear that the sweatiest student who earns extra credit is one who has put forth a lot of effort in class. There is no support in the passage for any of the other choices.

5. **Correct Choice: C.**

   PE teachers incorporate a lot of new material into their classes, including choices A, B, D, and E. Only choice C is not mentioned, so it is the correct answer.

6. **Correct Choice: B.**

   This question requires you to identify the author's purpose. Craig Buschner is the president of the National Association for Sport and Physical Education, so his words lend authority to the idea that PE classes need to change to place greater emphasis on general physical fitness. There is no support in the passage for any of the other answer choices.

Practice Set 9: Index Questions

Coffee, 156–226
    caffeine percentage [see nutritional information]
    consumption, 219–220
    countries of origin, 158–206
        Angola, 160–164
        Brazil, 165–170
        Colombia, 171–176
        Costa Rica, 177–182
        Guatemala, 183–187
        India, 188–192
        Indonesia, 193–197
        Mozambique, 198–202
        Nicaragua, 203–206
    cultural significance, 214–215
    filtration, 221–222
    nutritional information, 216–218
    processing, 223–226
    types, 207–210
    uses, 211–213
Coffee beans, 227–229
Coffee grinds, 230–231
Coffee shops, 232–235

GO ON TO THE NEXT PAGE.

1. On which pages should one look to find information about the percentage of caffeine in decaffeinated coffee?
   A. 211–213
   B. 223–226
   C. 216–218
   D. 221–222
   E. 227–229

2. On which pages should one look to find information about the removal of impurities in coffee?
   A. 223–226
   B. 227–229
   C. 230–231
   D. 219–220
   E. 221–222

Explanations to Index questions

1. **Correct Choice: C.**

   The index states that caffeine percentage is included under nutritional information.

2. **Correct Choice: E.**

   The removal of impurities means filtering. None of the other answer choices make sense.

Practice Set 10: Table of Contents Questions

1. In which part of the book would information about treating fleas most likely be found?
   A. Part One
   B. Part Two
   C. Part Three
   D. Part Four
   E. Glossary

2. A reader is looking for the formal definition of a schnauzer. The reader could probably find this information most quickly and easily by looking first in which of the following sections of the book?
   A. Part One
   B. Part Two
   C. Part Three
   D. Part Four
   E. Glossary

Explanations to Table of Contents Questions

1. **Correct Choice: B.**

   Part Two includes information on veterinary care.

2. **Correct Choice: E.**

   The glossary is the best place to look for formal definitions.

CHAPTER 9

THE CBEST WRITING TEST: THE ESSAYS

The California Basic Educational Skills Test (CBEST) for writing requires that you write two essays. This is the part of the test that test takers most often fail. If you are worried about the writing test, plan to spend some time working on your writing skills and writing practice essays. Practice will help you do better; so will feedback from others. Try to find friends, parents, colleagues, or teachers whom you will feel comfortable asking to read your practice essays and give you feedback.

THE BASICS

On the writing test, you will be given two topics; you must respond to both of the topics you are given. One topic will require you to write about a personal experience. The other topic will require you to take a position regarding a quotation or a situation. Both essays are graded using the same scoring standards. The techniques and strategies you should use are the same for each of the two essays.

Timing

Four hours are allocated for the entire CBEST, including reading, math, and writing. Since each part counts equally toward your CBEST score, plan to allocate equal time to all three sections. This means you have 1 hour and 20 minutes for the writing test. That gives you 40 minutes for each of the topics on the writing test.

Plan to spend at least 10 minutes thinking and planning before you start to write your essay. Then spend about 20 minutes doing the actual writing. The last 10 minutes should be spent rereading your essay and improving it by making edits and corrections.

How Much You Should Write

You are expected to write four to five paragraphs (with approximately two to six sentences per paragraph). Writing less will not allow you to develop your points and show your writing and reasoning skills. Writing more will probably also hurt your score. The scoring scale emphasizes quality, not quantity; your score won't be improved the more you write. Be direct and to the point without rambling on.

Make sure you answer all questions raised in the essay topic. There may be more than one part to the topic, and you'll need to address all issues raised. Read and reread the topic carefully before you begin to write. Identify the points you need to response to so that your essay is complete.

Legibility

It's important that you write legibly so that the scorers can read your writing. An essay that can't be read won't get any points. If necessary, print, rather than writing in cursive. It might take more time, but scorers will be less frustrated and likely to give you a better score. Try to leave a little space in the margins and in between lines so that after you've written the essay you can go back and make corrections and insertions that are also legible.

■ HOW THE ESSAYS ARE SCORED

Each essay is scored by two different people. If they can read your essay and it addresses the topic you were given, they will give it a score from 1 to 4, with 4 being the best score possible. The number of points you are given is based on the scoring standards set for the CBEST essays.

The Scoring Scale

The scoring standards are defined in the official CBEST Writing Score Scale, which can be viewed online at www.cbest.nesinc.com (go to the practice test and then go to the writing section). A summary of these scoring standards is provided on the next page.

If you understand how your essays will be graded, you will know what you need to do to get a good score. The scoring scale identifies six factors or criteria on which the essays are graded. Each factor is discussed in more detail below along with strategies and advice you can use to get a higher score on the writing portion of the CBEST.

The Central Idea of Your Essay

As you can see from the scoring chart above, the first criterion on which your essay will be judged is whether it presents a central idea or point of view and then how well it develops that idea or point of view. So, it is absolutely essential that you figure out the point of your essay before you begin to write. What position do you want to take? Each essay needs a central idea or point of view. Then it is important that your whole essay be focused on explaining and supporting the position or idea that you have chosen.

For the essay that is based on your personal experience, the biggest mistake you can make is to start writing about your personal experience without figuring what the central point of your essay will be. Decide on a point and then think about what experiences you can offer as examples to support or explain your point.

Similarly, for the essay that requires you to take a position on a statement or situation, you should decide exactly what position you are going to take before you begin to write. Spend a few minutes thinking about your position. These questions often give a quotation and ask you to develop an essay agreeing or disagreeing with the quotation. Remember, your position doesn't have to be entirely in agreement or entirely in disagreement with the statement you are given. You can partly agree and partly disagree, but you will need to clearly state the position you are taking.

Scoring the CBEST Writing Test	
Score	**Summary of Scoring Guidelines**
4	**A Score of 4 indicates a well-written essay that effectively develops an idea for the specified audience.**
	The essay has a central idea or point of view and the writer maintains the focus on the idea in a well reasoned essay.
	Ideas or points the author presents are logically arranged and the essay is clear and well-organized.
	Assertions are supported with relevant information and specific examples.
	Words usage is careful and precise.
	Sentences and paragraphs are well constructed and coherent; however, the essay may contain minor flaws in grammar, spelling, punctuation, etc.
	The essay completely addresses the topic and is appropriate for the given audience.
3	**A Score of 3 indicates an essay that for the most part, is adequately written and develops an idea for the specified audience.**
	The essay has a central idea or point of view and the writer, for the most part, maintains the focus on this idea in a well reasoned essay.
	The presentation of ideas and points, for the most, is adequately organized and clear.
	Most assertions are supported with relevant information and specific examples.
	Word usage is adequate; there may be some errors in usage but they are not bad enough to make understanding difficult.
	Sentences and paragraphs are generally well contructed and coherent; errors in sentence structure and grammar are not serious enough to cause confusion and misunderstanding.
	The essay addresses the topic and is appropriate for the given audience.
2	**A Score of 2 indicates an essay that attempts to communicate an idea but the idea is only partially formed and sometimess difficult to understand.**
	The essay may state a central idea or point of view but the focus is not maintained throughout the essay and the central idea is underdeveloped or simplistically reasoned.
	The organization of ideas lacks clarity and is only partially effective.
	Assertions are not always supported and the essay may contain irrelevant or insufficient details.
	Word usage is not always clear and may cause confusion or even misunderstanding.
	Sentences and paragraphs are not always well constructed and can be difficult to understand due to errors in sentence structure and grammar.
	The essay may not completely address the topic or be appropriate in style and content for the given audience.
1	**A Score of 1 indicates an essay that is difficult to understand and fails to communicate an idea to the intended audience.**
	The central idea or point of view of the essay is unclear and the essay is simplistically reasoned or contains serious flaws in reasoning.
	The essay lacks organization and coherence, leaving the reader confused.
	Assertions are not supported or are seriously underdeveloped and the essay contains irrelevant and/or insufficient details.
	Word usage is often unclear and confusing, leading to confusion or misunderstanding on the part of the reader.
	Sentences and paragraphs are not well constructed with many errors in paragraphing, sentence structure, and grammar that make understanding difficult.
	The essay may not completely address the topic or be appropriate in style and content for the given audience.
U	**This score indicates the essay cannot be scored. Reasons for this can be the essay was illegible, completely off topic, or not written in English.**
B	**This score indicates the essay response sheet was left blank.**

Remember, for the essay topics, there is no wrong or right position to take. You can take the position that you want to take. Your essay will be scored based on how well your position is explained and supported, not on whether you've taken the "right" position or said something the scorer agrees or disagrees with.

The Organization of Your Essay

Look at the chart, Scoring the CBEST Writing Test, again. The second factor on which you will be judged is the organization of your essay. Thus, it is vital that before you begin to write you have your thoughts organized and a plan for your essay. Jot down a list of things you want to cover or make a quick outline. Plan your essay before you begin to write. The scorers will be looking for an organized, well-planned essay.

The first paragraph should state the position or central idea that your essay will develop. Each paragraph that follows should give information or evidence to support your position or further explain and develop your position or central idea. Each paragraph should have its own main point or idea, and these paragraphs should work together to support and explain the central idea of the entire essay. The final paragraph should arrive at a conclusion and summarize your position or central idea.

There should be a logical flow from one paragraph to the next. Figure out the order that makes the most sense for the supporting examples and ideas you want to include. Transition words, such as *however, in addition, therefore,* and *for example,* will help you communicate the relationship of one paragraph to the next and improve the readability of the essay.

The Development of Your Essay

The third factor on which your essays will be scored is how well you support your points using examples, information, and logic. The scorers will be looking for your use of evidence to support your central idea or position. So, once you've defined the position or central idea of your essay, you need to figure out what evidence you can offer to support your position. The evidence can be from your own experiences, the experiences of other people you know, or from studies, situations, or events you have read about or heard about.

Word Usage

The fourth factor your essay will be judged on is your word usage. Are your words clear and precise or is the meaning muddled and the words confusing? Did you use all words correctly? It helps to have a large vocabulary so you have more words to choose from when you write and can clearly communicate your ideas. But it is not necessary to use big words just to use big words. If you are unsure of the meaning of a word, it's better not to use the word than make a mistake that can cause misunderstanding or confusion.

Sentence Coherence

The next factor on which your writing will be judged is the coherence of your sentences and paragraphs. Are they written correctly or do you have a lot of mistakes in sentence construction, grammar, punctuation, spelling, etc.? You are not required to be perfect; in fact, you can get the perfect score of 4 even if you have some mistakes in spelling, grammar, and punctuation. But you are required to compose sentences and paragraphs in a way that they are easily understood and easily read. If you need some review and practice with this, the next chapter contains a review of the rules and conventions of written English with a focus on common mistakes.

Audience

Finally, your essay will be judged on whether it completely addresses the topic you were given and whether it is appropriate for the audience you were told to address it to. In virtually all the essay topics on the CBEST, you are told to address your essay to an "audience of educated adults." Make sure you write to the intelligence level of educated adults and that the style and words you use are appropriate for them.

▪▪▪ STRATEGIES FOR WRITING YOUR ESSAYS

It's a good idea to have a plan of attack with which to approach the CBEST writing test. This will increase confidence and efficiency and help you score higher. Outlined below is a three-step approach that incorporates the strategies you should use.

Remember you have about 40 minutes for each essay. Use the first 10 minutes for Step I (Before You Start Writing). The next 20 minutes are for Step II, the actual writing of your essay, and the final 10 minutes should be allocated to Step III, polishing and proofing your essay. Use this same plan of attack for each essay.

Step 1: Before You Write

Many of the strategies listed below have already been discussed. The list below pulls everything together into a step-by-step approach. Here's what you need to do in Step 1 before you begin to write.

- Read and reread the topic. You need to make sure you understand what you are being asked to do; so, take your time to read as carefully as you can.
- Think about the topic. Particularly focus on what position you want to take or what central idea you want to develop. Jot down words or thoughts if this helps you to focus.
- Once you've decided what the point of your essay will be or what position you will take and defend, outline the things you want to cover. You can make a formal outline or just jot down a list of ideas. Do this writing on scratch paper or in the test booklet, not on the topic response sheet, which should be reserved for the essay itself.

- If you're having trouble getting started, brainstorm. To do this, jot down all the ideas that pop into your head and then look at what you have and see what looks most useful and promising.

Step 2: Writing

Once you've figured out your central idea and made a rough outline of what you want to cover, you can start writing.

- Write carefully and legibly, making sure your sentences make sense.
- Keep your focus on the central idea, rather than rambling off in other directions.
- Back up your assertions with examples and evidence.
- Start your essay with a statement of your central idea or position.
- Close your essay with a conclusion, which often includes a restatement (in different words) of the position or central idea you stated in the first paragraph.
- Don't get too creative or unconventional; this isn't a test of creativity, just a test of your ability to write and think clearly.

Step 3: Polishing and Proofing

Even though you may feel worn out after a long test, spend any time you have available at the end to polish your writing and proof your essay. A rereading of the essay after it's done will always result in identifying improvements that can be made.

- Reread your essay, making corrections to language mechanics, word usage, sentence structure, and similar areas where needed. It's a good idea to write in pencil so you can erase and more easily make corrections.
- As you reread your essay, you can also polish your language, fix mistakes, and make sentences and paragraphs clearer. When you write your essays, it's a good idea to leave some space in the margins or between lines for insertion of new words, phrases, or even sentences and other changes you want to make at this stage.
- Make sure your deletions and insertions are legible and that it's clear where everything goes.

▐▐▐▐ PRACTICE SETS

Practice the strategies above as you write essays on the topics in the practice sets below. Write your essays on the lined response sheets provided. Time yourself, allowing about 40 minutes per essay. Think through the topic and organize your thoughts first, then write the essay, and, finally, use the remaining time to polish and proof your essay.

When you are done, review the chart near the beginning of this chapter, Scoring the CBEST Writing Test, and use it to assign a score to each essay. Better yet, ask someone else—a teacher, parent, friend, or colleague—to score your essays based on this summary of the CBEST writing score scale.

Practice Set 1

Topic 1

Henry David Thoreau wrote, "Success usually comes to those who are too busy to be looking for it." To what extent do you agree or disagree with this statement? Write an essay for an audience of educated adults, stating your position. Use logical arguments and specific examples to support your position.

Topic 2

It's widely believed that we learn life's lessons by making mistakes. To what extent are mistakes necessary to learning or is it possible to avoid a costly mistake and still learn an important lesson? In an essay addressed to educated adults, discuss your position on this issue. Use your own personal experience to make your case. Use logical arguments and specific examples to support your position.

RESPONSE SHEET FOR TOPIC 1

WRITING ESSAY

WRITING ESSAY

_____

_____

_____

_____

_____

_____

_____

_____

_____

_____

_____

_____

_____

_____

_____

_____

_____

_____

_____

_____

_____

_____

_____

_____

_____

RESPONSE SHEET FOR TOPIC 2

WRITING ESSAY

RESPONSE SHEET FOR TOPIC 2 (CONTINUED)

WRITING ESSAY

Practice Set 2

Topic 1

Television actor Bill Cosby once said, "I don't know the key to success but the key to failure is trying to please everyone." To what extent do you agree or disagree with this statement? Write an essay for an audience of educated adults, stating your position. Use logical arguments and specific examples to support your position.

Topic 2

Much of the time students are in school, they work on their own, reading, writing, and doing assignments. Some of the time in school, however, students work as part of a team doing a task together rather than individually. Which type of learning is most effective? Based on your own experience as a student or a teacher, write an essay that takes a position on which method is most effective. Use logical arguments and specific examples to support your position. Address your essay to an audience of educated adults.

RESPONSE SHEET FOR TOPIC 1

WRITING ESSAY

_____
_____
_____
_____
_____
_____
_____
_____
_____
_____
_____
_____
_____
_____
_____
_____
_____
_____
_____
_____
_____
_____
_____
_____
_____
_____
_____
_____

RESPONSE SHEET FOR TOPIC 1 (CONTINUED)

WRITING ESSAY

RESPONSE SHEET FOR TOPIC 2

WRITING ESSAY

RESPONSE SHEET FOR TOPIC 2 (CONTINUED)

WRITING ESSAY

CHAPTER 10

THE CBEST WRITING TEST: REVIEW OF WRITING MECHANICS

As you know, the California Basic Educational Skills Test (CBEST) requires you to write two essays. In order to write well, you need an understanding of the rules and conventions of the English language. This chapter provides a quick review of those rules with a focus on rules and conventions that people often have trouble with.

The good news is that it is not necessary to write perfect essays to get perfect scores on the writing test. The scoring guidelines allow the highest score (4 points) even if you have a few mistakes in mechanical conventions (grammar, sentence structure, punctuation, capitalization, spelling, etc.). But if you have a lot of errors and these errors make reading or understanding your essay difficult, your score will decline. The CBEST scoring scale identifies "serious and numerous errors" in mechanical conventions with the lowest score (1 point).

If you do not have difficulty with the mechanical conventions of the English language, you can skip this chapter. However, if you need a quick review, read through this chapter and practice writing good sentences as you review the examples provided here. If this is an area in which you would like to spend some time and make major improvement, you may want to purchase a workbook covering English language grammar, sentence structure, punctuation, etc. Some suggested titles are *Schaum's Outline of English Grammar* and *English Grammar DeMystified*.

Covered in this chapter are some basic rules of grammar, suggestions to improve sentence composition, a guide to punctuation, and, finally, a brief guide to capitalization.

ENGLISH GRAMMAR

Adjectives and Adverbs

An **adjective** is a word that describes a noun. An **adverb** is a word that describes either a verb or an adjective (or possibly another adverb). To change most adjectives to adverbs, simply add "*ly*" to the end of the word.

Adjectives	*Adverbs*
He was caught up in the *swift* current.	He paddled *swiftly* through the current.
My clock shows the *correct* time.	I'm sure I set my clock *correctly*.
This *noisy* traffic is bothering me.	The traffic *noisily* made its way across town.
The gymnast's agility was *amazing*.	The gymnast was *amazingly* agile.

Most adverbs end with -*ly*, but some don't. In the next group of examples, notice that the adjective and adverb forms are the same.

Adjectives	*Adverbs*
The finished product looks *good*.	The finished product looks *good*.
This assignment is *hard* work.	I worked *hard* on my assignment.
Bob is a *fast* runner.	Bob can run *fast*.

Adjectives—Comparison and Superlative Forms

Use a **comparative** form of an adjective to compare two things. Use a **superlative** form to compare three or more things. For some adjectives, the comparative form ends in either "er" or "ier," and the superlative form ends in either "est" or "iest."

Comparative form (two things):	*Superlative form (three or more things):*
He sang much *better* than she did.	He was the *best* singer in the competition.
The sun is *brighter* than the moon.	The sun is the *brightest* star in the sky.
You look *prettier* with long hair.	You look your *prettiest* when you smile.

For longer adjectives, instead of adding a suffix to make a comparison, precede the adjective with a word such as *more* or *most*.

Comparative form (two things):	*Superlative form (three or more things):*
Math class is *more interesting* than I expected.	Christmas is the *most special* day of the year.
His new house is *less impressive* than his old one.	History is the *least demanding* subject in school.

For some adjectives, either form is correct. However, do not combine the two forms.

Wrong: My dog is *more furrier* than yours.
Correct: My dog is *furrier* than yours.
Correct: My dog is *more furry* than yours.

Subject–Verb Agreement

If a sentence's subject is *singular*, then the form of its verb should also be singular. Similarly, if a sentence's subject is *plural*, then the form of its verb should also be plural. In other words, there must be "agreement" between subject and verb.

Wrong: Beth are Tom's partner.
Correct: Beth is Tom's partner.
(The sentence's singular subject, *Beth,* should take the singular verb form *is.*)

Wrong: Beth and Tom is partners.
Correct: Beth and Tom are partners.
(The sentence's plural subject, *Beth and Tom,* should take the plural verb form *are.*)

In determining whether a verb form should be singular or plural, ignore words or phrases that come between the subject and verb.

Correct: The *play,* which consists of four acts, *is* very entertaining.
Correct: The *list* of chores *is* long.
Correct: The *students* in this class, but especially John, *need* to study harder.

The words *any, every, each, either,* and *neither* are considered singular. The words *all, some,* and *none* are plural.

Singular
Correct: Every person here *is* invited to the party.
Correct: Neither Dan nor Brad *has* a pen with *him.*
Correct: Each and *every* one of you *owes* me money.

Plural
Correct: All of you *are suspects* in the criminal investigation.
Correct: None of my teachers *are* well-liked.
Correct: Some believe that nothing ever happens accidentally.

Personal Pronouns and Case

A **personal pronoun** is a word that refers to a specific noun (person, place, or thing). A personal pronoun can either be singular (referring to one person, place, or thing) or plural (referring to two or more persons, places, or things). Personal pronouns take different forms ("cases") depending on how they're used in a sentence.

Subject-case pronouns: I, we, you, he, she, it, they

Example: I am going to the movies tonight.
Example: He/She is sitting in the front row of the theater.
Example: We/They were late for the movie.

Object–case pronouns: me, us, you, him, her, it, them

Example: Danita saw ____ at the restaurant.
Example: Danita will go with ____ to the restaurant.
(Any object-case pronoun would fill in the blank correctly.)

Object case–reflexive pronouns: myself, ourselves, yourself, yourselves, himself, herself, itself, themselves

Use a reflexive pronoun when describing an act performed upon the sentence's subject.
Example: I accidently cut *myself* while chopping vegetables.
Example: Hanna and Wendy should be ashamed of *themselves* for cheating on the test.
Example: If you don't behave *yourself (yourselves),* I'll report you to the school principal.

Possessive-case pronouns: my (mine), our (ours), your (yours), his, hers, its, their (theirs)

Use the possessive case to indicate ownership or possession.

Examples:
You just drove past *my (our/your/his/her/their)* house.
The second house on the left is *mine (ours/yours/his/hers/theirs)*.

Be careful to apply pronoun cases properly to compound subjects and objects.

Wrong: Me and Bruce plan to meet her at the mall later today.
Correct: Bruce and I plan to meet her at the mall later today.
(*Bruce and I* is the sentence's compound subject.)

Wrong: Janet met Bruce and myself at the mall yesterday.
Correct: Janet met Bruce and me at the mall yesterday.
(*Bruce and me* is the sentence's compound object.)

Relative Pronouns

Relative pronouns include the words *which, who, that, whose, whichever, whoever,* and *whomever.* You should know certain rules about how to use these words. Use *which* when referring to things, but use *who* when referring to people.

Correct: Jim's bike, *which* was brand new, was stolen yesterday.
Correct: Hector, *who* is Jim's neighbor, might have stolen the bike.
Correct: The only neighbor *who* saw Hector yesterday was Kathy.

Use *who* (or *whoever*) when referring to the sentence's subject. Use *whom* (or *whomever*) when referring to a direct or indirect object.

Correct: The person *who* ate all the cookies should confess.
Correct: Whoever ate all the cookies should confess.
Correct: Laurie, *who* has a sweet tooth, ate all the cookies.
Correct: Laurie is *who* ate all the cookies.

Correct: Oliver, with *whom* I spoke yesterday, won the first match of the tournament.
Correct: I'll play the next match against *whomever* wins this one.

Verb Tenses

A verb's **tense** indicates the time (past, present, or future) of the events described in a sentence. For many verbs, you indicate past tense by adding *-ed* to the verb (for example, *folded* or *watched*). Many verbs, however, have peculiar past-tense forms, which you must memorize. If you don't know the correct verb forms, trust your ear as to whether a verb sounds correct. The following examples show which form of the verbs *to see* and *to run* you should use, depending on the time frame.

simple present	see	run
simple past	saw	ran
simple future	will see	will run
present perfect	has seen (have seen)	has run (have run)
past perfect	had seen	had run
future perfect	will have seen	will have run

In some cases, mixing different tenses in a sentence can be confusing.

Confusing: Valerie *passed* the test, but Jerome *fails* the test.
Clear: Valerie *passed* the test, but Jerome *failed* the test.

In other cases, however, shifting from one case to another in the same sentence is perfectly alright—if the sentence's events shift from one time frame to another.

Examples:
Hattie *failed* the test, and she *will take* the test again next month.
(This sentence shifts from past tense to future-perfect tense)

Having failed the test, I *am* very discouraged.
(This sentence shifts from present-perfect tense to present tense)

He *had failed* the test twice before he finally *passed* it.
(This sentence shifts from past-perfect tense to past tense)

Sentence Fragments and Run-on Sentences

Every sentence must include a subject *and* a predicate. Otherwise, it is a **sentence fragment** (an incomplete sentence). A noun establishes a subject, while a verb establishes the predicate.

Wrong (Fragment): Strolling through the park without a care.
Correct: She strolled through the park without a care.
Correct: Strolling through the park at night can be dangerous.

A **main clause** is any clause that can stand alone as a complete sentence. Combining two main clauses into one sentence without properly connecting the two results in a **run-on sentence,** which is grammatically incorrect.

Wrong: Bill held the door open Nancy walked through the doorway.
Wrong: Bill held the door open, Nancy walked through the doorway.
Correct: Bill held the door open while Nancy walked through the doorway.
Correct: Bill held the door open, and Nancy walked through the doorway.
Correct: Bill held the door open; Nancy walked through the doorway.

SENTENCE STRUCTURE AND SENSE

Here are the specific topics this section covers:

- Parallelism
- Active and passive voices

- Placement of modifiers
- Redundancy (repetitiveness)
- Wordiness (unnecessary words)

Parallelism

If a sentence lists two or more things, they should be **parallel** (the same) in their grammatical structure.

Wrong: Gretchen bought eggs, milk, and bought meat at the store.
Correct: Gretchen bought eggs, milk, and meat at the store.

Wrong: The goose, hen, and the pig all lived happily ever after.
Correct: The goose, hen, and pig all lived happily ever after.
Correct: The goose, the hen, and the pig all lived happily ever after.

A parallel structure should be used when comparing two things.

Wrong: It's more fun to swim than running.
Correct: It's more fun to swim than to run.
Correct: It's more fun to swim than run.

The concept of parallelism also applies to **correlatives,** which are particular pairs of words used in special ways in sentences. The two most frequently used correlative word pairs are *either/or* and *neither/nor.* Whatever follows the first part of a correlative pair should be grammatically parallel to whatever follows the second part.

Wrong: You're *either* with me *or* you're against me.
Correct: You're *either* with me *or* against me.

Wrong: Either you're with me *or* against me.
Correct: Either you're with me *or* you're against me.

Active and Passive Voices

In the **active voice,** a sentence's subject is active, whereas in the **passive voice** the subject is acted upon. Using the passive voice often makes a sentence awkward and confusing, and so using the active voice is usually better.

Passive (Awkward): The sun's disappearance over the horizon was watched by us.
Active: We watched the sun disappear over the horizon.

In some cases, however, the passive voice sounds fine and actually helps get across the point of the sentence.

Examples:
The judge was appointed by President Clinton, not by Bush.
The defendant was tried and convicted by a jury of his peers.

Placement of Modifiers

A **modifier** is simply a word or phrase that describes or qualifies something else in the same sentence (usually the subject). Modifying phrases are often set off by commas. In general, you should place a modifier as close as possible to whatever it modifies; otherwise, the sentence might be confusing.

Confusing: This book is one of my favorites, written in 1990.
Clear: This book, written in 1990, is one of my favorites.
(The phrase *written in 1990* modifies *this book.*)

Confusing: Nearing the summit, the harsh wind began to take its toll on the mountain climbers.
Clear: The harsh wind began to take its toll on the mountain climbers as they neared the summit.
(The phrase *nearing the summit* modifies *the mountain climbers.*)

Confusing: Paula laughed at Janine as she left the room. (Who left the room: Paula or Jeanine?)
Clear: As she left the room, Paula laughed at Janine.
Clear: As Janine left the room, Paula laughed at her.

▄▄▄ REDUNDANCY (REPETITIVENESS)

Repeating the same essential idea is called **redundancy.** If a sentence contains a redundancy, often there's more than one way to correct the problem. (In the next examples, redundancies are italicized.)

Redundant: Gary is 20 years *old in age.*
Correct: Gary is 20 years old.
Correct: Gary's current age is 20 years.

Redundant: The *reason* I sat down is *because* I felt ill.
Correct: The reason I sat down is that I felt ill.
Correct: I sat down because I felt ill.

Redundant: I'm hungry, but I'm *also* tired, *too.*
Correct: I'm tired as well as hungry.
Correct: I'm tired, and I'm hungry, too.

Wordiness (Unnecessary Words)

Even if a sentence is free of grammatical errors, you might be able to improve it, especially if it uses too many words to get its point across. In general, briefer is better, as long as the sentence's meaning is clear. You might be able to improve a sentence by simply removing certain words because the sentence is more concise and graceful, yet still perfectly clear, without them.

Wordy: Danielle runs faster than Amy runs.
Concise: Danielle runs faster than Amy.

Wordy: I plan to arrive by the time of nine o'clock.
Concise: I plan to arrive by nine o'clock.

Wordy: This year it rained more than it ever rained before.
Concise: This year it rained more than ever before.

In other sentences, you might be able to replace wordy phrases with more concise, graceful ones.

Wordy: The view from the roof is better than the view from the first floor and the view from the second floor.
Concise: The view from the roof is better than from either the first or second floor.

Wordy: The band's guitarist, as well as the band's drummer, played too loudly.
Concise: The band's guitarist and drummer both played too loudly.

Wordy: I gave up for the reason that I was too tired to continue.
Concise: I gave up because I was too tired to continue.

Wordy: Ursula is a good student, but her sister is not a good student.
Concise: Ursula is a good student, but her sister is not.

▰▰▰ PUNCTUATION

This section covers the rules for using the following punctuation marks.

- Commas
- Colons, semicolons, and dashes
- Apostrophes—possessive nouns
- Apostrophes—contractions
- Quotation marks for dialogue
- Quotation marks and italics (or underlining) for titles

Commas

Use a comma followed by an appropriate connecting word (such as *and* or *but*) to connect two main clauses (which can stand alone as a complete sentence).

Wrong: Keith is a good swimmer and he is a good student as well.
Correct: Keith is a good swimmer, and he is a good student as well.

However, if the sentence contains only one main clause, do not use a comma to separate the main clause from the rest of the sentence.

Wrong: Keith is a good swimmer, and is a good student as well.
Correct: Keith is a good swimmer and is a good student as well.

Use commas when needed to make the logic and meaning of a sentence clear.

Confusing: An hour after you go call me.
Clear: An hour after you go, call me.

Use commas to separate three or more items in a list. Do not use a comma to separate only two list items.

Wrong: I plan to take algebra history and theater arts this year.
Correct: I plan to take algebra, history, and theater arts this year.

Wrong: I plan to take algebra, and history this year.
Correct: I plan to take algebra and history this year.

Use a pair of commas (not just one comma) as a substitute for a pair of parentheses—to set off a phrase that is not essential for the sentence to make sense and be grammatically correct.

Correct:
The tallest boy, whose name is Greg, is 12 years old.
Neil Armstrong, the first human to walk on the moon, is from Ohio.
The war, which occurred during the 1990s, resulted in many thousands of deaths.

Do not use commas to set off prepositional phrases in the middle or at the end of sentences.

Wrong: Beth loves to go to the beach, in the summer.
Wrong: Beth loves to go, to the beach, in the summer.
Correct: Beth loves to go to the beach in the summer.

Use a comma after a dependent clause (a clause that cannot stand alone as a complete sentence) at the beginning of a sentence to create a natural pause that helps the reader understand the sentence.

Correct: Upon arriving at the airport, Dru realized that he forgot his ticket at home.
Correct: During the summer, Beth loves to go to the beach.

Use a comma between two adjectives unless the first adjective is used to describe the second adjective—in which case you should not insert a comma.

Correct: It was a *hot, humid* day.
Correct: An *icy cold* beverage would be refreshing right now.

Colons, Semicolons, and Dashes

Use a **colon** (:) immediately preceding a list or a phrase that explains, paraphrases, or defines what came just before it. Do NOT use a colon if the sentence is grammatically correct without it.

Wrong: This summer I'm taking three classes, which include: geography, geometry, and art.
Wrong: The problem with my bike is: It has a flat tire.
Wrong: The only two ways to get to the island are: by boat and by small plane.

Correct: This summer I'm taking three classes: geography, geometry, and art.
Correct: There's a problem with my bike: It has a flat tire.
Correct: I know of two ways to get to the island: by boat and by small plane.

Use a **semicolon** (;) to combine two sentences whose ideas are very closely related. You do NOT need to use a connecting word (such as *and* or *but*) as well.

Correct: The middle school is very demanding; students must study hard to do well.
Correct: I ordered the hamburger; it was Gwen who ordered the hot dog.
Correct: I think I've sprained my ankle; could you please drive me home?

You can use a **dash** (—) instead of a comma just before a concluding phrase. You can also use a pair of dashes instead of commas or parentheses to set off a parenthetical phrase.

Correct: She looked straight ahead, as if she did not see him.
Correct: She looked straight ahead—as if she did not see him.

Wrong: The house across the street—the white one, is for sale.
Correct: The house across the street—the white one—is for sale.

Apostrophes—Possessive Nouns

Use an apostrophe to indicate possession or ownership.

Correct: Janice's book
Correct: my best friend's wedding
Correct: the women's choir

For plural nouns ending in the letter *s,* the apostrophe belongs after the *s.*

Correct: the four students' essays
Correct: the citizens' right to free speech

Possessive pronouns (for example, *his, hers, its*) do not take apostrophes.

Correct: The second car in the driveway is *ours.*
Correct: Among all the cars, *theirs* is the newest.

Apostrophes—Contractions

A **contraction** is a word made up of two or more words from which letters have been omitted. Insert an apostrophe where the letters have been omitted.

It's (It is) all up to you now.
If you'd (you would) like to go, just say so.
We've (we have) got three hours to finish this chore.
Why don't (do not) you like me?
There's (There is) nothing wrong with that.
My dog can't (cannot) do any tricks.
If they wouldn't (would not) have beat us, we'd (we would) have won first prize.

Be careful not to confuse contractions such as *they're* (they are), *who's* (who is), and *it's* (it is) with their homophones (words that sound the same).

I think *they're* (they are) traveling by plane.
I noticed that *their* luggage was missing.
I think I see the luggage over *there*.

If *it's* (it is) not too late, please don't eat the salmon.
The groundhog saw *its* shadow.

Who's (who is) up to bat next?
Whose bat is this?

Quotation Marks for Dialogue

Use quotation marks to begin and end written or spoken dialogue. An end-of-dialogue punctuation mark is part of the quotation (it should come *before* the second quotation mark). If the quotation comes at the end of a sentence, a comma should precede the quotation.

Wrong: Penny said "I like you."
Wrong: Penny exclaimed, "Of course I like him"!
Wrong: Penny asked me: Do you like her?

Correct: Penny said, "I like you."
Correct: Penny exclaimed, "Of course I like him!"
Correct: Penny asked me, "Do you like her?"

If the sentence continues after the quotation, punctuate the quotation. However, do not use a period.

Wrong: "We want a touchdown" said Jimmy.
Wrong: "We want a touchdown." said Jimmy.
Correct: "We want a touchdown," said Jimmy.

Correct: "We want a touchdown!" chanted Jimmy over and over.
Correct: After telling us, "Our team has no chance of winning," Jimmy got up and left.
Correct: "What are our chances of winning?" Jimmy asked.

Quotation Marks and Italics (or Underlining) for Titles

Use quotation marks for titles of poems, songs, speeches, and short stories. Use either italics or underlining for book titles and movie titles—whether or not you indicate the full title—as well as for names of specific ships and aircraft.

Correct:
The Beatles recorded "Hey Jude" in 1967.
Martin Luther King's "I Have a Dream" speech is familiar to most Americans.
The new book in the *Harry Potter* series arrived at bookstores this week.
Many movie critics rank *Citizen Kane* as the single best movie ever made.
The space shuttle *Discovery* is scheduled to launch again next month.

CAPITALIZATION

Capitalize all **proper nouns,** which are *specific* persons, places, events, and things. There are many categories of proper nouns, including:

- Names of specific persons and organizations
- Titles of specific persons (government and military officials)
- Titles of books, short stories, poems, songs, plays, and movies
- Geographic areas (streets, cities, states, regions, nations, continents)
- Special landmarks (parks, monuments, bridges, buildings, celestial bodies)
- Days of the week, months, holidays, and other special events
- Languages

Remember: You should NOT capitalize a noun unless it names a *specific* person, place, event, or thing. All of the following examples are correct.

Examples (official titles):
Who is the vice president of the United States in the year 2000?
Was Vice President Gore in office during the year 2000?
I wrote to Senator Smith about the proposed law.
You should write to your state senator about the proposed law.

Examples (places):
Mike lives on Madison Street in Brooklyn.
He was born in the state of New York, but he grew up in the Midwest.
I went to the Iowa State Fair last year, but I don't remember in which county the fair took place.
The continent of Africa is bordered by the Atlantic Ocean, the Indian Ocean, the Red Sea, and the Mediterranean Sea.

Examples (landmarks):
I've been to Yosemite National Park, but I've never been to Disneyland.
The Great Wall of China is visible from outer space but not from as far away as Mars.
It took us an nearly a half hour to drive from the Empire State Building to the George Washington Bridge.

Example (various types):
At Appomattox Courthouse in Virginia, General Lee officially surrendered to General Grant and the Union Army. This event marked the end of the Civil War, a bloody era in American history, and the beginning of the period called Reconstruction.

CHAPTER 11
PRACTICE TEST II

The practice test contained in this chapter will give you a very good idea of what you will face on test day. It includes separate tests for the three subject areas tested on the California Basic Educational Skills Test (CBEST): reading, mathematics, and writing. The questions for the reading and mathematics tests are in the multiple-choice format that you will encounter on the actual exam. For the writing test, you'll find two essay questions or writing prompts like the ones you'll be required to respond to on the real exam.

All the questions on this practice test are modeled after the questions on the actual CBEST. There are the same number of questions and the same type of questions as on the actual exam. They cover the same topics and are designed to be at the same level of difficulty. Explanations for the answers to the multiple-choice questions are given at the end of the practice test.

This test includes an answer sheet that you should remove from the book. Use this sheet to mark your answers to the multiple-choice questions.

When you are finished with the test, check your answers against the answer key provided at the end of this practice test. For any questions that you answered incorrectly or had difficulty with, carefully read the answer explanations at the end of this chapter. If you don't understand what you did wrong, you can use the review chapters of this book for review and further explanation.

This practice test best helps you prepare for the real test if you treat it as an actual examination. Here are some hints on how to take the test under conditions similar to those of the actual exam.

- Find a 4-hour time period when you will not be interrupted.
- Fill in the bubbles on the answer sheet with a no. 2 pencil; make sure the bubble is filled in completely and that there are no stray pencil marks on the sheet.
- Complete the entire test in one 4-hour session. If you want to take each subject area test contained in this practice test separately, you should allocate about 1 hour and 20 minutes per test. The actual test provides 4 hours, which you can allocate to the three tests in any way you wish.

Good luck!

■■■ **ANSWER SHEET**

PRACTICE TEST II
Answer Sheet for Multiple Choice Questions

READING TEST

1 Ⓐ Ⓑ Ⓒ Ⓓ Ⓔ	18 Ⓐ Ⓑ Ⓒ Ⓓ Ⓔ	35 Ⓐ Ⓑ Ⓒ Ⓓ Ⓔ
2 Ⓐ Ⓑ Ⓒ Ⓓ Ⓔ	19 Ⓐ Ⓑ Ⓒ Ⓓ Ⓔ	36 Ⓐ Ⓑ Ⓒ Ⓓ Ⓔ
3 Ⓐ Ⓑ Ⓒ Ⓓ Ⓔ	20 Ⓐ Ⓑ Ⓒ Ⓓ Ⓔ	37 Ⓐ Ⓑ Ⓒ Ⓓ Ⓔ
4 Ⓐ Ⓑ Ⓒ Ⓓ Ⓔ	21 Ⓐ Ⓑ Ⓒ Ⓓ Ⓔ	38 Ⓐ Ⓑ Ⓒ Ⓓ Ⓔ
5 Ⓐ Ⓑ Ⓒ Ⓓ Ⓔ	22 Ⓐ Ⓑ Ⓒ Ⓓ Ⓔ	39 Ⓐ Ⓑ Ⓒ Ⓓ Ⓔ
6 Ⓐ Ⓑ Ⓒ Ⓓ Ⓔ	23 Ⓐ Ⓑ Ⓒ Ⓓ Ⓔ	40 Ⓐ Ⓑ Ⓒ Ⓓ Ⓔ
7 Ⓐ Ⓑ Ⓒ Ⓓ Ⓔ	24 Ⓐ Ⓑ Ⓒ Ⓓ Ⓔ	41 Ⓐ Ⓑ Ⓒ Ⓓ Ⓔ
8 Ⓐ Ⓑ Ⓒ Ⓓ Ⓔ	25 Ⓐ Ⓑ Ⓒ Ⓓ Ⓔ	42 Ⓐ Ⓑ Ⓒ Ⓓ Ⓔ
9 Ⓐ Ⓑ Ⓒ Ⓓ Ⓔ	26 Ⓐ Ⓑ Ⓒ Ⓓ Ⓔ	43 Ⓐ Ⓑ Ⓒ Ⓓ Ⓔ
10 Ⓐ Ⓑ Ⓒ Ⓓ Ⓔ	27 Ⓐ Ⓑ Ⓒ Ⓓ Ⓔ	44 Ⓐ Ⓑ Ⓒ Ⓓ Ⓔ
11 Ⓐ Ⓑ Ⓒ Ⓓ Ⓔ	28 Ⓐ Ⓑ Ⓒ Ⓓ Ⓔ	45 Ⓐ Ⓑ Ⓒ Ⓓ Ⓔ
12 Ⓐ Ⓑ Ⓒ Ⓓ Ⓔ	29 Ⓐ Ⓑ Ⓒ Ⓓ Ⓔ	46 Ⓐ Ⓑ Ⓒ Ⓓ Ⓔ
13 Ⓐ Ⓑ Ⓒ Ⓓ Ⓔ	30 Ⓐ Ⓑ Ⓒ Ⓓ Ⓔ	47 Ⓐ Ⓑ Ⓒ Ⓓ Ⓔ
14 Ⓐ Ⓑ Ⓒ Ⓓ Ⓔ	31 Ⓐ Ⓑ Ⓒ Ⓓ Ⓔ	48 Ⓐ Ⓑ Ⓒ Ⓓ Ⓔ
15 Ⓐ Ⓑ Ⓒ Ⓓ Ⓔ	32 Ⓐ Ⓑ Ⓒ Ⓓ Ⓔ	49 Ⓐ Ⓑ Ⓒ Ⓓ Ⓔ
16 Ⓐ Ⓑ Ⓒ Ⓓ Ⓔ	33 Ⓐ Ⓑ Ⓒ Ⓓ Ⓔ	50 Ⓐ Ⓑ Ⓒ Ⓓ Ⓔ
17 Ⓐ Ⓑ Ⓒ Ⓓ Ⓔ	34 Ⓐ Ⓑ Ⓒ Ⓓ Ⓔ	

MATHEMATICS TEST

1 Ⓐ Ⓑ Ⓒ Ⓓ Ⓔ	18 Ⓐ Ⓑ Ⓒ Ⓓ Ⓔ	35 Ⓐ Ⓑ Ⓒ Ⓓ Ⓔ
2 Ⓐ Ⓑ Ⓒ Ⓓ Ⓔ	19 Ⓐ Ⓑ Ⓒ Ⓓ Ⓔ	36 Ⓐ Ⓑ Ⓒ Ⓓ Ⓔ
3 Ⓐ Ⓑ Ⓒ Ⓓ Ⓔ	20 Ⓐ Ⓑ Ⓒ Ⓓ Ⓔ	37 Ⓐ Ⓑ Ⓒ Ⓓ Ⓔ
4 Ⓐ Ⓑ Ⓒ Ⓓ Ⓔ	21 Ⓐ Ⓑ Ⓒ Ⓓ Ⓔ	38 Ⓐ Ⓑ Ⓒ Ⓓ Ⓔ
5 Ⓐ Ⓑ Ⓒ Ⓓ Ⓔ	22 Ⓐ Ⓑ Ⓒ Ⓓ Ⓔ	39 Ⓐ Ⓑ Ⓒ Ⓓ Ⓔ
6 Ⓐ Ⓑ Ⓒ Ⓓ Ⓔ	23 Ⓐ Ⓑ Ⓒ Ⓓ Ⓔ	40 Ⓐ Ⓑ Ⓒ Ⓓ Ⓔ
7 Ⓐ Ⓑ Ⓒ Ⓓ Ⓔ	24 Ⓐ Ⓑ Ⓒ Ⓓ Ⓔ	41 Ⓐ Ⓑ Ⓒ Ⓓ Ⓔ
8 Ⓐ Ⓑ Ⓒ Ⓓ Ⓔ	25 Ⓐ Ⓑ Ⓒ Ⓓ Ⓔ	42 Ⓐ Ⓑ Ⓒ Ⓓ Ⓔ
9 Ⓐ Ⓑ Ⓒ Ⓓ Ⓔ	26 Ⓐ Ⓑ Ⓒ Ⓓ Ⓔ	43 Ⓐ Ⓑ Ⓒ Ⓓ Ⓔ
10 Ⓐ Ⓑ Ⓒ Ⓓ Ⓔ	27 Ⓐ Ⓑ Ⓒ Ⓓ Ⓔ	44 Ⓐ Ⓑ Ⓒ Ⓓ Ⓔ
11 Ⓐ Ⓑ Ⓒ Ⓓ Ⓔ	28 Ⓐ Ⓑ Ⓒ Ⓓ Ⓔ	45 Ⓐ Ⓑ Ⓒ Ⓓ Ⓔ
12 Ⓐ Ⓑ Ⓒ Ⓓ Ⓔ	29 Ⓐ Ⓑ Ⓒ Ⓓ Ⓔ	46 Ⓐ Ⓑ Ⓒ Ⓓ Ⓔ
13 Ⓐ Ⓑ Ⓒ Ⓓ Ⓔ	30 Ⓐ Ⓑ Ⓒ Ⓓ Ⓔ	47 Ⓐ Ⓑ Ⓒ Ⓓ Ⓔ
14 Ⓐ Ⓑ Ⓒ Ⓓ Ⓔ	31 Ⓐ Ⓑ Ⓒ Ⓓ Ⓔ	48 Ⓐ Ⓑ Ⓒ Ⓓ Ⓔ
15 Ⓐ Ⓑ Ⓒ Ⓓ Ⓔ	32 Ⓐ Ⓑ Ⓒ Ⓓ Ⓔ	49 Ⓐ Ⓑ Ⓒ Ⓓ Ⓔ
16 Ⓐ Ⓑ Ⓒ Ⓓ Ⓔ	33 Ⓐ Ⓑ Ⓒ Ⓓ Ⓔ	50 Ⓐ Ⓑ Ⓒ Ⓓ Ⓔ
17 Ⓐ Ⓑ Ⓒ Ⓓ Ⓔ	34 Ⓐ Ⓑ Ⓒ Ⓓ Ⓔ	

1 ████████████████████████████ **1**

READING TEST

TEST DIRECTIONS: Read each passage and answer the multiple-choice questions that follow. For each question, choose the one best answer from the answer choices provided. Mark each answer on the answer sheet provided.

You may work on the questions in any order you choose. You have 4 hours to complete all three sections (reading, mathematics, and writing) of the CBEST.

1 ███████████████████████████████ **1**

Read the passage below and answer the five questions that follow.

Chess is the most intellectual, entertaining, and scientific of games, while at the same time more pleasingly absorbing than any pure science. With the possible exception of the simpler game of draughts, from which the modern game of checkers evolved, chess is also the most ancient of games. Oriental manuscripts, Eastern fables, and works of the early poets all *attest to* its antiquity. Although there is some disagreement concerning the origin of chess, most historians believe that the game originated in ancient India, then reached Persia from India in the first half of the sixth century, and from there eventually reached Europe and, subsequently, America.

Though chess has never been honored throughout its long life by any continuous written history or record, its traditions from time immemorial have been of the most noble and even royal character. In fact, for many ages, Europeans have referred to chess as "The Royal Game." Perhaps by coincidence, the key piece on a chessboard is the king, which is not surprising since chess takes its modern-day name from the Persian word *Schach,* or *Shah,* which in that language signifies "King." Interestingly, combining the Persian word *Matt,* meaning "dead," with *Schach* results in a two-word phrase meaning "the King is dead." It is from this phrase that the term *checkmate,* which English-speaking chess players now use, originated.

1. The author mentions "Oriental manuscripts" in order to make the point that
   A. the name "chess" comes from an oriental word.
   B. chess originated in Asia.
   C. chess has always been a game played by nobility.
   D. chess has a long, continuous written history.
   E. chess is an ancient game

2. As used in the passage, the phrase *attest to* most closely means
   A. mention.
   B. exclude.
   C. dispute.
   D. include.
   E. prove.

3. Why is it "hardly surprising" to the author that the key chess piece is the king?
   A. Chess has always been popular among royalty.
   B. The king is the largest piece on the chessboard.
   C. The player who captures the opponent's king wins the game.
   D. The Persian name for the game means "king."
   E. Chess originated from a group of kings in ancient India.

4. The author would probably agree that checkers
   A. was invented before chess.
   B. originated in ancient India.
   C. is known in Europe as "The Royal Game."
   D. is more popular today than chess.
   E. was the original game of chess.

5. A good title for the selection would be
   A. Chess and Checkers in Ancient Times
   B. A Brief History of the Game of Chess
   C. Why Chess is the World's Most Popular Game
   D. How the Game of Chess Changed Through the Ages
   E. How the Game of Chess Obtained Its Name

Read the passage below and answer the three questions that follow.

When most people think about taking a nap, they typically envision being down for the count for at least an hour or two. A German study, however, has shown that if you really want to refresh your brain, a 6-minute catnap will do it. Not only will you feel better afterward, but your ability to learn and remember will have improved as well.

Students at the University of Dusseldorf participated in experiments in which they had to memorize a list of words and then either take a nap or play a video game. The ones who napped consistently scored higher than those who stayed awake.

_____ .

A regular sleep schedule still plays an important role in overall well-being and health.

6. Which sentence, if inserted into the blank line in the passage, would best fit the development of the passage?
   A. The study may help scientists learn more about what happens when people sleep.
   B. Experts believe that sleeping helps the brain decide what memories from the day need to be placed in permanent storage and which ones don't need to be remembered.
   C. Of course, those catnaps may be wonderful but they can never replace the value of a solid 8 hours of sleep.
   D. There are dramatic shifts in brain chemistry during sleep.
   E. R.E.M. cycles are more productive than naps.

7. What is the main idea of this passage?
   A. Everyone has to have 8 hours of sleep each night.
   B. Brief naps help energize most people and help them learn better.
   C. There is a limited amount of room in the brain for storage.
   D. Memorizing lists of words is more difficult than you'd think.
   E. Playing video games has a negative effect on memory.

GO ON TO THE NEXT PAGE.

8. Napping apparently helps with everything EXCEPT

   A. fatigue.
   B. memory.
   C. learning.
   D. appetite.
   E. energy level.

Read the passage below and answer the five questions that follow.

The story of how the Roman armies conquered much of the ancient world is well known. But few people know the story of how Rome's language, Latin, conquered so many of the ancient world's languages. Most people would guess that the worldwide supremacy of Latin was a natural result of the worldwide supremacy of the Roman *legions* or of Roman law. But this guess ignores modern history.

Conquered people do not always accept their conqueror's *tongue*. At the turn of the twentieth century, after 150 years of British rule, only 1% of the population of India could read and write English. Also, the French language has never threatened to replace Arabic in Algeria.

The extent of Latin's supremacy throughout the ancient world is remarkable. From its narrow confines within an area initially covering less than 100 square miles, Latin spread through Italy and the islands of the Mediterranean, through France, Spain, England, northern Africa, and the Danubian provinces. The Latin language triumphed over all other tongues in those regions more completely than Roman arms triumphed over the peoples who spoke those tongues.

9. Throughout the passage, the author uses the word *tongue* to mean

   A. mouth.
   B. words.
   C. education.
   D. commands.
   E. language.

10. The author's main point in the passage is that

   A. the Latin language eventually died because the Roman Empire fell.
   B. the fact that Latin became so widely spoken is remarkable and worthy of understanding.
   C. people adopt a new language only when it is forced upon them.
   D. most people in India and Algeria cannot read or write Latin.
   E. the Latin language spread because the Romans forced it onto the peoples they conquered.

11. In describing Latin as a conqueror, the author means that Latin

   A. replaced many other languages.
   B. is a difficult language to learn.
   C. became India's official language.
   D. was the only language spoken in Rome.
   E. was the precursor to modern Romance languages.

12. As used in the passage, the word *legions* most nearly means

   A. diseases.
   B. the poor masses.
   C. civilizations.
   D. leaders.
   E. armies.

13. The author would probably agree that

   A. all languages evolved from Latin.
   B. all languages, like all roads, once led to Rome.
   C. a language can be mightier than an army.
   D. the language of war is the same as that of peace.
   E. Latin was the only language that spread heavily throughout the world.

Review the table of contents below and answer the two questions that follow.

14. In which part of the book would information about subject/verb agreement be found?

   A. Introduction
   B. Part I
   C. Part II
   D. Part III
   E. Part IV

15. A reader is looking for how to write up information for her bibliography about a book for a paper about a poem by Langston Hughes. Where is the best place in the book to look for this information?

   A. Introduction
   B. Part I
   C. Part II
   D. Part III
   E. Part IV

GO ON TO THE NEXT PAGE.

Read the passage below and answer the five questions that follow.

Put a dozen parents together in a room, and you will most likely have a dozen different theories of parenting. One of the most debated issues in raising kids is how to discipline them, especially when it comes to the question of to spank or not to spank. Some moms and dads are sure that it is an *integral* part of showing their kids what is right and wrong. Others are equally sure that spanking is a cruel act of violence against kids. Which is it?

According to new studies, spanking apparently increases the risk of future sexual problems such as violent and/or coercive sex with partners. Naturally, there are those who disagree as well. Some scientists believe that spanking two-to six-year-old children can be very helpful as long as parents are not angry or out of control emotionally.

_____ opinion on spanking remains divided, research continues on this contentious issue. _____, however, the American Academy of Pediatrics advises parents to use other methods of discipline.

16. Which word or phrases, if inserted *in order* into the blanks in the passage would best contribute to the development of the author's ideas?

    A. While; Nevertheless
    B. Although; In the meantime
    C. Even if ; Finally
    D. Because; Thus
    E. Since; On the other hand

17. What is the best title for this passage?

    A. Parents Have Different Ideas on Punishment
    B. Keeping Parental Emotions Under Control
    C. Spanking—Abuse or Appropriate?
    D. A Study on Spanking Effectiveness
    E. Spanking and Deviant Behavior

18. The word *integral* as used in the first paragraph of the passage can best be defined as

    A. central.
    B. initial.
    C. trifling.
    D. irrelevant.
    E. ancillary.

19. What can be inferred about spanking and future sexual problems?

    A. One leads directly to the other in every case.
    B. Spanking is a prelude to predatory sexual behavior and rape.
    C. The researchers who study this topic tend to have a bias against spanking.
    D. Studies have shown some correlation between the two.
    E. Any child that is spanked will engage in problematic sexual behavior as an adult.

20. What advice does the American Academy of Pediatrics give parents about spanking?

    A. Do it only if you are not feeling emotional.
    B. Find other alternatives to use before spanking.

C. Try to limit spankings to once a week or less.
D. Avoid it completely because it leads to other issues.
E. Spanking is a thoroughly acceptable form of discipline.

Read the passage below and answer the five questions that follow.

Anna May Wong was a Chinese-American actress from 1922 to her death in 1961. Born and raised in Los Angeles, she fell in love with movies at an early age and started asking filmmakers to cast her in movies that were being filmed, often in the same neighborhood where she grew up. Her first part in a movie was as an uncredited extra, carrying a lantern along with 300 other girls in *The Red Lantern*. Her first leading role was in *The Toll of the Sea*, which was loosely based on the story of Madame Butterfly.

Her acting received rave reviews that normally would have launched a young actress's career, but her ethnicity proved a stumbling block, mainly due to laws against minorities playing in romantic roles opposite Caucasian actors. Unfortunately, this pattern continued throughout her career. The most severe disappointment was when Wong was passed over for the leading part of O-lan in the film adaptation of Pearl S. Buck's novel, *The Good Earth*. Luise Rainer, the studio's choice for O-lan, won an Academy Award for the role.

21. According to the passage, Anna May Wong's first part in a movie

    A. won her critical acclaim.
    B. made her financially successful.
    C. did not even give her a listing in the movie credits.
    D. attracted the attention of filmmakers in her neighborhood.
    E. received rave reviews.

22. According to the passage, Luise Rainer

    A. should not have won an Academy Award.
    B. was chosen to play O-lan instead of Anna May Wong.
    C. was passed over in favor of Anna May Wong for several choice roles.
    D. should have refused the part of O-lan in *The Good Earth*.
    E. was passed over for an Academy Award.

23. With which of the following would the author of the passage most likely agree?

    A. If Anna May Wong had not been of Chinese descent, her acting career would have been more successful.
    B. Anna May Wong deserved an Academy Award for her role in *The Toll of the Sea*.
    C. Audiences at the time were not prepared to see a Chinese-American actress in a leading role.
    D. Anna May Wong was content with her acting career.
    E. Anna May Wong's first role jump-started her acting career.

GO ON TO THE NEXT PAGE.

24. The passage could best be described as a

    A. film critique.

    B. brief biography of one actress.

    C. cameo appearance.

    D. rant against casting directors of the early 1900s.

    E. rant against the racism of the film industry in the early 1900s.

25. Which of the following best states the main point of this passage?

    A. Many minorities in early Hollywood did not have enough opportunities to play major roles.

    B. Although Anna May Wong got good reviews in her earlier roles, critics later panned her work.

    C. Anna May Wong's career was limited because of her ethnicity and the laws of her time.

    D. Many teenagers who grow up in Los Angeles get to play minor roles in Hollywood movies.

    E. Anna May Wong managed to transcend the racism of the film industry in the early 1900s.

Review the excerpt from a book's index below and answer the two questions that follow.

> Retirement, 110–111
> Retirement age, 112–114
>   Social Security collection, 114
> Retirement planning, 115–180
>   Annuities, 152–158
>   Bonds, 143–151
>   corporate, 144–147
>   savings, 148–151
> Cash equivalents [see Liquid cash equivalents]
> CDs, 126–128
> Individual retirement accounts (IRAs), 121–130
>   Roth IRA, 123–126
>   contribution rates, 123–124
>   rules for early withdrawal, 124–125
>   tax laws, 125–126
>   Traditional IRA, 127–130
>   contribution rates, 127–128
>   rules for early withdrawal, 128–129
>   tax laws, 129–130
> Insurance, life, 170–174
> Insurance, medical, 175–180
> Investments, 135–142
> Liquid cash equivalents, 167–169
> Medicare [see Insurance, medical]
> Mutual funds, 131–134
> Pensions, 117–120
> Savings, 164–166
> Social security, 159–163
> Stocks [see Investments]

26. On which pages should one look to find information about how much a person can contribute to a Roth IRA in one year?

    A. 123–126

    B. 125–126

    C. 127–128

    D. 164–166

    E. 123–124

27. Which of the following best describes the organizational pattern used in the section of the book dealing with tax laws for IRAs?

    A. alphabetical

    B. by type of IRA

    C. by type of tax code

    D. by retirement planning option

    E. by page number

Read the passage below and answer the three questions that follow.

Millions of people all over the country choose to drink only bottled water because they are convinced that it is much better for them. In fact, according to the Beverage Marketing Corporation, the average person drinks 30 gallons of bottled water each year. Multiple companies are profiting from this new obsession, and the industry is currently worth $12 billion in the United States.

Bottled water and tap water have a lot in common, however. Both have set limits on how much chemicals, bacteria, and radiation are allowed to be in the water. Neither one of them, however, has any kind of limitation on acceptable levels of pharmaceuticals. The presence of pharmaceuticals in drinking water should be worrisome, but so far, no one is overly concerned. In fact, there are no U.S. standards set for pharmaceutical residue in any kind of water.

28. What is the main topic of this passage?

    A. The bottled water industry is currently worth $12 billion.

    B. The average person drinks more than 30 gallons of water annually.

    C. There need to be more laws regulating bottled water production.

    D. There are some ingredients in all drinking water that may be dangerous.

    E. There are limits to how much chemicals and bacteria can be in bottled water.

29. All of the following ingredients in water are monitored carefully EXCEPT

    A. pharmaceuticals.

    B. chemicals.

    C. bacteria.

    D. radiation.

    E. chlorine.

30. You might infer from this passage that

    A. bottled water is far safer than tap water.

    B. bottled water undergoes no testing at all.

    C. tap water and bottled water are similar in content.

    D. tap water has more pharmaceuticals than bottled water.

    E. tap water is a little safer than bottled water.

GO ON TO THE NEXT PAGE.

Read the passage below and answer the four questions that follow.

¹*West Side Story* is one of the best musicals of all time. ²It is the modern retelling of *Romeo and Juliet*, the famous play by William Shakespeare that tells of two teenagers from warring families who fall in love. ³In *West Side Story*, the teenagers are associated with different gangs in 1950s New York City. ⁴Tony is a former leader of the Jets, a Caucasian gang that rules the streets. ⁵Bernardo, Maria's older brother, is the leader of a Puerto Rican gang called the Sharks. ⁶As tensions between the two groups heat up, Tony and Maria fall in love and plan to run away to get married. ⁷But the violence that surrounds them eventually *engulfs* even Tony and Maria, and Tony is killed. ⁸My favorite song in the musical is a ballad called "Maria," which Tony sings as he wanders through the streets after meeting Maria.

31. Which of the following sentences is least relevant to the development of the paragraph?

    A. Sentence 3
    B. Sentence 4
    C. Sentence 5
    D. Sentence 6
    E. Sentence 8

32. Which of the following sentences expresses an opinion rather than a fact?

    A. Sentence 1
    B. Sentence 2
    C. Sentence 4
    D. Sentence 5
    E. Sentence 6

33. Who is the audience to which this paragraph is most likely addressed?

    A. People unfamiliar with *West Side Story*
    B. People who have seen *West Side Story* but not *Romeo and Juliet*
    C. People who have never read *Romeo and Juliet*
    D. People who are members of gangs
    E. People who have read Shakespeare

34. As it is used in the passage, what does the word *engulfs* mean?

    A. Drives away
    B. Transcends
    C. Brings death to
    D. Breaks up
    E. Overwhelms

Read the passage below and answer the four questions that follow.

The Texas Rangers are probably the best known, or at least the most mythologized, group of law officers in American history. Numerous references to the Texas Rangers can be found today in novels, television, and movies, and the Texas Rangers baseball team was named after them.

Although they are usually portrayed in popular culture as a band of renegade sharpshooters because of their *storied* history, they have actually have been a part of the

Texas Department of Public Safety since 1935. Their duties today are largely focused on detective work, and they have some of the best crime labs in the United States. Direct law enforcement is now under the control of the Highway Patrol; however, the Texas Rangers' legacy lives on as the force that took down Sam Bass, John Wesley Hardin, and Bonnie and Clyde in the Old West.

35. As it is used in the passage, what does the word *storied* mean?

    A. Narrative
    B. Having multiple floors
    C. For sale
    D. Fictional
    E. Legendary

36. According to the passage, which of the following would a Texas Ranger be LEAST likely to do today?

    A. Track down crime suspects
    B. Analyze evidence that is taken from a crime scene
    C. Compile facts about multiple crimes to find ones that might be related
    D. Stop and ticket speeding drivers
    E. Test evidence from a scene of a crime in a laboratory

37. Which of the following best presents the organizational structure of the main topics addressed in this passage?

    A. I. The myth of the Texas Rangers in history
       II. The reality of the Texas Rangers in history
    B. I. The Texas Rangers in history
       II. The Texas Rangers today
    C. I. The Texas Rangers in our popular culture today
       II. The reality of the Texas Rangers today
    D. I. Myths of the Texas Rangers in history
       II. Myths of the Texas Rangers today
    E. I. The reality of the Texas Rangers in history
       II. The myths of the Texas Rangers today

38. The author's main purpose in writing this passage is to

    A. debunk myths about the Texas Rangers' past.
    B. detail how some of the most notorious criminals in the Old West were caught.
    C. contrast the Texas Rangers' current role with their past reputation.
    D. trace the lineage of Texas Ranger clothing and gear.
    E. dispel the questionable reputation of the origins of the Texas Rangers

Read the passage below and answer the three questions that follow.

Until 1980, Mount St. Helens, a volcanic mountain between Portland, Oregon, and Seattle, Washington, had been dormant since the mid-1800s. But over a two-day period starting on March 25, it erupted with a series of 174 shocks registering at least 2.6 on the Richter scale, culminating in an explosion of ash that left a crater in the mountain 250 feet wide. Ash was spewed as high as 7,000 feet into the air and fell not only on the surrounding area, but also as far away as Bend, Oregon, and Spokane, Washington.

GO ON TO THE NEXT PAGE.

Among the immediate consequences of the eruption were a disruption of air travel in the region, power blackouts caused by ash collecting in electrical circuits, and numerous road closures, including Highway 90. Nearby cities such as Yakima were plunged into near-darkness for several days due to the fine ash that was suspended in the atmosphere.

39. The passage implies that in a natural disaster such as an earthquake or volcano, the Richter scale measures the

A. amount of lava released.
B. amount of energy released.
C. death toll.
D. financial consequences.
E. size of the affected area.

40. It can be inferred from the passage that Bend, Oregon, and Spokane, Washington, are

A. unlike Portland and Seattle.
B. considered far away from Mount St. Helens.
C. very close to Yakima.
D. not near any volcanoes.
E. at relatively high sea level.

41. What statement below best summarizes this passage?

A. The 1980 explosion of Mount St. Helens caused the loss of many jobs.
B. Before the 1980 explosion, Mount St. Helens was a big mountain.
C. The 1980 explosion of Mount St. Helens started on March 25.
D. The 1980 explosion of Mount St. Helens was huge in scale and had far-reaching consequences.
E. The 1980 explosion of Mount St. Helens had a negative impact on tourism.

Read the passage below and answer the three questions that follow.

[1]_____ that pepper is great for adding a little extra flavor to food, but a new study says that it may also have a medicinal value. [2]According to the study, black pepper can help treat a disfiguring skin condition known as vitiligo. [3]This is the disease that pop star Michael Jackson said was responsible for his skin color changes. [4]Vitiligo is a disease that kills the skin's melanin, the element that gives skin its color. [5]In the study, piperine, the compound in pepper that gives the spice its unique flavor, was found to be effective in stimulating pigmentation in people's skin. _____ scientists believe piperine offers a promising new treatment for vitiligo.

42. Which words, if inserted *in order* into the blank lines in the reading selection, would best help the reader understand the idea the writer wants to communicate?

A. Today we know; However
B. While we know; But
C. It's long been known; Now
D. It's obvious; Obviously
E. Although we know; On the other hand

43. Which of the following sentences is least relevant to the development of the paragraph?

A. Sentence 1
B. Sentence 2
C. Sentence 3
D. Sentence 4
E. Sentence 5

44. Which substance were the scientists conducting the study apparently studying?

A. Piperine
B. Pigmentation
C. Vitiligo
D. Disfiguring skin conditions
E. Melanin

Refer to the graph below to answer the question that follows.

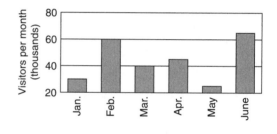

45. Which month showed the greatest increase in the number of park visitors over the month before?

A. February
B. March
C. April
D. May
E. June

Read the passage below and answer the five questions that follow.

Upon the mention of Afghanistan, most Westerners today think of a *forbidding* and severe wasteland at the western edge of the Himalayas, devastated by wave upon wave of strife and suffering. _____.

Should the rest of the world give up on this mostly agricultural nation, which is largely in ruins, and simply abandon it? True, invaders have left its agricultural lands barren, farm animals wiped out, and electricity and water systems destroyed. True, generations must pass before the deep-seated distrust its people must surely feel toward younger, mightier nations' subsides. But sweep away the land mines, gaze through the fog of war, and look deeply into the eyes of the Afghan people. You will see a colorful *pastiche* of clans almost too numerous to count, and a proud and strong-willed people with a long and varied heritage far too valuable to see wither from neglect.

GO ON TO THE NEXT PAGE.

46. Which sentence, if inserted into the blank line in the selection above, would best fit the development of the passage?

    A. Afghanistan is a landlocked country in central Asia.
    B. The 1979 Russian invasion and the U.S. bombings more than twenty years later are just two recent afflictions the Afghan people have endured in their long and bloody history.
    C. The people of Afghanistan come from many different tribes and speak many different languages.
    D. Foreign armies have often attempted—but never with success—to control this mountainous and isolated land.
    E. The land of Afghanistan is not conducive to farming.

47. As used in the selection, the word *forbidding* is best defined as

    A. prohibited.
    B. unfriendly.
    C. unpredictable.
    D. mountainous.
    E. law-oriented.

48. In the selection, the writer provides information that supports which of the following statements?

    A. No government exists in Afghanistan.
    B. The number of clans in Afghanistan is decreasing due to war.
    C. Producing food is difficult in Afghanistan.
    D. The crime rate is very high in Afghanistan.
    E. The Afghan people have little access to health care.

49. The selection can best be described as

    A. an explanation.
    B. a debate.
    C. a plea.
    D. a complaint.
    E. a diatribe.

50. As used in the selection, the word *pastiche* most nearly means

    A. village.
    B. assortment.
    C. generation.
    D. population.
    E. dearth.

2 ███████████████████████████ **2**

MATHEMATICS TEST

TEST DIRECTIONS: Carefully read the multiple-choice questions that follow. For each question, choose the one best answer from the answer choices provided. Mark each answer on the answer sheet provided.

You may work on the questions in any order you choose. You have 4 hours to complete all three sections (mathematics, reading, and writing) of the CBEST.

2　　　　　　　　　　　　　　　　　　　　　　　　2

1. If the amount of rainfall in one week was measured in centimeters per day and recorded as 3, 5, 0, 2, 1, 3, 0, then what was the average rainfall per day?

   A. 1.5 centimeters
   B. 2 centimeters
   C. 2.2 centimeters
   D. 3 centimeters
   E. 2.25 centimeters

2. In an election among three candidates—A, B, and C— candidate A received 20% of the votes, while candidate B received exactly three times as many votes as candidate C. What percent of the votes did candidate C receive?

   A. 20%
   B. 15%
   C. 60%
   D. 25%
   E. 30%

3. The legend on a map indicates a scale of 1 inch = 220 miles. Ava measures the distance between two cities, Harbortown and River City, and finds it to be 5.5 inches. How far apart are Harbortown and River City?

   A. 40 miles
   B. 1,240 miles
   C. 1,100 miles
   D. 1,420 miles
   E. 1,210 miles

4. Which of the following is the most appropriate unit for comparing the floor space of two different rooms?

   A. feet
   B. yards
   C. cubic feet
   D. square feet
   E. cubic yards

5. In takes Ludwig 45 minutes to paint a single figurine. At this rate, how long will it take him to paint 10 figurines?

   A. 2.5 hours
   B. 5 hours
   C. 7.5 hours
   D. 450 hours
   E. 5.5 hours

6. Heather bikes the course shown below every Saturday morning. If the entire course is 18 miles, what is the length of the unlabeled leg of the course?

   A. 4
   B. 5
   C. 2
   D. 3
   E. 1

7. A certain rectangular room has a length of 90 meters and a width of 85 meters. What is the area of the room?

   A. 350 square meters
   B. 1,250 square meters

C. 3,825 square meters
D. 7,650 square meters
E. 7,350 square meters

8. A package of 6 cookies is split between 2 children at snack time. How many cookies does it take to feed 12 children?

   A. 6
   B. 12
   C. 18
   D. 36
   E. 24

9. Michelle can paint two walls in 90 minutes. How long will it take her to paint six walls?

   A. 30 minutes
   B. 45 minutes
   C. 180 minutes
   D. 270 minutes
   E. 120 minutes

10. There are 12 marbles in a bag; 4 are red, 2 are blue, and the rest are green. The probability of randomly selecting a green marble from the bag is

    A. $^1/_3$.
    B. $^2/_3$.
    C. $^3/_4$.
    D. $^1/_2$.
    E. $^1/_4$.

11. The ratio of flour to sugar in a certain recipe is 3:2. If Don is making as much of the recipe as he can and he only has nine cups of flour, how much sugar will he use?

    A. 3
    B. 4.5
    C. 5.5
    D. 7.5
    E. 6

12. A salad costs $3.75, a beverage costs $1.50, and a bagel costs $2.25. Kevin, who has $5.50 to spend, can buy any of the following EXCEPT

    A. three beverages.
    B. two beverages and a bagel.
    C. a salad and beverage.
    D. a salad and bagel.
    E. a bagel and a beverage.

13. $3.902 \times 28 =$

    A. 1.09256
    B. 10.9256
    C. 109.256
    D. 1,092.56
    E. 10,925.6

GO ON TO THE NEXT PAGE.

14. What number subtracted from −1 is one greater than the sum of −1 and −1?

   A. 1
   B. 0
   C. 2
   D. −1
   E. −2

15. According to the score report, Matt's score on a standardized mathematics test was in the 63rd percentile. This score indicates that

   A. 63% of the students who took the test did as well as or better than he did.
   B. if he tries, he should be getting above-average scores in his math class.
   C. he got 63% of the questions correct.
   D. he did as well as or better than 63% of the students who took the test.
   E. he achieved a raw score of 63.

16. The expression below

$$68 + (-103) - 34$$

is equal to which of the following?

   A. −59
   B. 59
   C. −1
   D. 1
   E. −69

17. What is the average of −8, 12, 3, 4, and −1?

   A. 2
   B. 3
   C. 4
   D. 6
   E. 8

18. A team played 25 games in the season, losing 8 more games than it won. Three of the games resulted in ties. How many games did the team win?

   A. 15
   B. 12
   C. 7
   D. 10
   E. 13

19. Fill in the blank to complete the following equation:

$$11 - 10 \div (\_ \times 3) + 3 = 4$$

   A. $-^1/_3$
   B. 4
   C. −4
   D. $^1/_3$
   E. $^1/_4$

20. $1^2/_3 + ^4/_5 =$

   A. $^7/_{15}$
   B. $^{13}/_{15}$
   C. $^{37}/_{15}$
   D. $^{52}/_{15}$
   E. $^{11}/_{15}$

21. A full-time employee works 40 hours during a five-day week. The percentage of a five-day week that the employee is at work is

   A. 20%
   B. 33%
   C. 40%
   D. 50%
   E. 55%

22. The mixed number $4^5/_7$ expressed as a fraction is

   A. $^5/_7$
   B. $^{20}/_7$
   C. $^{33}/_7$
   D. $^{45}/_7$
   E. $^{55}/_7$

23. Including a 5% sales tax, what is the total cost of a sweater that costs $55 without tax?

   A. $57.50
   B. $60.00
   C. $57.25
   D. $62.50
   E. $57.75

24. A certain rectangular room has an area of 196 ft². If the length and width of the room are the same, how wide is the room?

   A. 12 ft
   B. 13 ft
   C. 14 ft
   D. 16 ft
   E. 18 ft

25. Rochelle is driving at 62 miles per hour. At 11:00 a.m. she sees the sign below:

Newton	45
Mayberry	80
Wilton	128

If she continues driving at the same speed, how far will she be from Wilton at 12:30 p.m.?

   A. 25 miles
   B. 35 miles
   C. 66 miles
   D. 97 miles
   E. 99 miles

26. Children are admitted to the movie theater at half the adult admission price. If one adult accompanies three children to the theater, paying $18.75 for all four tickets, what was the price of admission for each child?

   A. $4.50
   B. $4.00
   C. $3.75
   D. $7.50
   E. $4.75

GO ON TO THE NEXT PAGE.

27. For what value of x is it true that $x = 3(x + 2)$?

A. 2
B. −3
C. −2
D. 3
E. 6

28. Chuck goes to a farmer's market and sees tangerines, eggplant, carrots, plums, peaches, lettuce, bananas, cherries, strawberries, and squash for sale. He wants to buy lettuce, eggplant, cherries, tangerines, and peaches. A squash costs $1.95, a head of lettuce costs $1.85, a peach costs $0.45, bananas cost $0.85, a bunch of cherries costs $3.50, and a tangerine costs $0.35. If Chuck buys one of each item on his list and three additional bunches of cherries, how much money will he need?

What information is necessary to solve the problem above?

A. The cost of a bunch of cherries
B. The cost of strawberries
C. The cost of carrots
D. The cost of a head of lettuce
E. The cost of an eggplant

29. Dana works at a movie rental store that has 1117 movies that day. There are 351 action movies, 113 horror movies, 387 comedies, 243 dramas, and 23 foreign films. The store has rented out 732 movies that day.

Which of the following facts can be determined from the information given above?

A. The number of action movies rented
B. The number of comedies rented
C. The number of dramas rented
D. At least 1 horror movie or 1 drama was rented
E. At least 1 comedy was rented

30. Amy went to a shoe store to buy several pairs of shoes. She buys boots, sneakers, and sandals. If she has $150 to spend, what will be the average cost of a pair of shoes?

What information is required to solve this problem?

A. The price of each pair of shoes that Amy buys
B. The total cost of all of the pairs of shoes that Amy buys
C. The quantity of pairs of shoes that Amy buys
D. Both A and B
E. Both B and C

31. If Bob is paid $5,000 less than the sum of Al and Carl's salaries, which of the following mathematical statements expresses this relationship?

A. $B = A + C - 5,000$
B. $B = A \times C - 5,000$
C. $B = A + C + 5,000$
D. $B = A \times C + 5,000$
E. $B = A - C + 5,000$

32. Kyle needs to figure out $7/8$ of 176. Kyle can use all of the following methods EXCEPT:

A. Dividing 8 by 7 and then multiplying the answer by 176
B. Dividing 176 by 8 and then subtracting the answer from 176
C. Multiplying 7×176 and then dividing that number by 8
D. Dividing 176 by 8 and then multiplying that number by 7
E. Multiplying 176×7 and then dividing that number by 8

33. Willie volunteers at the library after school for 10 hours a week. One week he reshelves books for three quarters of that time and spends the rest of the time reading to kindergarten students. To figure out how much time he spends reading, he computes $3/4$ of 10 and subtracts that number from 10. Which expression below states another way he could compute the time he spends reading?

A. $1/4 \times 10$
B. $3/4 \times 10$
C. $3/4 \times 10 - 10$
D. $10 \times (1/4 \div 3/4)$
E. $3/4 \times 10 - 1/4$

34. The chart below shows a relationship between x and y. Refer to the chart to find the answer to the question that follows.

x	y
2	10
2.5	12.5
3	
3.5	17.5

Given the relationship between x and y shown above, what would be the number that fits in blank space in column y of the chart?

A. 14
B. 14.5
C. 15
D. 15.5
E. 16.5

35. Ashley earns $15 per hour and receives a 5% commission on all of her sales. How much did Ashley earn during an 8-hour day during which Ashley's sales totaled $400?

A. $160
B. $175
C. $150
D. $140
E. $155

36. Which of the statements below is correct?

A. $5^{11}/_{16} > 5^{7}/_{16} > 5^{3}/_{16}$
B. $5^{11}/_{16} < 5^{7}/_{16} < 5^{3}/_{16}$
C. $5^{3}/_{16} > 5^{11}/_{16} > 5^{7}/_{16}$
D. $5^{3}/_{16} > 5^{7}/_{16} > 5^{11}/_{16}$
E. $5^{3}/_{16} > 5^{13}/_{16} > 5^{15}/_{16}$

GO ON TO THE NEXT PAGE.

37. Which of the following lists is in order from smallest to largest?
    A. $1/8, 2/5, 1/2, 3/4$
    B. $2/5, 1/8, 3/4, 1/2$
    C. $3/4, 1/2, 2/5, 1/8$
    D. $2/5, 3/4, 1/2, 1/8$
    E. $1/8, 2/5, 3/4, 1/2$

38. $x + 2x + 3x =$
    A. $5x^3$
    B. $6x$
    C. $5 + 3x$
    D. $6x^3$
    E. $5x$

39. Which of the numbers below is between 6,589,188 and 6,782,136?
    A. 6,880,001
    B. 6,589,178
    C. 6,788,011
    D. 6,781,599
    E. 6,589,187

40. The value of m is between 0.0039 and 0.03. Which of the numbers below could represent the value of m?
    A. 0.01
    B. 0.001
    C. 0.1
    D. 0.00333
    E. 0.31

41. Alicia drove 233.2 miles on a business trip. She is told to round her mileage to the nearest 5 miles when she submits her expense report. How many miles should Alicia report?
    A. 230
    B. 233
    C. 233.5
    D. 235
    E. 233.3

42. Pablo is ordering books online. The first book costs $9.85, but there is a special offer of two books for $15.55. Pablo wants to figure out how much the second book will cost him. Rounding both prices to the nearest dollar, what is the price for the second book?
    A. $5.00
    B. $6.00
    C. $5.55
    D. $5.50
    E. $6.50

43. Christine must decide which camp activities in which she wants to participate.

    If she has an activity on Tuesday afternoons, she must participate in either kayaking or horseback riding.
    If she has an activity on Friday afternoons, she must participate in both boating and swimming.
    Bicycling is only offered on Monday or Wednesday mornings.
    There are no other activities offered.

If Christine has decided to participate in 2 activities and 1 of them is bicycling, then it must be true that

A. Christine participates in boating and bicycling.
B. Christine participates in kayaking and bicycling.
C. Christine participates in an activity on both Monday morning and Tuesday afternoon.
D. Christine participates in an activity on Tuesday afternoon.
E. Christine participates in an activity on Tuesday afternoon and Friday afternoon.

44. Larry and Joseph are choosing their college courses for the fall semester.

    If Larry takes chemistry, then Joseph takes anatomy.
    If Joseph takes calculus, then Larry takes finance.
    If Joseph takes finance, then Larry takes chemistry.

If Joseph does not take anatomy, which of the following must be false?

A. Larry does not take chemistry.
B. Larry takes finance.
C. Joseph does not take calculus.
D. Both Larry and Joseph take finance.
E. Larry takes anatomy.

45. Javier wants to join multiple sports teams at school.

    The baseball team meets during session 1 on Monday and Wednesday.
    The basketball team meets during session 2 on Tuesday and session 1 on Wednesday.
    The football team meets during session 1 on Tuesday and session 2 on Thursday.

Based on the information above, which of the following conclusions cannot be made?

A. If Javier joins the basketball team, he cannot join the baseball team.
B. Javier joins both the basketball and football teams.
C. Javier joins both the baseball and football teams.
D. If Javier joins the football team, he can also join the basketball team.
E. Javier can join both the baseball and basketball team

Refer to the table below to answer the question that follows.

Parent-Teacher Conferences

	Start	End
Session 1	7:00	7:18
Session 2	7:22	7:40
Session 3	7:44	
Session 4	8:06	8:24

46. The table shows the start and end time in a schedule for parent-teacher conferences. Assuming the pattern remains the same, what is the missing end time for session three?

GO ON TO THE NEXT PAGE.

A. 8:00
B. 8:02
C. 8:04
D. 8:06
E. 8:12

Refer to the mileage table below to answer the question that follows.

Distance Between Cities A, B, C, D, and E (in miles)

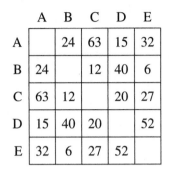

	A	B	C	D	E
A		24	63	15	32
B	24		12	40	6
C	63	12		20	27
D	15	40	20		52
E	32	6	27	52	

47. According to the mileage table above, which two cities are the furthest apart?

A. City D and City E
B. City C and the other City C
C. City A and City E
D. City A and City C
E. City A and City B

Refer to the line graph below to answer the question that follows.

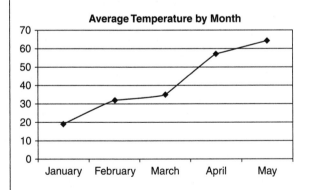

Average Temperature by Month

48. In the above chart, which month showed the smallest increase in temperature from the month before?

A. February
B. March
C. April
D. May
E. January

Refer to the pie chart below to answer the question that follows.

Composition of Final Grade in AP Biology Class

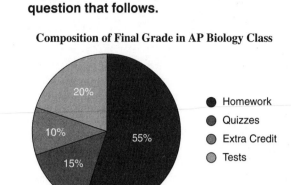

49. What percent of the final grade is determined by quizzes and tests together?

A. 30%
B. 35%
C. 45%
D. 55%
E. 60%

Refer to the bar graph below to answer the question that follows.

Watching Television on the Internet

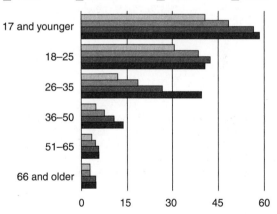

50. Which age group showed the greatest increase in watching television on the Internet in one year?

A. Ages 17 and younger
B. Ages 18–25
C. Ages 26–35
D. Ages 51–65
E. Ages 66 and older

GO ON TO THE NEXT PAGE.

3 **3**

WRITING TEST

TEST DIRECTIONS: The writing section of the CBEST includes two topics that assess your ability to write effectively. You must write essays responding to *both* topics.

Be sure to write about the given topics; essays on other topics will not be graded. Your answer must completely address all parts of the topic. Your response must be in your own words and not plagiarized from some other source. Write as legibly as possible; your answer can be scored only if it is legible.

Make sure you read each topic carefully. Before you begin to write, take several minutes to organize your thoughts. You may use any space provided in the test booklet to make notes or outline your response. Write your essay on the writing response sheets provided.

Topic 1

Academy-Award–winning actress Helen Hayes advised, "Always aim for achievement and forget about success." To what extent do you agree or disagree with this statement? Write an essay for an audience of educated adults, stating your position. Use logical arguments and specific examples to support your position.

WRITING ESSAY

RESPONSE SHEET FOR TOPIC 1 (CONTINUED)

WRITING ESSAY

Topic 2

There is widespread disagreement about the effect of television on learning. Does television encourage or discourage learning? Or does it do both of these things under different circumstances? State your position on this question in an essay addressed to educated adults. Use logical arguments and specific examples from your personal experience to support your position.

RESPONSE SHEET FOR TOPIC 2

WRITING ESSAY

RESPONSE SHEET FOR TOPIC 2 (CONTINUED)

WRITING ESSAY

 **ANSWER KEY**

PRACTICE TEST 2

	Reading				Mathematics	
1. E	26. E			1. B	26. C
2. E	27. B			2. A	27. B
3. D	28. D			3. E	28. E
4. A	29. A			4. D	29. E
5. B	30. C			5. C	30. E
6. C	31. E			6. C	31. A
7. C	32. A			7. D	32. A
8. D	33. A			8. D	33. A
9. E	34. E			9. D	34. C
10. B	35. E			10. D	35. D
11. A	36. D			11. E	36. A
12. E	37. C			12. D	37. A
13. C	38. C			13. C	38. B
14. B	39. B			14. B	39. D
15. E	40. B			15. D	40. A
16. B	41. D			16. E	41. D
17. C	42. C			17. A	42. B
18. A	43. C			18. C	43. D
19. D	44. A			19. D	44. D
20. B	45. E			20. C	45. E
21. C	46. B			21. B	46. B
22. B	47. B			22. C	47. D
23. A	48. C			23. E	48. B
24. B	49. C			24. C	49. B
25. C	50. B			25. B	50. C

Explanations for the Practice Test 2

Reading Test

1. **Correct Choice: E.** The author mentions "Oriental manuscripts, Eastern fables, and works of early poets" to support his claim that the game had origins in ancient times. There is no mention of the name of "chess" coming from an oriental word (choice A). In regards to answer choice B, the author also states that the game probably originated in India, but he does not mention "Oriental manuscript" to support that statement. Choices C and D are not correct because they contradict factual statements made by the author elsewhere in the passage.

2. **Correct Choice: E.** The phrase, *attest to*, as used in this sentence, most closely means prove. In the preceding sentence, the author tells us that chess is probably the world's second-oldest game. It makes sense that the three types of artifacts the author mentions in the next sentence would help "prove" the antiquity of chess, in other words, that chess is an ancient game.

3. **Correct Choice: D.** Given that the game's name literally means "King," it makes sense, and therefore is not surprising, that a chess piece designated as the king would play a key role in the game. According to the passage, it is this reason, not the other answer choices, why the author is not surprised the key chess piece is the king.

4. **Correct Choice: A.** In the first paragraph, the author tells us that except for draughts (an early form of checkers), chess is probably the world's oldest game, inferring that checkers predates chess.

5. **Correct Choice: B.** Aside from the first sentence, which introduces the topic, the passage is concerned with the history of the game of chess. Choice D is plausible since it also relates to history; however, because the author does not actually discuss how the game itself changed over time, this choice is not appropriate. The passage is about chess, not chess and checkers, making choice A incorrect. The author does not claim chess is the world's most popular game or give any information on that topic, making choice C incorrect. Choice E is incorrect because the author makes no mention of where the name "chess" originated.

6. **Correct Choice: C.** This sentence connects the paragraph before it with the sentence after it in a logical way. None of the other answer choices do this. Answer choices A, B, and D contain more information about sleep, but it is all about aspects of sleep not covered in this passage.

7. **Correct Choice: C.** Choices A, B, and E are statements on topics not covered in the passage. Choice D is an opinion and is not relevant to the main point of the reading selection.

8. **Correct Choice: D.** There was no mention in the passage about the effect of napping on appetite, making answer choice D the correct one. The passage stated effects that napping had on fatigue (choice A), memory (choice B), learning (choice C), and energy level (choice E), so all these answer choices are not correct responses to the question.

9. **Correct Choice: E.** One of the meanings of *tongue* is language. Substituting the word *language* for *tongue* throughout the passage makes perfect sense and does not change the meaning. None of the words in the other answer choices can be substituted for *tongue* without changing the meaning of the passage.

10. **Correct Choice: B.** In the first paragraph, the author asserts this point. Then, in the second and third paragraphs, the author further develops and explains the misunderstanding.

11. **Correct Choice: A.** In the third paragraph, the author describes how Latin spread throughout Europe and northern Africa, "triumphing over" (in other words, conquering) "all the other tongues of those regions," meaning that Latin replaced those tongues as the primary language spoken in those regions.

12. **Correct Choice: E.** *Legions* refers to Roman armies. As the author points out in the first paragraph, most people would assume that Latin spread throughout the Roman Empire because Roman legions imposed the language (through military force and Roman law) on the people they conquered. The word *armies* can be substituted for *legions* with no change in the meaning of this paragraph.

13. **Correct Choice: C.** In the passage's final sentence, the author points out that Latin triumphed over the languages of the regions that Rome conquered more completely than Roman arms triumphed over the peoples using those languages. In other words, ultimately, the Latin language was mightier than the Roman military.

14. **Correct Choice: B.** Part one is the correct answer because of the section titled "Most Common Grammatical/Spelling Mistakes."

15. **Correct Choice: E.** The appendices include information on how to write citations.

16. **Correct Choice: B.** "Although" correctly connects the content of this sentence with the discussion of opinion on spanking in the first two paragraphs. "In the meantime" correctly links the content of the final sentence with the preceding one. In regards to answer choice A, "While" is a plausible word to fill in the first blank; however, "nevertheless" does not work for the second sentence.

17. **Correct Choice: C.** Whether spanking is appropriate or not is the subject of this entire passage. Choice A is incorrect because "Punishment" is too broad; this passage only dealt with spanking, not other types of punishment. Choice B deals with one topic relating to the spanking debate but is not the main idea of the passage. Choice D is not the best answer because the passage is not about any one study of spanking effectiveness and only mentions studies in the broader context of laying out the grounds for both sides in the spanking debate. Choice E is incorrect because it is about deviant behavior instead of problematic behavior and is related to a topic that is not the main idea of the passage.

18. **Correct Choice: A.** The meaning of the word *integral* in this context is *central*. The other answer choices change the meaning of the sentence and make no sense in this context.

19. **Correct Choice: D.** Studies have shown some connection between spanking and future sexual problems. Choices A, B, and E are overly strong statements that are not supported by the passage. Choice C is not supported by anything in the passage.

20. **Correct Choice: B.** According to the passage, parents are advised to find other alternatives methods of discipline. Choices A, C, D, and E contradict the correct answer and do not accurately reflect the opinion of the American Academy of Pediatrics.

21. **Correct Choice: C.** According to the passage, her first part in a movie was "as an uncredited extra," making C the best choice. Answer choice A is mentioned but not in reference to her first part in a movie. Answer choice B is not discussed in the passage. Answer choices D and E are not correct statements of what the passage says.

22. **Correct Choice: B.** This fact was stated in the passage. In the reading selection, the author expressed no opinions about what should have happened, making answer choices A and D incorrect answer choices. Choice C was not mentioned in the passage, although it was mentioned that Anna May Wong was passed over in favor of Luise Rainer for a role in *The Good Earth*. Choice E is a false statement.

23. **Correct Choice: A.** Since the author states that Anna May Wong was a talented actress whose ethnicity was a stumbling block, he would almost certainly agree with answer choice A. Choice C sounds good at first, but the author actually makes no mention of *audiences* objecting to Anna May Wong, so it is unclear whether or not the author would agree or disagree with this statement. The author doesn't state his feelings regarding the statement in answer choice B and does not discuss Anna May Wong's own feelings (answer choice D). The author would disagree with answer choice E.

24. **Correct Choice: B.** The passage is a brief of Anna May Wong's life, making B the best answer choice. Although the author clearly raises questions about casting decisions of the time regarding Anna May Wong, the passage cannot accurately be described as a rant against casting directors (answer choice D) or against the film industry at large (answer choice E). Although several films are mentioned in the passage, it does not critique a film (answer choice A). Answer choice C describes a type of movie role, but not a type of passage or writing.

25. **Correct Choice: C.** Choice C sums up the ideas expressed in the passage. Answer choice A is a plausible answer, but is broader than the material covered by the passage. Answer choices B and D are not mentioned in the passage and do not describe any points made by the author in this passage. Answer choice E is contradicted by the passage.

26. **Correct Choice: E.** The index clearly shows that contribution rates for Roth IRAs are on pages 123–124.

27. **Correct Choice: B.** Tax laws for IRAs are divided by IRA type.

28. **Correct Choice: D.** The main point the article arrives at is that neither bottled water nor drinking water are tested for potential hazardous residues. Answer choices A, B, and E state facts provided in the article, but these are only selected facts, not the main point of the article. The opinion expressed in answer choice C is not expressed in the passage, making this answer choice incorrect.

29. **Correct Choice: A.** The article sates that pharmaceuticals are not monitored, making this the correct answer. The other answer choices were included in the article as examples of ingredients that are monitored in drinking water and bottled water.

30. **Correct Choice: C.** It is a reasonable conclusion that can be drawn from this article. The statements in answer choices A, B, D, and E are not supported by the passage.

31. **Correct Choice: E.** Sentence 8 states the author's opinion regarding a song in the musical, but this sentence is unrelated to the rest of the paragraph, which focuses on a brief explanation of the plot line of *West Side Story*. Sentence 8 can be removed from the passage without hurting the reader's ability to understand the passage. Removal of any of the other sentences listed in the answer choices would diminish the reader's understanding of *West Side Story*'s plot.

32. **Correct Choice: A.** Sentence 1 states the author's opinion that *West Side Story* is one of the best musicals of all time. Even if many others agree with the author on this opinion, it is still an opinion, rather than a fact. Each person has different likes and dislikes, and opinions on which are the best musicals of all time will vary depending on individual preferences. All the other answer choices link to sentences that factually describe the plot line of *West Side Story*.

33. **Correct Choice: A.** Since the passage describes the basics of the plot line of *West Side Story*, it can be inferred that this passage was written for an intended audience of people unfamiliar with the story. It is probably not intended for people who have seen the musical (answer choice B) since it would not provide any new information for them. The passage, in comparing *Romeo and Juliet* to *West Side Story*, assumes that at least some readers *are* familiar with *Romeo and Juliet*, making answer choice C incorrect. It is not addressed in any specific way to members of gangs, so answer choice D is not a good answer. The similarity to Shakespeare's *Romeo and Juliet* is only noted in passing and is not the main idea of the passage, so answer choice E is incorrect.

34. **Correct Choice: E.** In the context of this passage, *engulfs* means "to overwhelm." Substitution of any of the other answer choices for *engulfs* would change the meaning of the sentence.

35. **Correct Choice: E.** In the context of this passage, which describes how the Texas Rangers have been mythologized, the meaning of *storied* is "legendary." Substitution of any of the other answer choices for *storied* would change the meaning of the sentence.

36. **Correct Choice: D.** The passage states that today's Texas Rangers focus on detective work, while direct law enforcement is under the Highway Patrol. Therefore, giving speeding tickets would not be something a Texas Ranger would be likely to do. All of the other answer choices describe activities associated with detective work and are things a Texas Ranger might do today, making all of them incorrect answer choices.

37. **Correct Choice: C.** The first paragraph is not about history but about the myth of the Texas Rangers in our popular culture today. The second paragraph then focuses on the reality of the Texas Rangers today. Thus, answer choice C best describes the organizational structure of this passage. Answer choice B could be a plausible answer, but there is little description in the passage (and no description at all in the first paragraph) about what the Texas Rangers did in history.

38. **Correct Choice: C.** The bulk of the passage is spent drawing contrasts between the Texas Rangers' mythology and their current job responsibilities. There is nothing in the passage that debunks myths about the Texas Rangers' past (answer choice A), details how notorious criminals were caught (answer choice B), traces the lineage of Texas Ranger clothing and gear (answer choice D), or mentions a questionable reputation (answer choice E).

39. **Correct Choice: B.** The passage states that the Richter scale measures the "shocks" felt before the big explosion, so this implies that the Richter scale measures the amount of energy released. None of the other answer choices, including the amount of lava released (choice A), the death toll (choice C), the final consequences (choice D), and the size of the affected area (choice E), are even mentioned in the passage.

40. **Correct Choice: B.** The passage mentions that ash fell "as far away as Bend, Oregon, and Spokane, Washington." This implies that these cities are some distance from the volcano. None of the other answer choices are supported by any statements in the passage.

41. **Correct Choice: D.** The details described throughout the passage are presented to support the idea that the eruption of Mt. St. Helens was huge in scale and had far-reaching consequences. Answer choices A, B, and E are not supported by the passage and choice D is a minor detail, not the topic of the passage.

42. **Correct Choice: C.** The contrast between what's long been known about pepper and what is now being discovered frames this paragraph. Thus "It's long been known" best fills in the first blank and "Now" best fills in the second blank. The words and phrases in the other answer choices do not correctly relate the first and last sentence to the rest of the passage.

43. **Correct Choice: C.** Sentence 3 tells us interesting information about Michael Jackson's health but does not tell us anything about pepper (the main topic of this passage) or vitiligo (a secondary topic of this paragraph). Sentence 3 can be removed from the passage without hurting the reader's ability to understand the passage. Removal of any of the other sentences listed in the answer choices would diminish the reader's understanding of pepper as a treatment for vitiligo.

44. **Correct Choice: A.** The scientists were studying piperine, including its effects on skin pigmentation. Answer choice B would be a plausible answer, but skin pigmentation, or the colorization of the skin, is not a substance. According to the article, melanin is the substance that gives the skin its color, but melanin is not one of the answer choices provided for this question (answer choice E). Vitiligo (answer choice C) is a disease, not a substance, and disfiguring skin conditions (answer choice D) are a symptom of vitiligo, not a substance.

45. **Correct Choice: E.** The greatest increase in park visitors in one month over the previous month occurred in June. To answer this question we need to compare two consecutive months and look for the biggest difference in length of the bars in the graph. From a quick look at the bar graph, it is obvious that this increase too place in June. It is not necessary to compute numbers of visitors or figure out what the increase was in numbers of visitors.

46. **Correct Choice: B.** Answer choice B provides the only sentence that relates to the rest of the first paragraph. The sentence provides two examples of "recent afflictions the Afghan people have endured," connecting this sentence to "devastated by wave upon wave of strife and suffering" of the preceding sentence. Answer choices A and D provide information about Afghanistan, but this information is largely unrelated to the passage and its main point. Answer choice C provides additional information about Afghanistan that is relevant to the passage, but only to the second paragraph, not the first paragraph where the blank appears. Answer choice E is not stated in the passage.

47. **Correct Choice: B.** *Forbidding* in the context used here means "unfriendly." In this sentence, the author is attempting to impress the reader of how harsh the environment is throughout Afghanistan. The word *unfriendly* is often used to describe such an environment, and so substituting this word for *forbidding* makes sense. Substituting any of the other answer choices for *forbidding* would change the meaning of the sentence.

48. Correct Choice: C. The author tells us that Afghanistan's farmlands and farm animals have been destroyed. This information supports the statement that producing food is difficult in Afghanistan. No information is provided in the passage to support the statements that no government exists (answer choice A), that the number of clans is decreasing (answer choice B), that the crime rate is high (answer choice D), or that the Afghan people have little access to health care (answer choice E).

49. Correct Choice: C. In the selection, the author marvels at the rich traditions and pride of the Afghan people and wonders how the rest of the world can possibly allow this civilization to wither away. Implicitly, the speaker is appealing to those who are listening to help save Afghanistan and its people, a *plea* for help on their behalf.

50. Correct Choice: B. *Pastiche* means a variety or assortment. This meaning fits the context of the paragraph in which the author refers to the Afghan people as many, many different clans, each with its own distinct features and heritage. The other answer choices do not have the same meaning as *pastiche* and could not be substituted for *pastiche* without changing the meaning of the sentence.

Mathematics

1. Correct Choice: B. To compute the average, you add the amount of rainfall from each day (14) and divide that sum by the number of days (7). The answer is 2 centimeters.

2. Correct Choice: A. Together, candidates B and C received 80% of the votes (100% − 20%). Candidate C received 1/4 of that 80%, or 20% of the total number of votes. (Candidate B received 3 times as many votes: 3/4 of 80%, or 60%).

3. Correct Choice: E. If the cities are 5.5 inches apart and 1 inch equals 220 miles, then you multiply $5.5 \times 220 = 1,210$.

4. Correct Choice: D. Square feet can be used to measure the area covered by the floors in each room and give you an appropriate measurement to compare floor space in the two rooms. Feet and yards are only one dimensional; they can be used to measure length and/or width, but not compare floor space. Cubic feet measures three-dimensional volume, not area.

5. Correct Choice: C. Ludwig can paint one figurine in 45 minutes, which means he can paint 10 figurines in 450 minutes. Since the answer choices are in hours, you must divide by 60 to figure out how many hours that equals. $450 \div 6 = 7.5$ hours.

6. Correct Choice: C. The legs of the course that you can see are 3, 3, 4, and 6. They add up to 16, and the course is 18 miles total, so the remaining leg must equal to 2 because $18 − 16 = 2$.

7. Correct Choice: D. Because the problem is looking for the area of a rectangle, you need to multiply the length and the width. $90 \times 85 = 7,650$.

8. Correct Choice: D. If two children split a package of six cookies, each child gets three cookies. For 12 children, $12 \times 3 = 36$.

9. Correct Choice: D. Be sure to set up a proportion: 2 walls and 90 minutes are on the left and 6 walls and x are on the right. Cross-multiplying gives $2x = 540$. Divide both sides by 2 and you have $x = 270$.

10. Correct Choice: D. 6 of the 12 marbles are green. The probability of selecting a green marble is 6/12, or 1/2.

11. Correct Choice: E. Constructing a proportion, or two equal fractions, is again a good way to go. The fraction on the left has 3 in the numerator and 2 in the denominator, and the fraction on the right has 9 in the numerator and x in the denominator. Cross-multiply and get $3x = 9 \times 2$, and solve to get $3x = 18$, or $x = 6$.

12. Correct Choice: D. A salad and bagel would cost $3.75 + $2.25, or a total of $6.00, which is more money than Kevin has.

13. Correct Choice: C. Because the only difference between the answer choices in this problem is the number of places behind the decimal, all you really need to do is count. There are three places behind the decimal in the original problem; therefore, there are three places behind the decimal in the result.

14. **Correct Choice: B.** Work backward: The sum of −1 and −1 is −2. One greater than −2 is −1. What number subtracted from −1 = −1? The answer is 0. To set up an equation to figure the problem out: $−1 − x − 1 = −1 + (−1)$. Then solve for x.

15. **Correct Choice: D.** The meaning of percentile is correctly stated in answer choice D. Answer choice A would be correct only if it said "lower" rather than "better."

16. **Correct Choice: E.** Adding a positive 68 and a negative 103 gives you a negative 35. Subtracting 34 from a negative 35 gives you a negative 69.

17. **Correct Choice: A.** The total of the numbers is 10. Dividing 10 by the number of numbers (5) gives you 2.

18. **Correct Choice: C.** 22 games were either won or lost. You can find the number of games won by trying each answer choice in turn. Choice H works: $7 + 8 = 15$, and $15 + 7 = 22$. Or, you can solve the problem using algebra (let x equal the number of games won):

$$x + (x + 8) = 22$$
$$2x = 14$$
$$x = 7$$

19. **Correct Choice: D.** You can use the plug-in method, trying each answer choice in turn. Or, you can solve the problem using algebra, isolating the missing term on one side of the equation:

$$11 − 10 ÷ (\_ × 3) + 3 = 4$$
$$−10 ÷ (\_ × 3) = −10$$
$$−10 = −10(\_ × 3)$$
$$1 = (\_ × 3)$$
$$^1/_3 = \_$$

20. **Correct Choice: C.** First, you need to convert the mixed number $1^2/_3$ to an improper fraction. Multiplying the integer by the denominator, you get 3, which you then add to the numerator to get $^5/_3$. Using the bowtie method to add $^5/_3$ and $^4/_5$ gives $25 + ^{12}/_{15}$ [15 goes under $25 + 12$], which equals $^{37}/_{15}$.

21. **Correct Choice: B.** To solve this problem, you must first determine the number of hours in a five-day week. With 24 hours in a day and 5 days

in a work week, there are a total of 120 hours per week. The percentage that an employee is at work is:

40 hours/wk/120 hours/wk [this is a fraction] $× 100\% = 33.3\%$.

22. **Correct Choice: C.** The mixed number $4^5/_7$ can be converted into a fraction as follows:

$$4^5/_7 = 4 • 7 + ^5/_7 \text{ [the 7 goes under } 4 • 7 + 5]$$
$$= 23 + ^5/_7 \text{ [the 7 goes under } 23 + 5] = ^{33}/_7.$$

23. **Correct Choice: E.** The tax $= \$55 × 0.05 = \$2.75$. Add this tax to the sweater's price: $\$55 + \$2.75 = \$57.75$.

24. **Correct Choice: C.** If the length and width of the room are the same (and are integers, which they must be according to the answer choices), then a good knowledge of square roots helps solve the problem. The number 14 squared is 196, so 14 is the length and width of the room.

25. **Correct Choice: B.** In 1.5 hours she will go 93 miles ($1.5 × 62$) if she maintains her speed of 62 miles per hour. Subtract 93 from 128 and the answer is 35 miles.

26. **Correct Choice: C.** If the price of a child's ticket equals C, the price of an adult ticket equals $2C$. Set up an algebraic equation, then solve for C.

$$C + C + C + 2C = \$18.75$$
$$5C = \$18.75$$
$$C = \$3.75$$

27. **Correct Choice: B.** To answer the question, you can try plugging in each answer choice in turn. (With the correct number, the equation will hold true.) Or you can solve for x using algebra:

$$x = 3(x + 2)$$
$$x = 3x + 6$$
$$−2x = 6$$
$$x = −3$$

28. **Correct Choice: E.** Eggplant is on Chuck's list, but its cost is not included in the problem. The cost of cherries and the cost of lettuce are included in the problem. Strawberries and carrots are not on Chuck's list.

29. Correct Choice: E. Since 732 is a much larger number than the number of action comedies or drama movies, you can eliminate answer choices A, B, and C because there is no way to tell how many of any of these were rented. If you add the number of horror movies to the number of drama movies, you will see that it's possible that none of them were rented.

113 + 243 = 356. Answer choice D is incorrect.

If you subtract the number of rented movies from the total number of movies in the store, you will see that the total number of comedies exceeds the remainder of movies in the store. 1117 − 732 = 385. Therefore, answer choice E is correct. There are actually at least 2 comedies rented.

30. Correct Choice: E. You know that Amy has $150 to spend on shoes, but you don't know if she spent all of it. Answer choice B is required. While you know that Amy buys boots, sneakers, and sandals, you don't know how many of each pair she buys. Therefore, answer choice C is required. The individual cost of each pair of shoes is not needed to solve this problem.

31. Correct Choice: A. Translate: "Bob is 5,000 less than the sum of Al and Carl" (yes, the problem is actually talking about their salaries, but we are simplifying the language) translates to $B = -5,000 + A + C$, which can be rearranged to fit choice A.

32. Correct Choice: A. You can carry out the operations and see that they all yield the number 154 except answer choice A, making that the correct answer. Answer choice A would also yield 154 if it said "Divide 7 by 8" rather than "Divide 8 by 7."

33. Correct Choice: A. Willie spends 2.5 hours a week reading to kindergarten students. You can get that number by figuring out how much time he spends reshelving books and subtracting that number from 10 as Willie did. Or you can easily figure out if he spends three fourths of his time reshelving, that means he spends one fourth of his time reading. Then compute $1/4 \times 10$ (answer choice A).

34. Correct Choice: C. The chart shows the following relationship between x and y: $y = 5x$. Therefore, when x is 3, y is 15.

35. Correct Choice: D. At $15 per hour, Ashley earns $120 in wages during an 8-hour shift. Her 5% commission on $400 in sales is $20. Ashley's total earnings were $140 ($120 + $20).

36. Correct Choice: A. Since all choices contain the integer 5, you can eliminate—or at least ignore—the 5s and focus on the fractions. $^{11}/_{16}$ is larger than $^{7}/_{16}$, which is larger than $^{3}/_{16}$.

37. Correct Choice: A. This problem can be done by comparing individual fractions, but it is probably more time consuming than the alternate, which is converting the fractions into decimals so that they are easier to order. $^{1}/_{8} = 0.125$, $^{2}/_{5} = 0.4$, $^{1}/_{2} = 0.5$, and $^{3}/_{4} = 0.75$, so that is the order they should be in from left to right.

38. Correct Choice: B. Since all three terms share the same variable (x), you can combine terms by simply adding coefficients (1 + 2 + 3).

39. Correct Choice: D. Answer choices A and C are too large and choice B is too small to fit in the given range.

40. Correct Choice: A. Answer choices B and D are too small and choice C is too large to fit in the given range.

41. Correct Choice: D. Rounding to the nearest 5 miles means possible numbers are in intervals of 5: 5, 10, 15, etc. The number 233.2 is closer to 235 than to 230, so it should be rounded up to 235.

42. Correct Choice: B. Rounded to the nearest dollar, the first book costs $10 and the price for two books is $16. Now you can easily subtract in your head $16 − $10 is $6.

43. Correct Choice: D. You know that Christine participates in two activities and one of them is cycling, which is offered on either Monday or Wednesday mornings. Answer choice C is tempting, but remember that Christine could participate in bicycling on Wednesday mornings. She must participate in either kayaking or horseback riding, which are offered on Tuesday afternoon. Eliminate answer choice B because it *could* be true, but it doesn't *have* to be true. She cannot participate in an activity on Friday afternoon because she would then have to participate in both boating and swimming. Eliminate answer choices A and E.

44. Correct Choice: D. If Joseph does not take anatomy, then Larry does not take chemistry. Eliminate answer choice A. If Larry does not take chemistry, then Joseph does not take finance. This makes answer choice D the correct answer. Answer choices B, C, and E could all be true.

45. Correct Choice: E. Sketching out a quick chart would make this problem easy to complete.

	Monday	Tuesday	Wednesday	Thursday
Session 1	Baseball	Football	Baseball, Basketball	
Session 2		Basketball		Football

Answer choice E is clearly the correct choice. Javier cannot join both baseball and basketball.

46. Correct Choice: B. The table shows parent-teacher conferences are scheduled to last 18 minutes. 8:02 is 18 minutes later than 7:44.

47. Correct Choice: D. The number 63 is the largest number in the mileage chart and it appears at the intersection of the column/row for cities A and C. There is no "other" City C (answer choice B).

48. Correct Choice: B. The temperature between February and March only increased a slight amount—three degrees or so—compared with much larger increases between the other months.

49. Correct Choice: B. Quizzes count for 15% and tests count for 20%, giving a total of 35% for quizzes and tests.

50. Correct Choice: C. The 26–35 age group showed the biggest increase from 2007 to 2008.

Writing

After you take the actual CBEST, two human scorers will read your essay and assign a number score from 1 to 4. The score they give will be based on the scoring standards described in the official CBEST Writing Score Scale. This scale can be viewed online at www.cbest.nesinc.com (go to the practice test and then the writing section). A summary of the writing score scale is provided below.

Use this summary to score your own essay. Better yet, ask someone else— a teacher, parent, friend, or colleague—to score your essay based on this summary of the CBEST writing score scale.

Scoring the CBEST Writing Test	
Score	**Summary of Scoring Guidelines**
4	**A Score of 4 indicates a well-written essay that effectively develops an idea for the specified audience.**
	The essay has a central idea or point of view and the writer maintains the focus on the idea in a well reasoned essay.
	Ideas or points the author presents are logically arranged and the essay is clear and well-organized.
	Assertions are supported with relevant information and specific examples.
	Words usage is careful and precise.
	Sentences and paragraphs are well constructed and coherent; however, the essay may contain minor flaws in grammar, spelling, punctuation, etc.
	The essay completely addresses the topic and is appropriate for the given audience.
3	**A Score of 3 indicates an essay that for the most part, is adequately written and develops an idea for the specified audience.**
	The essay has a central idea or point of view and the writer, for the most part, maintains the focus on this idea in a well reasoned essay.
	The presentation of ideas and points, for the most, is adequately organized and clear.
	Most assertions are supported with relevant information and specific examples.
	Word usage is adequate; there may be some errors in usage but they are not bad enough to make understanding difficult.
	Sentences and paragraphs are generally well contructed and coherent; errors in sentence structure and grammar are not serious enough to cause confusion and misunderstanding.
	The essay addresses the topic and is appropriate for the given audience.
2	**A Score of 2 indicates an essay that attempts to communicate an idea but the idea is only partially formed and sometimess difficult to understand.**
	The essay may state a central idea or point of view but the focus is not maintained throughout the essay and the central idea is underdeveloped or simplistically reasoned.
	The organization of ideas lacks clarity and is only partially effective.
	Assertions are not always supported and the essay may contain irrelevant or insufficient details.
	Word usage is not always clear and may cause confusion or even misunderstanding.
	Sentences and paragraphs are not always well constructed and can be difficult to understand due to errors in sentence structure and grammar.
	The essay may not completely address the topic or be appropriate in style and content for the given audience.
1	**A Score of 1 indicates an essay that is difficult to understand and fails to communicate an idea to the intended audience.**
	The central idea or point of view of the essay is unclear and the essay is simplistically reasoned or contains serious flaws in reasoning.
	The essay lacks organization and coherence, leaving the reader confused.
	Assertions are not supported or are seriously underdeveloped and the essay contains irrelevant and/or insufficient details.
	Word usage is often unclear and confusing, leading to confusion or misunderstanding on the part of the reader.
	Sentences and paragraphs are not well constructed with many errors in paragraphing, sentence structure, and grammar that make understanding difficult.
	The essay may not completely address the topic or be appropriate in style and content for the given audience.
U	**This score indicates the essay cannot be scored. Reasons for this can be the essay was illegible, completely off topic, or not written in English.**
B	**This score indicates the essay response sheet was left blank.**

CHAPTER 12

PRACTICE TEST III

The practice test contained in this chapter will give you a very good idea of what you will face on test day. It includes separate tests for the three subject areas tested on the California Basic Educational Skills Test (CBEST): reading, mathematics, and writing. The questions for the reading and mathematics tests are in the multiple-choice format that you will encounter on the actual exam. For the writing test, you'll find two essay questions or writing prompts like the ones you'll be required to respond to on the real exam.

All the questions on this practice test are modeled after the questions on the actual CBEST. There are the same number of questions and the same type of questions as on the actual exam. They cover the same topics and are designed to be at the same level of difficulty. Explanations for the answers to the multiple-choice questions are given at the end of the practice test.

This test includes an answer sheet that you should remove from the book. Use this sheet to mark your answers to the multiple-choice questions.

When you are finished with the test, check your answers against the answer key provided at the end of this practice test. For any questions that you answered incorrectly or had difficulty with, carefully read the answer explanations at the end of this chapter. If you don't understand what you did wrong, you can use the review chapters of this book for review and further explanation.

This practice test best helps you prepare for the real test if you treat it as an actual examination. Here are some hints on how to take the test under conditions similar to those of the actual exam.

- Find a 4-hour time period when you will not be interrupted.
- Fill in the bubbles on the answer sheet with a no. 2 pencil; make sure the bubble is filled in completely and that there are no stray pencil marks on the sheet.
- Complete the entire test in one 4-hour session. If you want to take each subject area test contained in this practice test separately, you should allocate about 1 hour and 20 minutes per test. The actual test provides 4 hours, which you can allocate to the three tests in any way you wish.

Good luck!

■ **ANSWER SHEET**

PRACTICE TEST III
Answer Sheet for Multiple-Choice Questions

READING TEST

1 Ⓐ Ⓑ Ⓒ Ⓓ Ⓔ
2 Ⓐ Ⓑ Ⓒ Ⓓ Ⓔ
3 Ⓐ Ⓑ Ⓒ Ⓓ Ⓔ
4 Ⓐ Ⓑ Ⓒ Ⓓ Ⓔ
5 Ⓐ Ⓑ Ⓒ Ⓓ Ⓔ
6 Ⓐ Ⓑ Ⓒ Ⓓ Ⓔ
7 Ⓐ Ⓑ Ⓒ Ⓓ Ⓔ
8 Ⓐ Ⓑ Ⓒ Ⓓ Ⓔ
9 Ⓐ Ⓑ Ⓒ Ⓓ Ⓔ
10 Ⓐ Ⓑ Ⓒ Ⓓ Ⓔ
11 Ⓐ Ⓑ Ⓒ Ⓓ Ⓔ
12 Ⓐ Ⓑ Ⓒ Ⓓ Ⓔ
13 Ⓐ Ⓑ Ⓒ Ⓓ Ⓔ
14 Ⓐ Ⓑ Ⓒ Ⓓ Ⓔ
15 Ⓐ Ⓑ Ⓒ Ⓓ Ⓔ
16 Ⓐ Ⓑ Ⓒ Ⓓ Ⓔ
17 Ⓐ Ⓑ Ⓒ Ⓓ Ⓔ

18 Ⓐ Ⓑ Ⓒ Ⓓ Ⓔ
19 Ⓐ Ⓑ Ⓒ Ⓓ Ⓔ
20 Ⓐ Ⓑ Ⓒ Ⓓ Ⓔ
21 Ⓐ Ⓑ Ⓒ Ⓓ Ⓔ
22 Ⓐ Ⓑ Ⓒ Ⓓ Ⓔ
23 Ⓐ Ⓑ Ⓒ Ⓓ Ⓔ
24 Ⓐ Ⓑ Ⓒ Ⓓ Ⓔ
25 Ⓐ Ⓑ Ⓒ Ⓓ Ⓔ
26 Ⓐ Ⓑ Ⓒ Ⓓ Ⓔ
27 Ⓐ Ⓑ Ⓒ Ⓓ Ⓔ
28 Ⓐ Ⓑ Ⓒ Ⓓ Ⓔ
29 Ⓐ Ⓑ Ⓒ Ⓓ Ⓔ
30 Ⓐ Ⓑ Ⓒ Ⓓ Ⓔ
31 Ⓐ Ⓑ Ⓒ Ⓓ Ⓔ
32 Ⓐ Ⓑ Ⓒ Ⓓ Ⓔ
33 Ⓐ Ⓑ Ⓒ Ⓓ Ⓔ
34 Ⓐ Ⓑ Ⓒ Ⓓ Ⓔ

35 Ⓐ Ⓑ Ⓒ Ⓓ Ⓔ
36 Ⓐ Ⓑ Ⓒ Ⓓ Ⓔ
37 Ⓐ Ⓑ Ⓒ Ⓓ Ⓔ
38 Ⓐ Ⓑ Ⓒ Ⓓ Ⓔ
39 Ⓐ Ⓑ Ⓒ Ⓓ Ⓔ
40 Ⓐ Ⓑ Ⓒ Ⓓ Ⓔ
41 Ⓐ Ⓑ Ⓒ Ⓓ Ⓔ
42 Ⓐ Ⓑ Ⓒ Ⓓ Ⓔ
43 Ⓐ Ⓑ Ⓒ Ⓓ Ⓔ
44 Ⓐ Ⓑ Ⓒ Ⓓ Ⓔ
45 Ⓐ Ⓑ Ⓒ Ⓓ Ⓔ
46 Ⓐ Ⓑ Ⓒ Ⓓ Ⓔ
47 Ⓐ Ⓑ Ⓒ Ⓓ Ⓔ
48 Ⓐ Ⓑ Ⓒ Ⓓ Ⓔ
49 Ⓐ Ⓑ Ⓒ Ⓓ Ⓔ
50 Ⓐ Ⓑ Ⓒ Ⓓ Ⓔ

MATHEMATICS TEST

1 Ⓐ Ⓑ Ⓒ Ⓓ Ⓔ
2 Ⓐ Ⓑ Ⓒ Ⓓ Ⓔ
3 Ⓐ Ⓑ Ⓒ Ⓓ Ⓔ
4 Ⓐ Ⓑ Ⓒ Ⓓ Ⓔ
5 Ⓐ Ⓑ Ⓒ Ⓓ Ⓔ
6 Ⓐ Ⓑ Ⓒ Ⓓ Ⓔ
7 Ⓐ Ⓑ Ⓒ Ⓓ Ⓔ
8 Ⓐ Ⓑ Ⓒ Ⓓ Ⓔ
9 Ⓐ Ⓑ Ⓒ Ⓓ Ⓔ
10 Ⓐ Ⓑ Ⓒ Ⓓ Ⓔ
11 Ⓐ Ⓑ Ⓒ Ⓓ Ⓔ
12 Ⓐ Ⓑ Ⓒ Ⓓ Ⓔ
13 Ⓐ Ⓑ Ⓒ Ⓓ Ⓔ
14 Ⓐ Ⓑ Ⓒ Ⓓ Ⓔ
15 Ⓐ Ⓑ Ⓒ Ⓓ Ⓔ
16 Ⓐ Ⓑ Ⓒ Ⓓ Ⓔ
17 Ⓐ Ⓑ Ⓒ Ⓓ Ⓔ

18 Ⓐ Ⓑ Ⓒ Ⓓ Ⓔ
19 Ⓐ Ⓑ Ⓒ Ⓓ Ⓔ
20 Ⓐ Ⓑ Ⓒ Ⓓ Ⓔ
21 Ⓐ Ⓑ Ⓒ Ⓓ Ⓔ
22 Ⓐ Ⓑ Ⓒ Ⓓ Ⓔ
23 Ⓐ Ⓑ Ⓒ Ⓓ Ⓔ
24 Ⓐ Ⓑ Ⓒ Ⓓ Ⓔ
25 Ⓐ Ⓑ Ⓒ Ⓓ Ⓔ
26 Ⓐ Ⓑ Ⓒ Ⓓ Ⓔ
27 Ⓐ Ⓑ Ⓒ Ⓓ Ⓔ
28 Ⓐ Ⓑ Ⓒ Ⓓ Ⓔ
29 Ⓐ Ⓑ Ⓒ Ⓓ Ⓔ
30 Ⓐ Ⓑ Ⓒ Ⓓ Ⓔ
31 Ⓐ Ⓑ Ⓒ Ⓓ Ⓔ
32 Ⓐ Ⓑ Ⓒ Ⓓ Ⓔ
33 Ⓐ Ⓑ Ⓒ Ⓓ Ⓔ
34 Ⓐ Ⓑ Ⓒ Ⓓ Ⓔ

35 Ⓐ Ⓑ Ⓒ Ⓓ Ⓔ
36 Ⓐ Ⓑ Ⓒ Ⓓ Ⓔ
37 Ⓐ Ⓑ Ⓒ Ⓓ Ⓔ
38 Ⓐ Ⓑ Ⓒ Ⓓ Ⓔ
39 Ⓐ Ⓑ Ⓒ Ⓓ Ⓔ
40 Ⓐ Ⓑ Ⓒ Ⓓ Ⓔ
41 Ⓐ Ⓑ Ⓒ Ⓓ Ⓔ
42 Ⓐ Ⓑ Ⓒ Ⓓ Ⓔ
43 Ⓐ Ⓑ Ⓒ Ⓓ Ⓔ
44 Ⓐ Ⓑ Ⓒ Ⓓ Ⓔ
45 Ⓐ Ⓑ Ⓒ Ⓓ Ⓔ
46 Ⓐ Ⓑ Ⓒ Ⓓ Ⓔ
47 Ⓐ Ⓑ Ⓒ Ⓓ Ⓔ
48 Ⓐ Ⓑ Ⓒ Ⓓ Ⓔ
49 Ⓐ Ⓑ Ⓒ Ⓓ Ⓔ
50 Ⓐ Ⓑ Ⓒ Ⓓ Ⓔ

1   1

READING TEST

TEST DIRECTIONS: Read each passage and answer the multiple–choice questions that follow. For each question, choose the one best answer from the answer choices provided. Mark each answer on the answer sheet provided.

    You may work on the questions in any order you choose. You have 4 hours to complete all three sections (mathematics, reading, and writing) of the CBEST.

1 ▮▮▮▮▮▮▮▮▮▮▮▮▮▮▮▮▮▮▮▮▮▮▮▮▮▮▮▮▮▮▮▮▮▮ **1**

Read the passage below and answer the five questions that follow.

Lemurs are small primates native to Madagascar and its surrounding islands. There are about 50 species of lemur of varying sizes, and all but one species live in trees and use all four limbs to climb and leap from tree to tree, using their long tails for balance. They eat mainly plants and some insects, but the tiny dwarf and mouse lemurs also eat some smaller animals. Lemurs also differ in their living habits. Some of them are nocturnal, and some are active during the day. Nocturnal lemurs usually live alone, while *diurnal* lemurs tend to live in groups.

Most of the existing species of lemur are considered endangered or threatened. Some larger species of lemur have already gone extinct, before lemurs were as protected as they are now by anti-hunting laws. However, the survival of many remaining lemurs is still threatened by deforestation.

1. Some lemurs are *diurnal*. The meaning of the word is best defined as

    A. active during the night.
    B. active during the day.
    C. living primarily in trees.
    D. living in groups.
    E. eat mainly plants.

2. According to the passage, one benefit of a lemur's long tail is

    A. it helps them carry their young.
    B. it helps them move easily in trees.
    C. it helps them ward off predators.
    D. it helps them pick food.
    E. it helps them attract a mate.

3. According to the passage, deforestation

    A. is a bigger threat than hunting.
    B. cannot be stopped in Madagascar.
    C. only affects one species of lemur.
    D. is the sole cause of the lemurs being endangered.
    E. threatens the lemurs' ability to survive.

4. Which of the following best presents the organizational structure of the main topics addressed in this passage?

    A. I. Where to find lemurs
        II. Why it is so hard to find them now
    B. I. The habitat of lemurs
        II. Deforestation threatens their habitat
    C. I. Animals of Madagascar
        II. Survival of wildlife on Madagascar
    D. I. Basic facts about lemurs
        II. Their endangered status today
    E. I. Where to find lemurs
        II. The habitat of lemurs

5. The author's intent in writing this passage is to

    A. extol how entertaining it can be to watch lemurs.
    B. outline the precise scientific classifications of lemurs.
    C. describe how lemurs are the dominant form of wildlife in Madagascar.
    D. plead for action to save the lemurs.
    E. tell about the living habits and threats faced by lemurs.

Read the passage below and answer the three questions that follow.

The Centers for Disease Control and Prevention (CDC) is always busy monitoring health issues and sending out regular warnings to make sure people know of any impending threats. One of the most recent warnings, however, caught Americans by surprise. The CDC announced that one of today's most under recognized public health problems is sleep loss. It is estimated that between 50 and 70 million Americans suffer from this problem.

_____.

If you do not get enough sleep on a regular basis, you run an increased risk of obesity, diabetes, high blood pressure, stroke, cardiovascular disease, depression, cigarette smoking, and excessive drinking.

6. Which sentence, if inserted into the blank line in the passage, would best fit the development of the passage?

    A. Unfortunately, instead of sleeping, many kids stay up late at night to surf the Internet or watch television.
    B. Adequate sleep is essential to good mental and physical health.
    C. Children need more sleep than adults.
    D. People get less sleep in summer when days are longer.
    E. Sleep loss is more prevalent in populations with lower income.

7. The main idea of this passage is

    A. the CDC keeps all eye out for new, potentially threatening health issues.
    B. that the number Americans who don't get adequate sleep is 50 to 70 million.
    C. adults need seven to nine hours of sleep a night.
    D. a lack of adequate sleep is becoming a major national health problem.
    E. sleep loss is the most underrecognized public health problem today.

8. All of the following are potential risks from inadequate sleep EXCEPT

    A. high blood pressure,
    B. obesity.
    C. diabetes.
    D. depression,
    E. cancer.

GO ON TO THE NEXT PAGE.

Read the passage below and answer the five questions that follow.

Until the twentieth century, art in America was dominated by romanticism. In the nineteenth century, the Hudson River Valley school of painters turned for their inspiration almost entirely to the beauty of nature—the wilderness, mountains, and sea.

During the first decade of the twentieth century in the United States, a group of artists known as the progressives revolted against romanticism and its focus on *idyllic* scenes of nature. Led by Robert Henri, the progressives tried to capture the architectural and industrial ugliness of America's urban landscapes in the industrial age. But it was the impact of this new age on human beings that the progressives were most interested in portraying.

Initially, the political and art establishments refused to accept the progressives. But the progressives finally gained acceptance in the art world with New York City's Armory Show in 1913. It was at this show that their paintings, along with those of the European painters Picasso, Matisse, and Gauguin, who were already widely known in Europe, launched the modernist era of art in the United States.

9. In this passage, the author's attitude toward progressives is

   A. factual.
   B. supportive.
   C. critical.
   D. passionate.
   E. argumentative.

10. As used in this passage, the word *idyllic* most nearly means

    A. abstract.
    B. brilliant.
    C. spiritual.
    D. thoughtful.
    E. idealized.

11. A progressive painter of the early twentieth century in the United States was most likely to paint

    A. a seascape.
    B. a beautiful landscape.
    C. a person working in a factory.
    D. a religious work of art.
    E. a portrait.

12. Paintings created by the progressives

    A. appeared in the Armory Show of 1913.
    B. immediately appealed to the art establishment, which was eager for change.
    C. were unlike those of Robert Henri.
    D. focused more on scenery than people.
    E. portrayed idealized scenes.

13. This passage is mainly about the

    A. ugliness of the American urban landscape as an inspiration for art.
    B. influence of the Hudson River Valley school on modern art.
    C. progressive movement and the rise of modern American art.
    D. influence of the Armory Show of 1913.
    E. elitism of the Hudson River Valley school.

Read the passage below and answer the two questions that follow.

Although helium is one of the most common elements in the universe, it makes up only a small fraction of the Earth's composition. The element can be found in natural gas deposits as well as in the atmosphere. In the atmosphere it accounts for only about 5 parts per million of the air. Because helium is so light, it is constantly escaping from the atmosphere and drifting into space.

14. Which of the following pieces of additional information about helium is NOT relevant to the main idea expressed in this passage?

    A. Helium makes up 0.00052% of the earth's atmosphere.
    B. Helium is used to cool superconducting magnets.
    C. Helium accounts for 24% of the mass of our galaxy.
    D. Helium is one of the primary components of the stars, including the sun.
    E. Helium exists in gas form.

15. The author's purpose in writing the paragraph was most likely to

    A. convince readers to conserve helium.
    B. encourage more funding for research regarding helium.
    C. explain why helium balloons rise.
    D. inform nonscientific readers about helium.
    E. assure readers that the percentage of helium in the air is so small that it is not toxic to humans.

Read the passage below and answer the five questions that follow.

The main function of a building is to provide a safe shelter and living space. Beyond this function, however, what should be the goal of architecture? To impress people? To glorify the architect or owner? To create something new for its own sake? An increasing number of architects today—myself included—believe that the *overriding* goal should be to elevate the human spirit. Architecture designed with this goal in mind is known as organic architecture. While the "organic" label is new, the principle is centuries old. The current revival of *organic* architecture actually began in the twentieth century with the work of architects such as Frank Lloyd Wright and Spain's Antonio Gaudi.

GO ON TO THE NEXT PAGE.

Organic architecture should not be confused with *green* architecture, in which the primary design concern is with a structure's environmental cost in terms of the natural resources used to build and maintain it. Also, unlike *feng shui* design, which dictates that a building should conform to certain rules of proportion and direction, there's no objective test for whether a building is organic. If people feel more alive in and around it, or even just looking at pictures of it, then it can be called organic.

16. In the passage, the author's primary concern is to
   A. compare various forms of architecture.
   B. explain the meaning of "organic architecture."
   C. describe a typical organic building.
   D. criticize green architecture.
   E. give examples of architects whose work was organic.

17. Which of the following would the author agree should be the most important factor in designing a building?
   A. Its environmental cost
   B. Its energy efficiency
   C. Its overall appearance
   D. How much it costs to build
   E. Its effect on a person's mood

18. As it is used in the passage, the word *overriding* is best defined as
   A. most aggressive.
   B. accidental.
   C. quickest.
   D. simplest.
   E. primary.

19. A building designed to use energy only from the sun is an example of
   A. organic architecture.
   B. green architecture.
   C. natural architecture.
   D. elemental architecture.
   E. *feng shui* architecture.

20. Which of the following would probably be most important to an architect applying *feng shui* to a building's design?
   A. How to heat and cool the inside of the building
   B. Whether the building looks like nearby structures
   C. A room's ceiling height compared to its length and width
   D. The personal tastes and preferences of the building's owner
   E. How many floors the building should have

Read the passage below and answer the three questions that follow.

For years, aromatherapy has been touted as a safe and natural way to relax and even heal. Essential oils from a variety of scents have been added to candles and sprays to help people feel better. However, a recent study performed at Ohio State University says that these smells, as nice as they may be, do not do a thing to improve people's health.

To find out if aromatherapy actually works, the researchers tested two of the most popular scents: lemon and lavender. First, test subjects had their heart rate, blood pressure, stress hormones, and immune function measured and noted. Next, they were subjected to mild stressors and then told to sniff one of the scents to see if the scent would help them to relax. Finally, all the subjects were tested again to look for improvement. There were no significant changes noted.

Of course, this does not necessarily prove that aromatherapy is worthless, either. It was just one study, pitted against the opinions of thousands of consumers who swear by peppermint on their pillow for an upset stomach or vanilla for a headache. More tests will be done, but, in the meantime, a whiff of lavender, lemon, or other scents will certainly do no harm—and can be quite pleasant at the same time.

21. What is the best title for this passage?
   A. Lavender Help for Headaches
   B. The Importance of Avoiding Aromatherapy
   C. Great Aroma Yes, Health Boost No
   D. The Benefits of Lemon Pillow Spray
   E. Aroma and Mood

22. Why did the researchers decide to test lemon and lavender?
   A. They were the two easiest scents to find.
   B. They were two of the most popular scents.
   C. They were the two scents that helped with headaches.
   D. They were the two least expensive scents available.
   E. They were the two most common scents available in stores.

23. Which of the following is the best conclusion you can draw from this passage?
   A. Aromatherapy is not a legitimate therapy by anyone's standards.
   B. Lemon and lavender are not healthy scents to inhale or use.
   C. More studies are needed to determine if aromatherapy is truly beneficial.
   D. Adding aromatherapy to regular treatment will help speed healing.
   E. The scent of vanilla can never help a headache.

Read the passage below and answer the five questions that follow.

Sometimes, a child loses interest in a toy or a game—even one with which he/she was obsessed—and moves on to a new stage in life. This can happen suddenly and inexplicably.

During my ninth and tenth years, I became obsessed with playing buttons. We would flip around brass buttons from the uniforms of soldiers on some patch of unpaved ground with a little pit for a billiard pocket. —————————————————. I would spend hours in some secluded spot developing skill for the sport. I gambled *passionately* and was continually counting how many buttons had won.

GO ON TO THE NEXT PAGE.

But one day I wearied of it all and traded my entire hoard for a pocket knife. "Don't you care for buttons any more?" my mother inquired.

"I can't bear the sight of them," I replied.

24. Which sentence, if inserted into the blank line in the selection above, would best fit the development of the passage?

A. My mother was very patient.
B. My father didn't have time to play with me.
C. My own pockets were usually filled with these buttons.
D. It was mainly the boys who played buttons, but some girls played, too.
E. Playing buttons was a popular game among my friends.

25. When was the author obsessed with the game of buttons?

A. In ninth and tenth grades
B. When he was nine and ten years old
C. Throughout his childhood
D. For nine or ten years
E. When he was nineteen years old

26. As a youngster the author probably

A. played buttons on the floor of his house.
B. became a skilled button player without practice.
C. wagered his buttons when playing against others.
D. played buttons against his mother's wishes.
E. played buttons only with boys.

27. As it is used in the passage, the word *passionately* is best defined as

A. angrily.
B. endlessly.
C. happily.
D. greedily.
E. enthusiastically.

28. Which of the following best describes the technique the author uses in this passage to make his point?

A. Explaining through the use of a personal example
B. Asking a question and then answering it
C. Using different examples to back up a point
D. Stating arguments on both sides of an issue
E. Providing a series of statistics about a topic

Read the passage below and answer the five questions that follow.

Humanity has only just begun its conquest of nature. As astronomy assures us, in all probability we have, not centuries or even thousands of years, but millions of years of earthly destiny to realize.

Barely 3,000 years of scientific research have brought the ends of the earth, and even the solar system, to our doorstep. Just 300 years of research have made us masters where we were slaves—of distance, of the air and oceans, of space, and of many of the most dreaded aspects of disease and suffering. Isn't it odd that life today would seem inconceivable without airplanes, which practically unheard of a century ago?

What will the future bring humankind? Things too vast to grasp today. Things that would make the imaginings of today's most *eminent* scientists and science-fiction novelists seem ordinary by comparison. The future will bring us amazing control over things that seem to us almost sacred—over life and death and development and thought itself. Although this prospect might seem disturbing, through all that may happen to humankind, we can be sure that we will remain human, and so we can face the future confident that it will be better than the present.

29. The author's overall attitude toward science is

A. fearful.
B. critical.
C. enthusiastic.
D. skeptical.
E. thoughtful.

30. As used in the selection, the word *eminent* is best defined as

A. unusual.
B. distinguished.
C. intelligent.
D. articulate.
E. popular.

31. The author would be most likely to agree that it is human nature to

A. want to improve our lives.
B. dwell too much on the past.
C. believe we are smarter than we really are.
D. ignore scientific evidence.
E. predict scientific developments.

32. In the third paragraph of the selection, the author uses which of the following techniques?

A. Asking a question and then answering that question
B. Describing the impact of certain historical events
C. Asking a rhetorical question
D. Evaluating opposing views
E. Asking a series of questions

33. Which of the following is the best title for the selection?

A. Scientific Advancements of the Last 3,000 Years
B. The Great Promise of Scientific Research
C. Why Society Must Encourage Scientific Progress
D. A Bleak Past but a Bright Future for Scientific Research
E. What We Should Fear from Scientific Research

GO ON TO THE NEXT PAGE.

Refer to the table below to answer the question that follows.

Train Schedule

Train destinations	Charleston	Aiken	Greenville
Departure times	9:03 a.m.	9:30 a.m.	10:00 a.m.
Arrival times	11:07 a.m.	10:46 a.m.	12:11 a.m.

34. If you caught the train to Aiken, about what time would you need to ask someone to meet you at the station in Aiken?

    A. 10:00 a.m.
    B. 11:00 a.m.
    C. 12:15 p.m.
    D. 10:00 p.m.
    E. 10:45 p.m.

Review the excerpt from a book's index below and answer the two questions that follow.

```
Credit, 225–236
Credit bureau, 237–241
Credit card, 259–290
        Types, 261–277
                American express, 263–266
                Discover, 267–270
                Mastercard, 270–273
                Visa, 274–277
        Credit card fees, 278–290
                annual fee, 280–281
                cash advance fee, 282
                international transaction fee, 282–283
                late fee, 284–288
                overdraft fee, 289–290
Credit rating, 256–258
Credit reporting companies, 242–255
        Equifax, 244–247
        Experian, 248–251
        Transunion, 252–255
Credit score, 291–298
Credit union, 299–302
```

35. On which pages should one look to find information about credit reports?

    A. 225–236
    B. 237–241
    C. 256–258
    D. 242–255
    E. 291–298

36. A reader wishes to find information about a fee for making an ATM withdrawal in Mexico. On which pages should the reader look for this information?

    A. 259–290
    B. 278–290
    C. 280–281
    D. 282
    E. 282–283

Read the passage below and answer the four questions that follow.

Human organs available for transplants are in short supply in the United States. The waiting list exceeds 100,000 people who desperately need a healthy organ to replace one of their own that is failing.

Some U.S. lawmakers propose legalizing the selling of human organs in some way to encourage more people to donate. —————, one proposed law would allow death-row prisoners to avoid execution by donating bone marrow or a kidney. Supporters of these kind of laws often *invoke* what they believe is a fundamental right to make decisions regarding one's own body. —————, many opponents are concerned that legalizing sale of organs would result in just one more way for the rich to exploit the poor. Other opponents argue that selling human body parts is morally wrong because it reduces humans to saleable commodities.

37. Which words, if inserted *in order* into the blank lines in the reading selection, would best help the reader understand what the writer wants to communicate?

    A. For example; However
    B. However; Therefore
    C. So; Nevertheless
    D. Therefore; Finally
    E. In addition; Furthermore

38. As it is used in the passage, the word *invoke* is best defined as

    A. believe in.
    B. oppose.
    C. call attention to.
    D. legalize.
    E. question.

39. Which statement is best supported by data in the reading selection?

    A. The demand for human organs increases with each passing year.
    B. The supply of human organs is far smaller than the demand for organs for transplanting.
    C. The supply of human organs is increasing.
    D. The demand for human organs will always outpace supply.
    E. There will always be a demand for organs for transplanting.

40. In the passage, the author

    A. supports legalization of the selling of human organs.
    B. criticizes U.S. lawmakers for outlawing sales of human organs.
    C. proposes a law to help the supply of human organs meet demand.
    D. identifies arguments for and against a proposed law.
    E. laments that there is no solution to the shortage of organs available for transplanting.

GO ON TO THE NEXT PAGE.

Read the passage below and answer the four questions that follow.

[1]Funnel cake, a staple of outdoor summer activities, originated in the Pennsylvania Dutch region of the United States. [2]This region is located in southeastern Pennsylvania. [3]Depending on the region in which a person grew up, one may or may not have seen funnel cake in concessions stands as a child. [4]——————, almost everyone who has been to a baseball game or carnival has seen elephant ears or fried dough, which are similar. [5]The difference between these desserts and funnel cake is that funnel cake is made with batter, not dough. [6]The batter is poured in a circular pattern into hot oil, where it is cooked very quickly. [7]—————— it is generally covered with powdered sugar or chocolate and served hot on a paper plate. [8]It's a delicious treat and large enough to share with at least one friend.

41. Which words, if inserted *in order* into the blank lines in the reading selection, would best help the reader understand the idea the writer wants to communicate?

    A. However; Then
    B. Without a doubt; So
    C. Obviously; However
    D. Of course; When
    E. Furthermore; On the other hand

42. Which of the following sentences of the passage best expresses an opinion rather than a fact?

    A. Sentence 3
    B. Sentence 4
    C. Sentence 5
    D. Sentence 7
    E. Sentence 8

43. Which of the following sentences is least relevant to the main idea the author is communicating?

    A. Sentence 2
    B. Sentence 3
    C. Sentence 5
    D. Sentence 6
    E. Sentence 7

44. What was the main purpose of the author in writing this paragraph?

    A. To get more people to buy his funnel cakes
    B. To explain what a funnel cake is
    C. To inform people of the Pennsylvania Dutch region
    D. To explain the difference between elephant ears and funnel cake
    E. To convince people that funnel cake is a delicious treat

Read the passage below and answer the four questions that follow.

Almost anyone who lives in a place where the winter months are mostly dark and rainy or snowy knows what it is like to yearn longingly for "just a few *rays*." For some people, however, this feeling is much more than a simple longing; it is a physical and emotional need. These people suffer from seasonal affective disorder (SAD).

Although in the past the experience has been put down to nothing more than "winter blues," more and more physicians are recognizing the fact that for some, it is much more than a mood swing. Those with SAD not only get depressed, they struggle with *lethargy* and chronic fatigue, often to the point of impairing their daily lives. Other symptoms include anxiety, social withdrawal, appetite changes, weight gain, and insomnia.

If untreated, SAD can actually lead to substance abuse or even suicide. Treatment focuses primarily on light therapy but may be supplemented with medications and psychotherapy.

45. What is the best title for this passage?

    A. Treatments for SAD
    B. The "Winter Blues" Are Exaggerated
    C. When Sadness Comes with the Season
    D. Symptoms of SAD
    E. SAD: Mood Swings

46. What does the word *rays* mean as used in the passage?

    A. Waves
    B. Energy
    C. Sunshine
    D. Warmth
    E. Breezes

47. The word *lethargy* as used in the second paragraph of the passage can best be defined as

    A. sluggishness.
    B. irritability.
    C. energy.
    D. starvation.
    E. clumsiness.

48. Based on this passage, what is the primary treatment for SAD?

    A. Medication
    B. Surgery
    C. Psychotherapy
    D. Light therapy
    E. Physical therapy

GO ON TO THE NEXT PAGE.

Review the table of contents below and answer the two questions that follow.

49. In which part of the book would information about commas, colons, and semicolons be found?

   A. Part One
   B. Part Two
   C. Part Three
   D. Part Four
   E. The Index

50. A reader wants to know the differences between the words "there," "they're," and "their." Where would the reader find this information?

   A. Part One
   B. Part Two
   C. Part Three
   D. Part Four
   E. The Index

2 2

MATHEMATICS TEST

TEST DIRECTIONS: Carefully read the multiple-choice questions that follow. For each question, choose the one best answer from the answer choices provided. Mark each answer on the answer sheet provided.

You may work on the questions in any order you choose. You have 4 hours to complete all three sections (mathematics, reading, and writing) of the CBEST.

2 ▬▬▬▬▬▬▬▬▬▬▬▬▬▬▬▬▬▬ **2**

1. John obtained scores of 90, 85, 78, 83, 91, 89, and 86 on a series of seven assignments. What was his average score on the assignments?

   A. 86
   B. 85
   C. 84
   D. 83
   E. 82

2. Boys comprise 60% of the graduating class of North High School. If there are a total of 430 students in the class, how many girls are in the graduating class?

   A. 74
   B. 86
   C. 172
   D. 215
   E. 223

3. A plane flew over the city of South Bay at 3:00 and over Mountain City at 3:30. Maria measures the distance between the two cities on her map and finds it is 2 inches. The map's scale is 1 inch = 150 miles. How fast must the plane be going?

   A. 600 miles per hour
   B. 450 miles per hour
   C. 300 miles per hour
   D. 150 miles per hour
   E. 100 miles per hour

4. Paulo wants to find out what kind of gas mileage his new car is getting. Which of the following is the most appropriate unit of measure for computing this?

   A. Mileage
   B. Miles
   C. Miles per gallon
   D. Square miles
   E. Miles per hour

5. Ms. Bennett is going to buy ribbon to tie around packages the students in her class are making. There are 27 students in Ms. Bennett's class and each is going to wrap a ribbon around a box that is 2 feet around. An additional 10 inches are need for a bow for each box. How much ribbon will Ms. Bennett need to buy?

   A. 76 feet, 6 inches
   B. 64 feet, 10 inches
   C. 64 feet, 4 inches
   D. 49 feet, 6 inches
   E. 49 feet, 4 inches

6. The school's lunchroom is being extended. An addition being built will extend the rectangular lunchroom so that the length is 28 feet longer than it was. The width will remain the same. How much larger will the perimeter of the new room be compared to the old one.

   A. 28 feet longer
   B. 56 feet longer
   C. 112 feet longer
   D. 14 feet longer
   E. 44 feet longer

7. The area of a rectangular sandbox in the school playground is 66 square feet. The width of the sandbox is 6 feet. What is the length?

   A. 36 feet
   B. 14 feet
   C. 12 feet
   D. 11 feet
   E. 9 feet

8. If donut holes cost 45 cents for two, how much does it cost to buy 10 donut holes?

   A. $0.90
   B. $1.45
   C. $2.25
   D. $4.50
   E. $4.65

9. If Jacob spends 45 minutes per day playing video games, how long does he play in one week?

   A. 3 hours, 45 minutes
   B. 4 hours
   C. 4 hours, 15 minutes
   D. 5 hours
   E. 5 hours, 15 minutes

10. On a single roll of a die, what is the probability of NOT getting a 2?

    A. $1/6$
    B. $2/6$
    C. $3/6$
    D. $4/6$
    E. $5/6$

11. Linda is making a smoothie recipe that calls for five parts berries to four parts yogurt. If she is putting in 10 cups of yogurt for a big party, how many cups of berries will she need?

    A. 2.5
    B. 5
    C. 7
    D. 10
    E. 12.5

12. Michelle and Rhonda take two different paths through a canyon. If Rhonda's path is 5,167 feet and Michelle's path is 7,298 feet, how many feet longer is Michelle's path?

    A. 1,091 feet
    B. 2,131 feet
    C. 2,366 feet
    D. 3,036 feet
    E. 12,465 feet

GO ON TO THE NEXT PAGE.

13. Compute 35.2×4.16. The correct answer is:
   A. 1464.32
   B. 146.432
   C. 176.212
   D. 197.12
   E. 1971.2

14. The Sandy River was 7.8 feet above flood stage on May 4. On June 4, the river was 5.9 feet below flood stage. How many feet did the water level drop between May 4 and June 4?
   A. 1.9 feet
   B. 2.1 feet
   C. 2.9 feet
   D. 13.7 feet
   E. 14.7 feet

15. The median score on the final exam in Mr. Lee's class was 72. This score indicates that
   A. the average score was 72.
   B. more students got a score of 72 than any other score.
   C. half the students scored higher and half scored lower than 72.
   D. the score of 72 was midway between the highest score in the class and the lowest.
   E. half the students got a score of 72.

16. The expression below

$$-8 - (-45) + 12$$

   is equal to which of the following?
   A. -41
   B. 41
   C. 49
   D. -65
   E. 65

17. Eight friends have challenged each other to see who can lose the most weight. The table below shows the change in each person's weight one month later.

Name	Weight Change
Madison	+2 pounds
Miles	−5 pounds
Tatiana	−1.5 pounds
Jude	+0.5 pounds
Avery	−0.5 pounds
Isablella	−2.5 pounds
Scott	0 pound
Rose	−3 pounds

   What was the average weight loss among the group?
   A. 1.25 pounds
   B. 1.5 pounds
   C. 1.75 pounds
   D. 2.25 pounds
   E. 2.5 pounds

18. If shirts at a garage sale cost $0.75 each, how many shirts can Abby buy for $15?
   A. 10
   B. 20
   C. 30
   D. 40
   E. 50

19. Find the tens digit in the multiplier below.

$$240 \times \underline{\quad}8 = 13{,}920$$

   What number correctly fills in the blank?
   A. 3
   B. 4
   C. 5
   D. 6
   E. 7

20. A member of the cross-country team ran $22^{1/5}$ miles last week and $26^{3/8}$ miles this week. How many more miles did she/he run this week than last?
   A. $3^{3/4}$
   B. $4^{1/8}$
   C. $4^{2/3}$
   D. $4^{7/40}$
   E. $4^{13/40}$

21. Express $^{60}/_{12}$ as a percentage.
   A. 0.05%
   B. 0.5%
   C. 5%
   D. 50%
   E. 500%

22. If you add 2 ounces of water to a 16-ounce mixture consisting of equal amounts of milk and water, what portion of the resulting mixture is water?
   A. $^{3}/_{5}$
   B. $^{5}/_{9}$
   C. $^{5}/_{8}$
   D. $^{4}/_{9}$
   E. $^{7}/_{9}$

23. Which of the following expresses 65% as a decimal?
   A. 0.065
   B. 0.65
   C. 6.5
   D. 65
   E. 650

24. A box is 10 inches long, 8 inches wide, and 6 inches high. Claire needs to wrap two pieces of tape completely around the box—one piece will encircle the length of the box and one piece will encircle the width. How many inches of tape does she need? (Assume no overlap of tape.)
   A. 30 inches
   B. 48 inches
   C. 60 inches
   D. 64 inches
   E. 68 inches

GO ON TO THE NEXT PAGE.

25. Samantha is driving at 55 miles per hour. She sees the sign below:

Upham	25
Downing	59
Riverton	120

If she continues on the highway driving at the same speed, how far will she be from Upham in two hours?

A. 0 mile
B. 30 miles
C. 55 miles
D. 65 miles
E. 85 miles

26. If Ryan is 2 years older than four times the age of his dog, Pixie, which expression represents that relationship?

A. R = 4 + 2P
B. R = (2 + 4)P
C. R = $\dfrac{2+4}{P}$
D. R = 2 + 4P
E. R = $\dfrac{P}{2+4}$

27. Jamie's parents give her $10 for every A on her report card and $5 for every B. If she received $30 for her report card today and she made on A, how many Bs did she make?

A. 2
B. 3
C. 4
D. 5
E. 6

28. Henry ran 2 miles to the track, ran around the track 4 times, and then ran home, arriving at 8:00 p.m. He had run 13 miles total. What was Henry's average speed?

What information is necessary to solve the problem above?

A. The amount of time it took for him to run to the track
B. The amount of time it took for him to run from the track back home
C. The total length of the track
D. His average number of strides per minute
E. The time Henry left home

29. Anya ordered 20 sandwiches for her staff's meeting. The options were roast beef, ham, turkey, tuna, and roasted vegetable. Anya ordered 3 roasted vegetable, 6 tuna, and 3 ham sandwiches. How many turkey sandwiches did Anya order?

What information is required to solve this problem?

A. Whether Anya also ordered roast beef sandwiches
B. Whether Anya ordered more roast beef than turkey sandwiches
C. The number of roast beef sandwiches that Anya ordered

D. The number of tuna sandwiches that Anya ordered
E. Whether Anya ordered more roast beef sandwiches than roasted vegetable sandwiches

30. An orchard has 4 trees. The first tree has 46 apples, the second tree has 34 lemons, the third tree has 29 mangoes, and the fourth tree has 31 oranges. By the end of the day, 95 pieces of fruit have been picked.

Which of the following facts can be deduced from the information provided above?

A. More apples were pieked than oranges.
B. More lemons were picked than mangoes.
C. At least 1 lemon was picked.
D. At least 1 of each kind of fruit was picked.
E. At least 1 apple was picked.

31. The chart below shows a relationship between x and y. Refer to the chart to find the answer to the question that follows.

x	y
2	−7
3	−11
4	−15
5	−19

Given the relationship between x and y shown above, what would be the number that fits in the blank space in column y of the chart?

A. −14
B. −15
C. −16
D. 14
E. −17

32. Kendra swam one lap in S seconds, faster than Paul by 4 seconds. Which of the following represents the average lap time of the two swimmers?

A. S + 2
B. S − 2
C. S − 1
D. S + 4
E. S + 1

33. Ruth needs to tind ¾ of 3120. She takes (3120 ÷ 4) × 3. She could also have done which of the following:

A. .75 × 3120
B. 75 × 3120
C. .075 × 312
D. 3120 + ¾
E. 3120 + ¼

34. The expression 2¾ ÷ ⁷/₈ can also be written:

A. 2 × ¾ ÷ ⁷/₈
B. 2 × ¾ ÷ ⁸/₇
C. 1¼ × ⁷/₈
D. 1¼ ÷ ⁸/₇
E. 2¾ × ⁸/₇

GO ON TO THE NEXT PAGE.

35. The expression $x(y + z) + 5$ can also be written as
    A. $xy + (z + 5)$
    B. $xy + xz + 5x$
    C. $xy + xz + 5$
    D. $5xy + 5z$
    E. $5xy + z$

36. If there are three foreign cars for every two domestic cars in a parking lot, what percentage of the cars in the parking lot are domestic cars?
    A. 20%
    B. 33.3%
    C. 40%
    D. 60%
    E. 65%

37. The number 8 is what percent of 5?
    A. 62.5%
    B. 160%
    C. 160.5%
    D. 162.5%
    E. 200%

38. Compute $-407 \div 7.4$.
    A. -55
    B. -18
    C. -5.5
    D. 5.5
    E. 18

39. Which of the following is less than $^{13}/_{40}$?
    A. $^1/_3$
    B. $^7/_{20}$
    C. $^2/_5$
    D. $^3/_{10}$
    E. $^3/_7$

40. Which of the following numbers is between 782,056.99 and 782,833.11?
    A. 782,833.2
    B. 783,056.0
    C. 782,833.1
    D. 782,833.111
    E. 782,863.02

41. If the value of x is between $-2^3/_4$ and $1^1/_2$, which of the following could be x?
    A. $2^1/_2$
    B. $1^3/_4$
    C. $-2^1/_2$
    D. $-2^7/_8$
    E. $-2^{13}/_{16}$

42. Which of the following numbers is changed by rounding it to the nearest one-tenth?
    A. .28
    B. 25.0
    C. $3^1/_{10}$
    D. $14^2/_5$
    E. ???

43. Round each term to the nearest hundred and subtract 294,293 from 582,651. The answer is:
    A. 288,460
    B. 289,000
    C. 288,300
    D. 288,360
    E. 288,400

44.
> Keith orders take-out for lunch every day.
> - Keith orders Chinese food every Tuesday.
> - If it's raining any day of the week, he will order from the deli.
> - On Mondays and Fridays, he orders either Italian or sushi.

If it is not raining and it is Monday, which of the following statements could be true?
    A. Keith orders sushi.
    B. Keith orders Chinese.
    C. Keith orders from the deli.
    D. Keith orders either Italian or sushi.
    E. Keith does not order from the deli.

45.
> Beth has homework to complete in five subjects: social studies, math, science, English, and Spanish.
> - Beth must complete her science homework first.
> - Beth cannot complete her English homework before her math homework.
> - If Beth completes her Spanish homework second, then she completes her social studies homework last.

If Beth completes her math homework fourth, then it must be true that
    A. Beth completes her Spanish homework second.
    B. Beth completes her English homework first.
    C. Beth completes her science homework third.
    D. Beth completes her English homework last.
    E. Beth completes her social studies homework last.

46.
> - The pharmacy is five miles from the gas station.
> - The gas station is six miles from the burger joint.

Based on the information above, which of the following conclusions can be made?
    A. The pharmacy is 11 miles from the burger joint.
    B. The burger joint is not more than 11 miles from the pharmacy.
    C. The pharmacy is exactly 1 mile from the burger joint.
    D. The pharmacy is exactly 5 miles from the burger joint.
    E. The burger joint is exactly 6 miles from the pharmacy.

GO ON TO THE NEXT PAGE.

Refer to the table below to answer the question that follows.

Wine Sales for Vineyard X

	Cases Sold	Bottles Sold	Total Bottles
1997 Pinot Noir	5,437	15,229	80,473
1994 Pinot Gris	4,913	18,445	77,401
1991 Chardonnay	6,110	14,757	88,077
2001 Bordeaux	7,226	11,934	98,646

47. Which wine sold the largest percentage of bottles in cases?

A. 1997 Pinot Noir
B. 1994 Pinot Gris
C. 1991 Chardonnay
D. 2001 Bordeaux
E. Both A and D

Refer to the bar graph below to answer the question that follows.

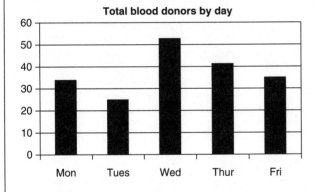

48. What is the approximate percent increase between the number of donors on Tuesday and the number of donors on Wednesday?

A. 25%
B. 50%
C. 100%
D. 150%
E. 200%

Refer to the pie chart below to answer the question that follows.

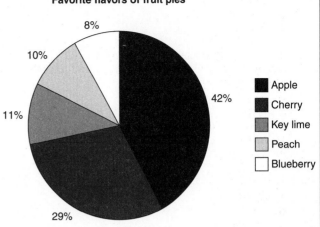

49. Which flavors of pies together are greater in popularity than apple?

A. Key lime, cherry
B. Peach, key lime, cherry
C. Peach, key lime, blueberry
D. Peach, cherry
E. Blueberry, cherry

Refer to the bar graph below to answer the question that follows.

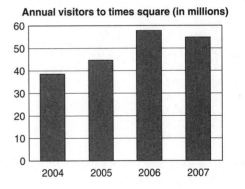

50. Based on the chart above, approximately how many more visitors went to Times Square in 2007 than in 2005?

A. 10 thousand
B. 100 thousand
C. 10 million
D. 20 million
E. 1 million

GO ON TO THE NEXT PAGE.

3 ■■ **3**

WRITING TEST

TEST DIRECTIONS: The writing section of the CBEST includes two topics that assess your ability to write effectively. You must write essays responding to *both* topics.

Be sure to write about the given topics; essays on other topics will not be graded. Your answer must completely address all parts of the topic. Your response must be in your own words and not plagiarized from some other source. Write as legibly as possible; your answer can be scored only if it is legible.

Make sure you read each topic carefully. Before you begin to write, take several minutes to organize your thoughts. You may use any space provided in the test booklet to make notes or outline your response. Write your essay on the writing response sheets provided.

Topic 1

U. S. historian and commentator Christopher Lasch said, "Nothing succeeds like the appearance of success." To what extent do you agree or disagree with this statement? Write an essay for an audience of educated adults, stating your position. Use logical arguments and specific examples to support your position.

RESPONSE SHEET FOR TOPIC 1

WRITING ESSAY

RESPONSE SHEET FOR TOPIC 1 (continued)

WRITING ESSAY

Topic 2

Schools are institutions dedicated to learning, but nearly everyone would agree that much—may be even most—learning takes place outside the classroom. In an essay addressed to educated adults, discuss how much of your own learning happened in the classroom and how much took place outside it. Which is most important? Use logical arguments and specific examples to support your position on this question.

RESPONSE SHEET FOR TOPIC 2

WRITING ESSAY

RESPONSE SHEET FOR TOPIC 2 (continued)

WRITING ESSAY

ANSWER KEY

PRACTICE TEST 3

Reading			Mathematics		
1. B	26. C		1. A	26. D
2. B	27. E		2. C	27. C
3. E	28. A		3. A	28. E
4. D	29. C		4. C	29. C
5. E	30. B		5. A	30. E
6. B	31. A		6. B	31. B
7. D	32. A		7. D	32. A
8. E	33. B		8. C	33. A
9. A	34. E		9. E	34. E
10. E	35. D		10. E	35. C
11. C	36. E		11. E	36. C
12. A	37. A		12. B	37. B
13. C	38. C		13. B	38. A
14. B	39. B		14. D	39. D
15. D	40. D		15. C	40. C
16. B	41. A		16. C	41. C
17. E	42. E		17. A	42. A
18. E	43. A		18. B	43. E
19. B	44. B		19. C	44. A
20. C	45. C		20. D	45. D
21. C	46. C		21. E	46. B
22. B	47. A		22. B	47. B
23. C	48. D		23. B	48. C
24. C	49. B		24. C	49. B
25. B	50. C		25. E	50. C

Explanations for the Practice Test 3

Reading Test

1. **Correct Choice: B.** Diurnal means active during the day or the opposite of nocturnal, which means active at night.

2. **Correct Choice: B.** The passage says they "leap from tree to tree, using their long tails for balance." Other uses for the tails were not mentioned in the passage.

3. **Correct Choice: E.** The last sentence of the passage states that deforestation is a threat to lemurs' survival.

4. **Correct Choice: D.** The first paragraph gives basic facts about lemurs—where they live, what they eat, their social habits, etc. The second paragraph discusses their endangered status including what's being done to protect them and why they are still endangered. This makes D the best answer choice. The first paragraph includes much more than where to find lemurs (answer choices A and E) or what their habitat is (answer choice B). Answer choice C is too broad—the passage is only about lemurs.

5. **Correct Choice: E.** The author explains how lemurs live and are now threatened with extinction. Answer choice D would be plausible in that the author probably wants to save the lemurs, but the author just gives facts and never makes a plea for action, making this answer choice incorrect.

6. **Correct Choice: B.** This sentence introduces the topic of how sleep relates to health and leads to the next sentence which names health risks associated with lack of sleep. Answer choices C, D, and E contain sentences not directly related to the content of the passage. The rant about kids watching too much TV or surfing the Internet (answer choice A) doesn't fit the development of the passage, which is entirely factual in nature and doesn't get into the topic of how people should or should not spend their time.

7. **Correct Choice: D.** The passage is about the lack of sleep being a major health problem. Answer choices A and B are supporting facts used by the author to make his point, but not the main idea of the passage. Exactly how much sleep people should get (answer choice C) is related to the passage's main idea, but not mentioned in this passage. Answer choice E is an exaggeration; sleep loss is *one* of the most underrecognized public health problems today, not the most.

8. **Correct Choice: E.** Cancer is not mentioned in this passage as a risk resulting from inadequate sleep. All the other answer choices are identified in the last sentence of the passage as being health risks related to the lack of sleep.

9. **Correct Choice: A.** The article gives factual information about the development of the progressive art movement. The author never says anything about whether she supports the movement or not (answer choice B). The author does not criticize progressives (answer choice C). She maintains a factual approach without ever becoming passionate (answer choice D) or argumentative (answer choice E).

10. **Correct Choice: E.** *Idyllic* in this context most closely means idealized. The progressives revolted against the romanticists, who chose to paint an idealized picture of the world, in which all appeared beautiful, ignoring life's ugly and unpleasant aspects.

11. **Correct Choice: C.** The author states that progressives were most interested in portraying the impact of the new industrial age on human beings. Beautiful landscapes and seascapes (answer choices A and B) are examples of "idyllic scenes of nature" that the author says the progressives were rebelling against, so it is unlikely they would paint these. Nothing in the passage indicates that the progressives were interested in religious subjects (answer choice D) or a portrait (answer choice E).

12. **Correct Choice: A.** The author tells us that the progressives gained a foothold into mainstream art at the Armory Show of 1913, where their paintings helped launch a new era in art. Other information in the passage contradicts the other answer choices, making all of them incorrect.

13. **Correct Choice: C.** The author talks about how the progressive movement emerged as a reaction to established art of the time and then how it gained prominence in the art world and launched the modernist era in American art. In regard to answer choice A, the ugliness of the American urban landscape was mentioned in the first paragraph as an inspiration for the progressive movement, but the passage is not mainly about

this topic. Similarly, the influence of the Armory Show of 1913 (answer choice D) is discussed in the second paragraph, but the passage is not mainly about this show. The influence of the Hudson River Valley school of painters (answer choice B) on modern art is not discussed. There is no mention of any elitism on the part of the Hudson River Valley school (answer choice E).

14. **Correct Choice: B.** The fact that helium is used to cool superconducting magnets has nothing to do with the central idea of the passage, which is that helium is rare on Earth although it is among the most abundant elements of the universe.

15. **Correct Choice: D.** The author's main purpose is to inform readers about helium. He is talking primarily to nonscientific readers who know nothing about helium. The author does not mention conservation or any dire consequences if we fail to conserve helium (answer choice A). Nor does the author mention either scientific research (answer choice B), helium balloons (answer choice C), or the aspect of toxicity (answer choice E).

16. **Correct Choice: B.** In the first paragraph, the author provides a basic definition of the term "organic architecture." Then, in the second paragraph, the author distinguishes organic architecture from green architecture and *feng shui* to help the reader understand what organic architecture is, and what it is not. Comparison of various forms of architecture (answer choice A) is not her objective; she does this only in the second paragraph and only to better define organic architecture. The example of architects whose work was organic (answer choice E) is mentioned only in passing.

17. **Correct Choice: E.** In the first paragraph, the author informs us that she is an architect who, like a growing number of architects today, believes that one of the chief goals of architecture is to elevate the human spirit. Accordingly, the author would probably agree that how a building affect's a person's mood is very important.

18. **Correct Choice: E.** In the context of this passage, overriding can best be defined as primary. This is the only word among the answer choices that makes sense in the context of the sentence as well as the passage as a whole.

19. **Correct Choice: B.** The goal of green architecture is to design a building in a way that helps conserve natural resources. Using solar energy would be consistent with that goal. It would be possible for such a building also to be an example of organic architecture (choice A). But this is not as good an answer as choice B since energy conservation is a defining characteristic of green architecture, not organic architecture.

20. **Correct Choice: C.** The author tells us that one of the principles of *feng shui* has to do with a building's proportions. The height of a room's ceiling compared to its other dimensions is a good example of proportion.

21. **Correct Choice: C.** The study showed no improvement in people who used aromatherapy, making choice C an accurate reflection of the results of the study. However, the passage never makes a case for avoiding aromatherapy (answer choice B) and the author seems to say that you should do aromatherapy if you want, just don't expect much in the way of an improvement for your health. Neither lavender (answer choice A) nor lemon (answer choice D) were found to have an effect on people's heath, making these proposed titles inconsistent with the passage. The passage does not discuss aroma and mood (answer choice E).

22. **Correct Choice: B.** The passage states that lemon and lavender were tested in the study because they are two of the most popular scents used in aromatherapy. The ease of finding scents (answer choice A), the expense in obtaining them (answer choice D), and their availability (answer choice E) are not mentioned in the passage, making these answer choices incorrect. The passage only mentions vanilla in connection with headaches—not lemon or lavender, making answer choice C incorrect.

23. **Correct Choice: C.** The study described in the passage is not necessarily absolutely conclusive, so choice C is the only conclusion you can legitimately draw from the passage. The passage itself states this conclusion in the last paragraph. The results of the study do no support any of the other answer choices.

24. **Correct Choice: C.** Only this sentence fits with the topic of the paragraph, which is the author's obsession with the game of buttons. The other

answer choices provide information on other topics. Answer choice D provides more information about the game of buttons, but even this sentence doesn't fit under the topic of this paragraph, which is only about the author's own obsession.

25. **Correct Choice: B.** The passage says that the author became obsessed with the game of buttons during his "ninth and tenth years."

26. **Correct Choice: C.** In recounting the sport of buttons, the author tells us that he "gambled passionately" and would continually count his "treasure" (his buttons). From this account, we can infer that in a game of buttons, the winner's prize was the opponent's buttons.

27. **Correct Choice: E.** As used in this sentence, *passionately* most closely means enthusiastically. Substituting any of the other answer choices for *passionately* would change the meaning of the sentence.

28. **Correct Choice: A.** In this passage the author takes a position—here it is stated in the first sentence of the first paragraph—and then explains and backs it up using an example from his own life. None of the other answer choices apply to the technique used here.

29. **Correct Choice: C.** The passage's author is very optimistic about the future of science and how it will benefit humankind. Of the five choices, the word *enthusiastic* best describes such optimism.

30. **Correct Choice: B.** The word *eminent* is best defined as distinguished. The author's point here is that even our most prominent and respected—our most distinguished—scientists and science-fiction writers couldn't dream up what the future of science will actually hold.

31. **Correct Choice: A.** In the final sentence, the author expresses confidence that, thanks to science, the condition of humankind will be better in the future than it is today. The underlying assumption is that humans want to improve their lives and that this is a goal we all share.

32. **Correct Choice: A.** In the third paragraph, the author poses, and then answers, a question. This is a common technique used by writers. In contrast, a rhetorical question (answer choice C) is a question asked solely for effect with no answer expected.

The question itself is designed to make the author's point. An example of a rhetorical question is the last sentence of the second paragraph.

33. **Correct Choice: B.** The passage's main idea is that the great scientific advancements of the past give us reason to believe that more great advancements will occur in what's sure to be a long future for humankind. Answer choice C could also be a plausible answer, but the author never makes the case that we need to encourage scientific research; to some extent at least, he seems to think scientific progress happens unexpectedly and naturally. Answer choice A focuses solely on the past while the article focuses mostly on the future, making this option not a good choice for a title. There is nothing in the passage to indicate that past was bleak in terms of scientific research, making answer choice D incorrect.

34. **Correct Choice: E.** This table requires that you look down the column labeled "Aiken" to find the arrival time in Aiken. The train to Aiken departs at 9:30 and arrives at 10:46 a.m., making 10:45 the best answer.

35. **Correct Choice: D.** Pages 242–255 indicate information on credit reporting companies, which one can infer are affiliated with credit reports.

36. **Correct Choice: E.** Pages 282–283 include information on international transactions. Page 282 (answer choice D) might have been tempting if you didn't know what a cash advance was, but the reference to Mexico clearly shows the reference to an international transaction.

37. **Correct Choice: A.** "For example" correctly relates the sentence containing the first blank with the preceding sentence. The sentence provides a specific example of the proposals mentioned in the preceding sentence. "However" correctly relates the sentence containing the second blank with the sentence that precedes it. This sentence presents an argument opposed to the one presented in the preceding sentence.

38. **Correct Choice: C.** The word *invoke*, as used here, is best defined as "call attention to." Supporters of laws legalizing trade in human organs are calling upon what they believe is a fundamental right to justify their position. None of the other answer choices correctly describes the meaning of *invoke* in this context.

39. Correct Choice: B. According to the passage, there is a long waiting list for organ donations. This means that the supply of organs is not keeping up with demand. There is no evidence in the passage to support any of the other answer choices.

40. Correct Choice: D. In the second paragraph the author states the arguments made by both supporters and opponents of laws to legalize the selling of human organs. The author does not take a position himself, a fact which makes the other answer choices incorrect.

41. Correct Choice: A. "However" correctly relates sentence 4 with sentence 3. "Then" correctly relates sentence 7 with sentence 6; sentence 7 gives the next step in the process of making funnel cakes.

42. Correct Choice: E. Sentence 8 states that funnel cake is delicious. What tastes good is very subjective and depends on the likes and dislikes of each individual person. This statement is the author's opinion and not a fact. All the other sentences provided as answer choices are factual statements.

43. Correct Choice: A. This sentence provides information that is not important to the development of the passage. This sentence could be eliminated without any problem. None of the other answer choices are sentences that could be eliminated without affecting the development of the passage.

44. Correct Choice: B. The passage explains what a funnel cake is, including how it is made and how it compares to similar products. There is no indication the author is selling funnel cakes (answer choice A) and nothing in the passage provides much information about the Pennsylvania Dutch region (answer choice C). The author's statement that a funnel cake is a delicious treat (answer choice E) is not the main idea of the passage. The passage does discuss the difference between elephant ears and funnel cake (answer choice D), but the purpose of this is to help develop the reader's understanding of what a funnel cake is (answer choice B).

45. Correct Choice: C. This title best summarizes the main idea of the passage, which is to explain seasonal affective disorder (SAD). Only the last sentence discusses treatments (answer choice A) and only two sentences in the second paragraph discuss the symptoms of SAD (answer choice D). Answer choices B and E are incorrect because they contradict the position taken by the author that SAD is a real disorder that needs to be treated.

46. Correct Choice: C. The word *rays*, in this context, refers to sunshine. Warmth (answer choice D) could be a plausible answer but does not work in the context of this passage since SAD is not caused by a lack of warmth, but by a lack of light, particularly sunlight.

47. Correct Choice: A. Lethargy means sluggishness. The meaning can be inferred from the connection with depression, social withdrawal, and chronic fatigue. None of the other answer choices correctly define *lethargy*.

48. Correct Choice: D. The passage states that treatment of SAD focuses on light therapy, making it the primary treatment. Medication (answer choice A) and psychotherapy (answer choice C) are identified as supplemental treatments, but not primary treatments. There is no mention of surgery (answer choice B) or physical therapy (answer choice E) in the passage.

49. Correct Choice: B. Part Two includes content about punctuation.

50. Correct Choice: C. Part Three includes a section about commonly misspelled words.

Mathematics Test

1. **Correct Choice: A.** Add all the scores to get 602. Divide by the number of terms (7). $602 \div 7 = 86$.

2. **Correct Choice: C.** If boys comprise 60%, then girls comprise 40%. 40% of 430 is expressed as $.40 \times 430$. The answer is 172.

3. **Correct Choice: A.** The cities on the map are 2 inches apart and each inch is equivalent to 150 miles. So the cities are 300 miles apart ($2 \times 150 = 300$). It took the plane ½ hour to go 300 miles. There are two half hours in one hour, so in an hour the plane would go 600 miles at that speed ($2 \times 300 = 600$). The plane is going 600 miles per hour.

4. **Correct Choice: C.** Miles per gallon will tell the gas mileage the car is getting. Mileage is not a unit of measure, but a concept measured by miles per gallon.

5. **Correct Choice: A.** First we need to figure out how much ribbon is needed by each student. It is 2 feet + 10 inches. We need to convert this to either feet or inches and add; inches will be easier to use. Two feet = 24 inches. $24 + 10 = 34$ inches. Each student will need 34 inches of ribbon. There are 27 students so we need to multiply 27 by 24 inches. 27×24 is 918 inches. Since the answer choices are in feet, we need to divide this total by 12 to get feet. $918 \div 12 = 76.5$ feet. This is equivalent to 76 feet, 6 inches, or answer choice A.

6. **Correct Choice: B.** Two sides of the rectangle will be extended 28 feet to create a new, longer lunchroom. $2 \times 28 = 56$. So the perimeter, or length of the walls around the room, will increase by 56 feet.

7. **Correct Choice: D.** Length × width = area. $x \times 6 = 66$. Dividing both sides of the equation by 6, we get $x = 11$.

8. **Correct Choice: C.** Set up a basic proportion with 45 (cents) over 2 (holes) on the left and x over 10 (holes) on the right. Then you can cross-multiply to get $45 \times 10 = 2x$ and solve to get $225 = x$. Of course, you then need to express that in dollars to fit the answer choices, and 225 cents = $2.25.

9. **Correct Choice: E.** This question is mostly a basic proportion, with 45 minutes over 1 day on the left and x over 7 days (remember to convert!) on the right. Cross-multiply and you get $315 = x$. However, the answer choices are expressed in hours *and* minutes, so you must divide 315 by 60 (the number of minutes in one hour) to get 5r15, or 5 hours, 15 minutes.

10. **Correct Choice: E.** The probability of not getting a 2 on the roll of the dice can be found using the equation $q = f/n = \dfrac{n - s}{n}$, where n is the total number of possible outcomes ($n = 6$) and s is the number of outcomes considered a success ($s = 1$). So

$$q = \frac{n - s}{n} = \frac{6 - 1}{6} = \frac{5}{6}$$

11. **Correct Choice: E.** Creating two equal fractions for your proportion, you could put 5 (berries) in the numerator and 4 (yogurt) in the denominator on the left, then 10 (yogurt) in the denominator on the right and x in the numerator. Cross-multiplying gives you $50 = 4x$, so $12.5 = x$.

12. **Correct Choice: B.** To calculate how many feet longer Michelle's path is, just take the difference between the two paths. $7298 - 5167 = 2131$, so answer choice B is the correct answer.

13. **Correct Choice: B.** To determine the product of 35.2 and 4.16, the numbers should be arranged as:

$$
\begin{array}{r}
35.2 \\
\times 4.16 \\
\hline
2{,}112 \\
3{,}520 \\
+140{,}800 \\
\hline
146.432
\end{array}
$$

14. **Correct Choice: D.** To compute the difference between two numbers, we subtract. Here, however, one of the numbers is negative. $7.8 - (-5.9)$. Subtracting a negative number is the same as adding a positive number. $7.8 + 5.9 = 13.7$. The difference between the high and low level is 13.7 feet.

15. **Correct Choice: C.** Half of the students got a higher score and half got a lower score. This is not the same as the average score. It is also different from the midpoint of the range of scores (answer choice D).

16. **Correct Choice: C.** Since subtracting a negative number is the same as adding a positive number, we can rewrite the expression as $-8 + 45 + 12$. The result is 49.

17. **Correct Choice: A.** To compute the average we add the numbers and divide by the number of terms. Adding a negative number is the same as subtracting a positive number. So we can write the expression: $2 - 5 - 1.5 + 0.5 - 0.5 - 2.5 + 0 - 3$. This equals -10, or a total loss of 10 pounds. There are eight persons so we divide this number by 8. 10 divided by 8 = 1.25. This is the average weight loss of the eight friends.

18. **Correct Choice: B.** You simply need to figure out how many times $.75 goes into $15.00. Divide 15 by .75. To get rid of the decimal point in the divisor, move the decimal 2 places to the right in both numbers. Now divide 75 into 1,500. The answer is 20.

19. **Correct Choice: C.** Divide 13,920 by 240 and you get 58. The tens digit is 5. Or, since you know that one of the answer choices is correct, you can plug one in until you get the correct answer. The number 5 works.

20. **Correct Choice: D.** To subtract fractions, you need a common denominator. The common denominator for $1/5$ and $3/8$ is 40 ($5 \times 8 = 40$). Five goes into 40 eight times so $1/5 = 8/40$. Eight goes into 40 five times and 5×3 is 15. So $3/8 = 15/40$. Subtract $22^{8/40}$ from $26^{15/40}$. The answer is $4^{7/40}$.

21. **Correct Choice: E.** The fraction $60/12$ divides out to 5, which is the same as 500%.

22. **Correct Choice: B.** The new, 18-ounce mixture contains 10 ounces of water. Thus, water accounts for $10/18$, or $5/9$, of the next mixture.

23. **Correct Choice: B.** Converting a percent to a decimal involves removing the percent sign and moving the decimal point two places to the left. Therefore, 65% becomes 0.65.

24. **Correct Choice: C.** The length of the piece of tape going around the length of the box can be computed as $10 + 6 + 10 + 6$, which equals 32 inches. The length of the piece of tape going around the width of the box can be computed as $8 + 6 + 8 + 6$, which equals 28 inches. Then to get the total for the two pieces of tape add 28 and 32.

25. **Correct Choice: E.** In two hours she will travel 110 miles. Going this distance, she will pass Upham and Downing and be 10 miles from Riverton. This problem asks how many miles she will be past Upham at that point. To compute that number, subtract 25 from 110 to get 85 miles.

26. **Correct Choice: D.** You can translate this statement directly into algebra. The statement "Ryan is 2 years older than four times Pixie's age" becomes $R = 2 + 4P$, which is answer choice D.

27. **Correct Choice: C.** The report card had one A, so you can subtract $10 from the $30 total. That means Jamie got $20 for her Bs, and since she gets $5 for every B and $20 \div 5 = 4$, she got four Bs.

28. **Correct Choice: E.** You have Henry's end time, but also need his start time to calculate his average speed. Answer choices A and B are incorrect because each of them only provides part of the time of Henry's complete trip. The length of the track and average strides per minute are irrelevant (answer choices C and D).

29. **Correct Choice: C.** You need to know how many roast beef sandwiches Anya ordered. Answer choices A, B, and E don't provide enough information to solve the problem. Answer choice D is information given in the problem.

30. **Correct Choice: E.** If you add up the number of lemons, mangoes, and oranges, you have 94 pieces of fruit. Therefore, at least 1 apple was picked.

31. **Correct Choice: B.** The chart shows the following relationship between x and y: $y = -4x + 1$. Therefore, when $x = 4$, $y = -15$.

32. **Correct Choice: A.** Apply the arithmetic mean (simple average) formula:

$$AM = \frac{S + (S + 4)}{2} = \frac{2S + 4}{2} = S + 2$$

33. **Correct Choice: A.** The fraction $3/4$ expressed as a decimal is .75. You probably already know this, but if you don't, you could divide 3 by 4 ($3 \div 4 = .75$). Therefore, she can compute the answer by multiplying $.75 \times 3120$.

34. **Correct Choice: E.** To divide by a fraction, you invert the fraction and multiply. Thus $2^{3/4} \div 7/8$ is equivalent to $2^{3/4} \times 8/7$.

35. **Correct Choice: C.** The expression $x(y + z)$ means hat both terms in the parenthesis are multiplied by x. So $x(y + z)$ is the equivalent of $xy + xz$ and $x(y + z) + 5 = xy + xz + 5$.

36. **Correct Choice: C.** We don't know how many cars are in the lot, but we do know that out of every five cars, two are domestic. Compute the percent by dividing the number of domestic cars (2) by the number of cars (5). $2 \div 5$ is .4 or 40%.

37. **Correct Choice: B.** A little translation is a big help on this problem: The question "8 is what percent of 5?" translates to "$8 = {}^{x}/_{100} \times 5$." To solve, $8 \times 100 = {}^{5x}/_{100}$ (100, which comes out to $800 = 5x$, which becomes ${}^{800}/_{5} = {}^{5x}/_{5}$, or $160 = x$.

38. **Correct Choice: A.** To get rid of the decimal in the divisor, move both decimal points one space to the right. $4070 \div 74 = 55$. When dividing a positive number by a negative number, the quotient is negative, so the answer is -55.

39. **Correct Choice: D.** To compare with ${}^{13}/_{40}$, convert the denominators in choices B, C, and D to 40:

$$\frac{7}{20} \times \frac{2}{2} = \frac{14}{40} > \frac{13}{40}$$
$$\frac{2}{5} \times \frac{8}{8} = \frac{16}{40} > \frac{13}{40}$$
$$\frac{3}{10} \times \frac{4}{4} = \frac{12}{40} < \frac{13}{40}$$

For choice A, you can compare this way:

$$\frac{1}{3} \times \frac{13}{13} = \frac{13}{39} > \frac{13}{40s}$$

40. **Correct Choice: C.** 782,833.1 is slightly less than 782,833.11, meaning that it is within the range identified here. Answer choice B is too small to fit into this range and choice A, D, and E are too large.

41. **Correct Choice: C.** Choices A and B are too large to fit into the specified range and D and E are too small.

42. **Correct Choice: A.** .28 rounded to the nearest one-tenth would be .3. Choices C and D are equivalent to 3.1 and 14.2, respectively, both of which cannot be further rounded to the nearest one-tenth.

43. **Correct Choice: E.** Rounding to the nearest hundred, we get 582,700 – 294,300, which equals 288,400.

44. **Correct Choice: A.** Keith could order sushi. Answer choices B and C are impossible. Answer choices D and E must be true. The question asks what could be true.

45. **Correct Choice: D.** Beth cannot complete her English homework before her math homework, so she must complete her English homework last. Answer choices B and C are clearly wrong because the problem states that she completes her science homework first. Answer choices A and E describe the same scenario, with Spanish as second and social studies as last. This is impossible because English must go last.

46. **Correct Choice: B.** We don't know if the three places are in a straight line, or if the paths from the gas station of the pharmacy and burger joint overlap. Eliminate answer choice A. Answer choices C, D, and E state exact locations. Eliminate.

47. **Correct Choice: B.** To find what percentage of sales was in individual bottles, just consider the number of individual bottles divided by the number of bottles total. Because the math on this one is pretty time consuming, "ballpark" first to see if you can eliminate any answer choices. For the 1997 Pinot Noir, approximately 15,000 divided by approximately 80,000 is a little less than 20%. For the 1994 Pinot Gris, approximately 18,000 divided by approximately 77,000 is about 23%, or almost 25%. For the 1991 Chardonnay, approximately 15,000 divided by approximately 90,000 is about 20%. For the 2001 Bordeaux, approximately 12,000 divided by approximately 100,000 is about 12%. So the 1994 Pinot Gris has definitely the largest percentage of sales in individual bottles.

48. **Correct Choice: C.** The number of donors on Tuesday was about 25 and from Tuesday to Wednesday, that number increased by about 25. That is a 100% increase from Tuesday to Wednesday.

49. **Correct Choice: B.** Simply add the percents the pie graph attributes to each flavor to find which combination surpasses the 42% share held by apple. All the other answer choices represent less than 42%.

50. **Correct Choice: C.** In 2005, about 45 million visited Times Square, compared to 55 million in 2007. 55 million – 45 million = 10 million.

Writing Test

After you take the actual CBEST, two human scorers will read your essay and assign a number score from 1 to 4. The score they give will be based on the scoring standards described in the official CBEST Writing Score Scale. This scale can be viewed online at www.cbest.nesinc.com (go to the practice test and then the writing section). A summary of the writing score scale is provided below.

Use this summary to score your own essay. Better yet, ask someone else—a teacher, parent, friend, or colleague—to score your essay based on this summary of the CBEST writing score scale.

Scoring the CBEST Writing Test	
Score	**Summary of Scoring Guidelines**
4	**A Score of 4 indicates a well-written essay that effectively develops an idea for the specified audience.**
	The essay has a central idea or point of view and the writer maintains the focus on the idea in a well reasoned essay.
	Ideas or points the author presents are logically arranged and the essay is clear and well-organized.
	Assertions are supported with relevant information and specific examples.
	Words usage is careful and precise.
	Sentences and paragraphs are well constructed and coherent; however, the essay may contain minor flaws in grammar, spelling, punctuation, etc.
	The essay completely addresses the topic and is appropriate for the given audience.
3	**A Score of 3 indicates an essay that for the most part, is adequately written and develops an idea for the specified audience.**
	The essay has a central idea or point of view and the writer, for the most part, maintains the focus on this idea in a well reasoned essay.
	The presentation of ideas and points, for the most, is adequately organized and clear.
	Most assertions are supported with relevant information and specific examples.
	Word usage is adequate; there may be some errors in usage but they are not bad enough to make understanding difficult.
	Sentences and paragraphs are generally well contructed and coherent; errors in sentence structure and grammar are not serious enough to cause confusion and misunderstanding.
	The essay addresses the topic and is appropriate for the given audience.
2	**A Score of 2 indicates an essay that attempts to communicate an idea but the idea is only partially formed and sometimess difficult to understand.**
	The essay may state a central idea or point of view but the focus is not maintained throughout the essay and the central idea is underdeveloped or simplistically reasoned.
	The organization of ideas lacks clarity and is only partially effective.
	Assertions are not always supported and the essay may contain irrelevant or insufficient details.
	Word usage is not always clear and may cause confusion or even misunderstanding.
	Sentences and paragraphs are not always well constructed and can be difficult to understand due to errors in sentence structure and grammar.
	The essay may not completely address the topic or be appropriate in style and content for the given audience.
1	**A Score of 1 indicates an essay that is difficult to understand and fails to communicate an idea to the intended audience.**
	The central idea or point of view of the essay is unclear and the essay is simplistically reasoned or contains serious flaws in reasoning.
	The essay lacks organization and coherence, leaving the reader confused.
	Assertions are not supported or are seriously underdeveloped and the essay contains irrelevant and/or insufficient details.
	Word usage is often unclear and confusing, leading to confusion or misunderstanding on the part of the reader.
	Sentences and paragraphs are not well constructed with many errors in paragraphing, sentence structure, and grammar that make understanding difficult.
	The essay may not completely address the topic or be appropriate in style and content for the given audience.
U	**This score indicates the essay cannot be scored. Reasons for this can be the essay was illegible, completely off topic, or not written in English.**
B	**This score indicates the essay response sheet was left blank.**